T0323259

ADVENTURES IN TRIPOLI

First published in 1924 by Philip Allan & Co.
This Reprint published by
Darf Publishers Limited

First edition, 1924

New impression, 1984

To my friend
Griffin
Tripoli 1912.
Seppings
Wright

THE AUTHOR

By Seppings Wright

ADVENTURES IN TRIPOLI

A Doctor in the Desert

BY

ERNEST H. GRIFFIN

D.S.O., M.C.

LONDON
DARF PUBLISHERS LTD
1984

TO

MAY, GEORGE AND PHYL
IN MEMORY OF HAPPY DAYS

ISBN 1 85077 010 7

Printed in Great Britain by
A. Wheaton & Co. Ltd., Exeter

PREFACE

I COMPLETED the manuscript of this book just before the outbreak of the Great War, and was already looking for a publisher when Italy drew the sword and took her stand on the side of the Allies. As I was then at the front myself, I felt it was no time to print anything that might cause the slightest annoyance even to the humblest of my Italian comrades, so I relegated the sheets to a cupboard where they lay for nearly nine years. A few months ago, a letter by me in one of the evening papers brought me an offer from my present firm of publishers. I am having the narrative printed in almost its original form, merely cutting out descriptions of battles and scenes of bloodshed with which everyone has recently been completely satiated.

If it appears that I have taken, rather quixotically, a view entirely favourable to the Arab and the Turk, I will ask my readers to remember how naturally one sympathizes with a small nation in conflict with a more powerful one, and how spontaneously one sides with the team for which one may be playing, even if it be only for the afternoon. I feel quite sure that the Italian officers with whom I made firm and lasting friendships in the prison camp at Karlsruhe will understand my point of view.

It is a great pleasure for me to be able to state that the present Italian Government are treating the inhabitants of their new colony in a generous fashion. They have given the natives of Tripolitana citizenship, with all the civic and political liberties that the word implies. She is colonizing not only with her sword, but also with the aid of her doctors and her teachers. In accordance with the traditions of that great statesman, Francesco Crispi, she is covering the Mediterranean coast with schools and hospitals. Zymotic disease is being stamped out and the hotbeds of infection are being cleaned up.

It would not perhaps be out of place if I said a few words about the British Red Crescent Society, under whose flag I served in Tripolitana. This organization, to succour the Moslem victims of war, was founded by that distinguished Orientalist, the Right Honourable Syed Ameer Ali, P.C. A faithful and devoted servant of the King Emperor, he has ever been anxious to promote good feeling between the Mussulman States and our own country, and not the least of his good works has been the founding of the British Red Crescent Society, which has carried out its mission of mercy in many parts of the world and proved to distressed Moslems that the peoples of our Empire do not confine their charity to the disciples of one faith alone.

In close association with Mr. Ameer Ali in his work has been H.H. Aga Khan, whose purse has always been open to assist his less fortunate co-religionists. As a firm friend of Turkey and in constant touch with prominent men both in Constantinople and Angora, I can only say that a reinvigorated and rejuvenated Turkey owes an enormous debt of gratitude to these two distinguished Indians, who, labouring under the greatest difficulties, have obtained for her a fair hearing in the Council of Nations.

A few words as to some of the people I have mentioned. Bahrouni like a wise man and sturdy patriot has bowed to the inevitable and has accepted honourable service under the King of Italy. I am sure all surviving members of our Mission will wish him the best of luck. My good friend, Sheikh Sassi, also made his submission, and I greatly regret to say that the staunch fidelity he showed to his oath of allegiance cost him his life. At the beginning of the Great War, the savage tribesmen from the interior swept up to the coast and called upon Sassi to lead them to victory. True to his pledged word to his King, he stood firm and was stoned to death by an infuriated mob. The rifle he gave me hangs above my writing-desk, and I shall ever keep it in memory of a very gentle and gallant Arab gentleman.

Dr. Martin Turnbull died a victim to duty in the War. It is pleasant for me to remember that when we met in London after the campaign we both agreed that any little friction we might have had was to be put down to the effects of chronic malaria, from which we both suffered. He was an excellent surgeon and took great pains in his work. Many an Arab walking the desert owes the use of arm or leg to his skill and care.

Mohammed, my faithful servant, has settled down in Algeria, where appropriately enough he keeps a cookshop. He writes to me from time to time, usually to announce the arrival of an addition to his family. As Madame Mohammed recently sent me an elaborate piece of needlework, executed by her own fair hands,

I imagine these frequent incidents do not trouble her over much. Mustapha has married a very charming French lady and was recently touring England as a commercial traveller. An amazing coincidence took place when he met another of our interpreters, Muktar, in the lift at a hotel in the Highlands of Scotland!

E. H. G.

48 UPPER BERKELEY STREET,
    PORTMAN SQUARE,
        LONDON.

CONTENTS

AT–A*

LIST OF ILLUSTRATIONS

xi

INTRODUCTION.

In 1877 a German traveller named Rohlfs, who had done some good work in exploring the lesser-known tracts of North Africa, returned from Tripolitana with an attractive phrase on his lips:—Tripoli is the key to Africa; he who possesses Tripoli is master of the whole Sudan.

In those days the German bubble had not been pricked, and the oracular words of Rohlfs went the round of clubs and chancelleries. Amid the general scramble for European expansion in Africa, here was a nice tit-bit to be swallowed by some Great Power. Only one consideration held back prospective grasping hands, and that was that Tripoli belonged to Turkey; and both France and England were guided by a golden rule of diplomacy—that the integrity of the Ottoman Empire was to be maintained. It was over thirty years later when the abandonment of the policy of our great Ministers, Palmerston and Beaconsfield, enabled Italy to seize Tripoli, and thus send Europe sliding a little further down the abyss which led to the Great War.

Erroneous as they were, let us look for a moment at the facts and ideas that Rohlfs put forward in support of his extraordinary statement.

A chain of mountains and plateaux runs along the north coast of Africa, from Egypt to Morocco, shutting out the interior from European penetration. Behind this formidable barrier lies the immense desert; the monotony of the mournful, burning sands being broken, here and there, by green and fruitful oases. Tapping this vast interior are the grand caravan routes, along which camels toil bearing the produce of the country, ultimately dropping their loads in the market-place of Tripoli.

But if Tripoli is the natural port of the "ships of the desert," so is it a port for ocean-going vessels, which will bring manufactured goods to its wharves in exchange for the oils, feathers, ivory and gold of the interior.

Unfortunately, however, the trade from the interior was very small from a European point of view. The people were content to live after the manner of their fathers, and did not wish to be exploited for the enrichment of manufacturers. The government of the Turks sat lightly on the people, and the trifling tribute demanded did not force the natives to sustained work in order to satisfy the tax-gatherers.

But, said Rohlfs, let there only come to Tripoli a progressive European Power, who will pacify the tribes, open the roads, and push forward the telegraph, and commerce will improve by leaps and bounds. The construction of railways will be the simplest of engineering tasks; no bridges to build, no tunnels to excavate, with the sand of the desert forming a natural ballast to the rails and sleepers.

The picture thus attractively painted by the German

traveller caused many greedy eyes to be cast upon the *vilayet*; but it was Italy, perhaps, who was chiefly interested. A glance at the map and a brief consideration of European politics and economics prior to the Great War will show why.

The pride of Italy had been hurt at the French occupation of Tunis, and she was by no means content with the small amount of territory that she had secured in the general scramble for Africa. Tripoli was the last bone left, and to restore her prestige Italy determined to get it. Moreover, she was hemmed in by her neighbours and scarcely had space to breathe. On the north was her hereditary enemy Austria, spreading down the coast of the Adriatic and Germanizing the ancient Gulf of Venice. On the south she saw the British firmly entrenched at Malta, with France in possession of Tunis, with a naval base at Bizerta. She asked herself where was a natural outlet, and found the answer in Tripoli.

From an economic point of view Tripolitana was also necessary to the Italians. Italy was making vast strides in commerce, and already her silk and cotton goods were competing successfully with the products of Manchester and Lyons. But at the same time parts of Italy were being emptied by emigration. A new colony was badly needed to receive these emigrants, whence they would be able to send home raw material in return for manufactured goods.

The fact that the inhabitants of Tripolitana were perfectly satisfied with the Ottoman rule and utterly detested the idea of Christian domination was, of course, not considered for a moment.

How Tripolitana passed eventually from the hands of the Turks to those of the Italians is well described by Lord Eversley in his interesting work, *The Turkish Empire*, and I will quote the passage in *extenso*:—"The next blow to the Ottoman Empire came from a very unexpected quarter, from Italy, which made a sudden and unprovoked attack on Tripoli. This province in Africa had never been autonomous. It was an integral part of the Ottoman Empire, governed directly from Constantinople. Its population was purely Moslem—Turks and Moors in the city of Tripoli and other places on the coast, and with semi-independent Arabs in the hinterland. There was no demand on the part of these natives for a change of government. Italy had no valid cause of complaint on behalf of its few subjects who resided in the province, though it trumped up something of the kind. It was a case of pure aggression, prompted by jealousy of France in respect of Tunis, to which, geographically and economically, Italy had a stronger claim. It may be confidently assumed that the French Republic gave its consent to the seizure of Tripoli by Italy, and that Great Britain acquiesced in it, if it did not formally approve.

"Up to the end of 1910 the Italian Government had constantly professed the desire to maintain the integrity of the Turkish Empire. When rumours arose of an intention to grab Tripoli, its Foreign Minister, so late as December 2, 1910, emphatically denied them in the Italian Chamber. 'We desire,' he said, 'the integrity of the Ottoman Empire, and we wish Tripoli to remain Turkish.' Nothing had since occurred to disturb the relations between the two countries. But in September, 1911, the Italian Government sprang a mine on the Porte by declaring its intention to occupy Tripoli. On October 26th it notified to the Powers of Europe its intention to annex that province. It sent an army of 50,000 men for the purpose. Its fleet bombarded the Turkish town of Prevesa, in the Adriatic, and drove the Turkish Fleet to seek refuge within the Dardanelles. It took possession of several of the islands in the Ægean Sea.

"The Porte was caught at a disadvantage. Abdul Hamid had for many years completely neglected his navy. He owed it a grudge for having taken part in the deposition of his predecessor. He feared that its guns might be trained on his palace. He had allowed the Minister of Marine, the most corrupt and greedy of all his Pashas, to appropriate to his own use the money allotted by the Budget for the repair of warships. For many years the battleships never left the Golden Horn. But for this, the Ottoman Navy, which in the time of Abdul Aziz had been the third most powerful in Europe, might have made the landing of an Italian army in Africa impossible. The garrison in Tripoli, which Abdul Hamid had always maintained in strength, had been greatly reduced by the Young Turks. The reinforcement of it after the declaration of war, when Italy had command of the sea, was a very difficult task, the more so as the British Government proclaimed the neutrality of Egypt, though it was still tributary to the Porte, and forbade the passage of Turkish troops into Tripoli.

" In spite of these obstacles, the Porte made a gallant fight for its African province, with the aid of the Arabs of the hinterland.   Both Turkish and Italian armies committed the most horrible atrocities in this war; and there was little to choose between them in this respect.[1] The war lasted till October, 1912, and was only brought to an end when the Porte found itself confronted by danger from a quarter much nearer home."

[1] AUTHOR's NOTE.—It is only fair to state that no member of our Mission and no British war correspondent saw any atrocities committed either by the Turkish troops or by their Arab auxiliaries.

CHAPTER I.

To those of us who were spending a vacation in England after a few years' grilling in the Tropics, the summer of 1912 proved somewhat of a disappointment. I well remember the day I decided I had had enough of London. A dismal drizzle, alternating with heavy showers, made an overcoat and umbrella indispensable. The continued absence of the sun gave a gloomy appearance to the streets, and the motor traffic, ploughing through the slush-filled road, bespattered the people on the side-walks. Hoping that the climate of Paris would prove more agreeable, I packed up and left by the evening train; but alas! there the weather was, if anything, even worse. However, my journey did not prove altogether fruitless, for there it was I first heard that the British Red Crescent Society was on the lookout for surgeons to assist the wounded Turks and Arabs in Tripolitana. Thinking of the tales I had heard of the pleasant warmth of the desert, the clearness of the sky, and the beauty of the nights, I returned to London, and soon closed with an offer to go out, little thinking that before I returned to England I was going to see samples of some of the worst weather it is possible to imagine.

As I was carrying with me to Tripolitana twenty large cases of surgical and medical stores, in addition to my personal luggage, and not wishing to have acrimonious discussions with the Custom officers in France and Tunisia, I took the precaution of making a sworn declaration as to the contents of the boxes before the Lord Mayor, whose signature was afterwards attested at the French Consulate. Despite these precautions, however, my journey from London to Sfax was one continuous battle with inquisitive officials, who wished, under some pretext or other, to satisfy themselves that I was not carrying contraband.

I left Charing Cross on the 7th September, 1912; but before the train steamed out of the station I was annoyed to notice that my cases had been marked with the sign of the Cross, instead of the Red Crescent, which is the emblem of the Society I was serving. This may seem a small matter; but it must be borne in mind that to the Turk, with his vast experience of Balkan fighting, the Cross does not stand out as the supreme symbol of love and mercy. It will be sufficient if the reader looks up the report of the Carnegie Commission on the atrocities committed in the last Balkan War to understand this attitude of the Turks. However, having an hour to spare at Paris, an energetic porter succeeded in planing off the offending marks, and then painting on the necessary Red Crescent.

The train arrived at Marseilles late at night, but, as the French seem to have solved the great licensing question better than we have, I was able to linger over my supper on the terrace of a café on the Canobière, watching the animated crowd that passed before me.

MEDININE, TUNISIA

ANCIENT ARAB FORTRESS

To face p. 8

It was a relief to have escaped from the cloud-patched sky of London; here was the blue " inverted bowl " with the diamond-like stars scattered therein with lavish hand.   What a pleasure it was to finger a liqueur glass in the open air and once again to blow cigar smoke into air that was decently warm!

I left Marseilles for Tunis on the *Carthage*, a boat belonging to the General Transatlantic Company.   It was a comfortable and well-appointed ship; the cabins were kept scrupulously clean, and the food on board could not be grumbled at.   My fellow-passengers were mostly French people who lived in the Tunisian Protectorate, and they all seemed glad to be returning home.   On the 10th September we reached Tunis, and the decks were immediately invaded by a rabble of gesticulating Arabs, who wished to carry our luggage ashore.

As the train left the next morning, I had little opportunity of " doing " Tunis.   I certainly took a drive round the town, but only got a vague impression of a stuffy and odorous native quarter, of rows of gleaming white houses, and broad streets planted with palm trees.

From Tunis to Sfax is about a day's trip, and the railway authorities are apparently not unaware of the tedious nature of the journey, for the accommodation was quite comfortable.   There were four of us in the little drawing-room car—a thin Frenchman and his wife, returning, as they took an early opportunity of informing me, from their honeymoon in Paris, and a stout man from St. Etienne, apparently selling a new line in agricultural implements, for long before the

train had started I held his card in my hand and was
listening to a long dissertation on the advantages of a
patent plough.

The country through which we travelled was not
very interesting, although here and there Arabs could
be seen working in the fields, in many cases their
ploughs being pulled by camels. Occasionally ancient
ruins loomed up, notably at El Djem, where the
imposing remains of a huge coliseum could be glimpsed
in the fading light. This noble ruin, second only in
size to the Coliseum at Rome, is one of the most
striking relics of the Roman sway in Northern Africa.

Glancing over the list of my outfit, I found the only
thing I had forgotten was an Arab fez, which I had
been advised by an official in London to wear in
Tripolitana in order to avoid giving offence to our
Moslem patients. As I gathered the thin man
was a draper by trade, all unknowing of the
commercial importance of Sfax, I asked him if I
could purchase an Arab headdress in that town.
He smiled and told me that that would not be
a difficult business, and then proceeded to ask me
what I wanted it for. I told him, and he at once
agreed that it was most essential, and illustrated the
point by pulling out of his pocket a current number
of a local paper which contained the exhilarating
news that the Arabs had captured some more or less
inoffensive person wearing a helmet, and had deprived
him of his ears and slit his nose before returning him
to the Italian camp. Needless to say, this item of news
emanated from an enemy source. The stout gentleman
now took up the cudgels on behalf of the helmet,

asserting that to wear a fez in the desert was to court a fatal sunstroke, while the Arabs reported that the Italians shot at sight all persons caught wearing them. I was loth to believe either tale; but the way in which Arab and Italian mutually accused each other of atrocities during the campaign might have led one to believe that it was the unevangelized denizens of the cannibal islands fighting, instead of two highly religious peoples. This, however, was my first introduction to "propaganda," a phase of war little understood by English people prior to the Great War.[1]

The discussion on helmet *versus* fez between my two companions became rather heated; and, although I politely listened with a show of interest, the rapid French exceeded my powers of comprehension, and I was delighted when a halt was called at Sousse, where dinner was served in the refreshment room. On returning to the car I was pleased to find that an end had been put to the dispute by the overpowering noise from the next coach, which was filled with a company of soldiers who were shouting loudly the choruses of songs that had been popular in the cafés of Montmartre six months previously.

We ran into Sfax at half-past eleven, where in the

[1] When a German intelligence officer interrogated me as a prisoner of war in 1918, he asked me especially if I knew what object British soldiers had in violating German burial places ! On my indignant denial that this had ever been done, he showed me some photographs in a paper, intended for neutral consumption, of cemeteries where the crosses had been thrown down. It is more than probable that this had been done by the Germans themselves, and it shows to what lengths the unscrupulous propagandist will go, to throw discredit on the enemy.

midst of a heated argument with the *octroi* officer I was rescued by Mr. William Leonardi, brother of the British Consul, who quickly released my boxes and remained with me until he had seen me comfortably settled at the Grand Hôtel de France.

In the morning I found to my annoyance that the weekly boat for Ben-Gardane, the starting-point for the caravans into Tripoli, had left the previous evening. As my orders were to push on to the Turkish camp at Zavia with all possible speed, as the stores I carried were urgently needed, I requested Mr. Leonardi to find me some other means of transport. He therefore took a passage for myself and Ali—an interpreter who was an expert at turning bad Arabic into worse French —on a little sailing boat of some 30 tons burden. As the Arab captain informed me he was starting " To-morrow, please God!" I hastened to get my papers in order and pack up my things. My haste in doing this was due to the fact that as yet I did not know that the words " To-morrow, please God," in the mouth of an Arab could best be translated by the Spanish word *mañana*.

Sfax is a town containing some 25,000 Arabs, who live in the native quarter, which is surrounded by imposing-looking walls; on to this the French conquerors have grafted a miniature Paris of restaurants, boulevards, cafés and cinemas. There is an active trade in dates, olive oil, esparto grass, wool, fruits and sponges, and nearly 2000 vessels are docked in the port annually.

The colonizing genius of France is seen, not only in the construction of large docks and other important public works, but also in the manner in which they have preserved the Oriental character of the architecture in the municipal buildings, displaying on every side that love of elegance and good taste which as a nation they learned in the days of the *Roi Soleil*. The bandstand on the Boulevard de France, with its elegant cupola and screen of palms, is worthy of more than a passing glance.

Business in connection with Ali's passport took me to the building devoted to the control of civil affairs, where I had a pleasant interview with the French Consul. I found him, like all other officials I met in Tunisia, courteous and obliging, and anxious to assist in every way. I got out of the Consul's office just in time to see some Colonial troops swing past—a handful of Spahis and a company of infantry. During the time I spent in Tunisia my respect for the French Army went up by leaps and bounds. There one saw none of the pasty-faced *piou-pious* that were familiar objects in large French towns, but bronzed, workmanlike soldiers, who marched as though they thoroughly enjoyed it, led by officers with a glint of confidence in their eye and a pleasing degree of swagger common to soldier-men who know their value. Later on, when thrown into contact with both officers and men, I could not avoid remarking a species of fanatical zeal that animated all ranks of the French Army. To English eyes, accustomed to the stiff bearing of our troops, a certain *flottement* in the ranks of a French regiment on the march gives the impression of a degree of slackness; but this light touch is merely a national characteristic, and the same thing may be noticed permeating their methods of colonial government. In the public buildings the Arab ushers and police, clad in their loose Oriental robes, carry out their business with commendable alacrity, tinged, however, with the easiness of Eastern people; while other Arabs having business with officials loll about in the entrance smoking and even eating unchecked. One can hardly imagine the stiff, starchy, all-important black constable on duty in the entrance-hall of the Court of Justice in one of our West Indian islands permitting anyone to smoke or eat unrebuked within the sacred precincts. He would consider it an insult to his own dignity.

Before returning to the hotel for dinner I drank an *apéritif* at the Café de la Régence with some of the customers to whom I had been introduced. There was the military surgeon, tall and immaculate; a war correspondent returning home, shattered in health after a few months in Tripoli; the torpedo-boat commander with a Captain Kettle beard, a pleasant enough fellow to take a drink with, but the stamp of man to make me highly nervous were I in command of a battleship and I knew his vicious craft to be in the vicinity, with those blue Breton eyes squinting along the torpedo tube. It seemed strange to see officers in all the glory of their uniforms sitting at the little tables, while at their elbows private soldiers and bluejackets were enjoying their glass of beer. I always admire the amazing sobriety of the French people; they appear to have learned the correct use of alcohol. The cafés seem to be allowed to keep open as long as they wish, and yet one never sees a drunken person—a sight all too familiar to our English eyes. At Sfax it seemed

almost impossible to get an officer to take a second
glass of beer, while even the ordinary seaman seemed
to know when he had had enough.   Perhaps it is a
matter of education, for I have often seen in France
what would throw one of our own fanatical temperance
advocates into convulsions—a French mother mixing
a glass of wine and water for each of her young
children.

The torpedo-boat commander had apparently done a
good day's work. A small steam yacht flying the British
colours had been chased into Tunisian waters by the
Italian cruisers, and, on the Custom authorities paying
the boat a visit, it was found that the hold contained
an assortment of magazine rifles, automatic pistols and
cartridges, evidently intended for the Ottoman troops
across the frontier.   The torpedo-boat escorted the
yacht into harbour, where the captain had to face the
music with the authorities.

The Turks, with criminal folly, had starved and
neglected their fleet to such an extent that the Italians
were masters of the sea, and free to bring a vast army
into Tripolitana without let or hindrance, while the
Turkish Army had to depend on a stray contraband
to fill their depleted arsenals.   To this neglect of their
fleet it is easy to trace Turkey's downfall, not only in
Tripoli but also in the Balkans.   This object-lesson in
the value of sea power should not be forgotten by our
own country, whose vast Empire depends entirely on
the supremacy of the Navy.

On returning to the hotel I was addressed by a
gentleman in faultless English, marred (or improved)
by a slight American accent.   He was a Turk who had

come to Sfax to look after Ottoman interests in connection with the seized yacht. He told me he understood I was going into Tripolitana under the Red
Crescent, and proceeded to make himself very pleasant.
He introduced me to the commander of the contraband
yacht, and also to that officer's wife, who had accompanied her husband throughout what had been a perilous
voyage. They had experienced very bad weather on
the trip; and although, as I learned by personal inspection later, comfort on board had given place to arms
and there seemed little place for a woman, the lady
was turned out in that irreproachably neat fashion which
one always associates with French women.

In wartime it is well to avoid the society of
smugglers, unless you wish to draw down on yourself
the suspicion of the authorities; and I am afraid I
must date a good many of my subsequent misfortunes
from that night. When I entered the dining-room and
was looking round for a seat I caught the eye of
Madame. She motioned me to a seat at their table,
and—well, I do not think she would have to beckon
twice to the majority of men. I sat down, and found
myself in most interesting company. On one side was
the Turk, Aziz Sabit Bey, to give him his name and
title; on the other the gallant captain, the hero of the
occasion; while in front of me were the bright eyes
of his wife. Aziz Bey proved to be a polished man
of the world; all languages seemed to come alike to
him. During the course of the evening I heard him
converse fluently in Turkish, Arabic, French, English
and Spanish. He had, it seemed, been attached to the
Turkish Embassy at Washington, among other places,

THE "BOUDELBLOUS" AT SFAX

BEN-GARDANE

To face p. 16

and was married to an American woman. Brought up, as I had been, to look upon the Turks as a barbarous and uneducated race, I had to begin to revise my ideas.

The captain, too, proved an entertaining companion, and his conversation roamed from China to Peru. He had but lately returned from Easter Island on some expedition or other, and gave us an account of the gigantic statues and other ancient monuments so puzzling to archæologists which are to be found on this little isle, plunged in the heart of the Pacific. He seemed rather depressed over the loss of his cargo; but thanks probably to the cunning of the local Arabs, months afterwards I saw rifles and cartridges from his ship in active use at the seat of war.

After dinner we went into the native quarter and took coffee in an Arab café. I ought to add that Madame came too, to see that we did not get into mischief. The coffee was excellent; but as much could not be said for the native music which was provided for our amusement. It is possible, however, that, once the ear is trained to it, it is pleasant enough. I remember when first I went to Venezuela how barbarous the native music seemed, produced as it is by the twanging of guitars and the turbulent agitation of the strings of mandolines. However, after a few weeks' residence in the country we thought no festival complete unless we called in the local band.

In this connection a good story is told about ex-President Cipriano Castro. In order to do him honour, a European band of international repute had been summoned to Caracas. El Cabito (Little Corporal) listened disdainfully for a time to their

efforts, and then, telling the musicians he would show
them what really good music was like, he called in four
of his fellow-villagers from the Andes, who regaled
their rivals with a few jingling airs.

The next morning, after laying in a stock of provisions for the voyage, I sent all my luggage down to
the docks and told Ali to bring back word at what time
the boat was sailing. He returned about lunch time,
telling me that the skipper said he was unable to set
sail that day, but he should start " To-morrow, please
God," adding that the Custom officials would not
allow my goods to be taken on board until they had
been examined. I immediately went down to the
docks, and found that my association with my friends
of the previous night had made the Italian agents suspicious, and they had denounced me to the authorities.
I allowed the officers to examine my personal luggage,
which they did with a thoroughness I could but admire.
A week's washing was shaken out of my dirty-linen
bag on to the quay for the delectation of a crowd, who
audibly commented on the fact that many of my garments required mending as well as washing. However,
when the cases of hospital stores were approached with
hammer and chisel, I did not feel it consistent with my
duty to allow them to be opened without strong protest,
as I doubted if anyone in Sfax could repack the bottles
in such a manner that they would stand uninjured the
several days' journey they would have to make later
on, on the backs of camels. I took a cab to the French
Consul's, and after another long perusal of my papers
I got a permit to take them on board unopened.

The next day saw me treading the deck of the

Boudelblous, which was to carry me to Ben-Gardane, taking stock of my surroundings. First of all I noticed the boat was very heavily burdened, so much so that there was very little free-board, and by leaning over the side I could quite easily dip my hands into the water. The hold was apparently quite full, and room therein had only been found for two boxes of hospital stores and one of my tin cases; the other boxes were piled up with sundry merchandise on the deck. The accommodation was certainly not palatial; at one end the captain, Abboussalam Boussin, had a tiny cabin, to enter which was an athletic feat, rewarded on its performance by an intense feeling of nausea, brought on by the smelliness and stuffiness that prevailed therein.

My provisions for the voyage, consisting of a variety of tin foods, a dozen bottles of wine, a supply of bread, some large pots of water and a jar of rum, were put by Ali in as safe a position as he could find.

The crew consisted of a cutthroat-looking lot of Arabs, who, however, improved vastly on acquaintance. A man in gaudy raiment, who might well have just walked out of the cast of the Forty Thieves in a provincial pantomime, was going to join the Turkish Army; a pessimistic-looking individual, dressed in rags, was making a pilgrimage to some holy spot. Altogether, I was not too pleased with the company, and it was not without some misgiving that I saw the *Boudelblous* pushed off from the docks.

Having got nearly outside the harbour, the skipper decided that the wind was not in the right direction; and, whilst eating a frugal lunch, I was annoyed to find the anchor was being lowered. I asked when a fresh start would be made, and got the answer, to which I was rapidly becoming accustomed, " To-morrow, please God." So from midday, until I rolled myself in a blanket for an attempted night's rest, I had nothing to do but promenade up and down the lumber-strewn deck and scrutinize the harbour with my field-glasses. Privacy of course there was none. One ate, slept and washed on the deck. The captain certainly invited me into his hutch once or twice; but there are circumstances even on the most up-to-date liners that render the most luxurious cabins insupportable, and I only once availed myself of the kind offer. Later, however, I was glad I had deposited a suit-case with my papers in a cupboard where Boussin kept his own valuables.

I soon made a most unpleasant discovery about my fellow-passengers, and that was that they nearly all suffered from a form of skin disease which called for vigorous and frequent scratching. The hunting expeditions the Arabs so zealously performed in their robes left little doubt in my mind as to the nature of the complaint; nor indeed was it long before discoveries on my own person clinched the diagnosis.

The next morning I was awakened at daybreak by the creaking of the windlass as the anchor was being drawn up. The wind had freshened in the night, and with the bowsprit turned towards the south the *Boudelblous* began to pitch, roll and toss her way towards Ben-Gardane.

The day opened inauspiciously. An Italian tramp, with rusty plates and screw half out of the water, passed so close to us that the water squirted from her bilges nearly fell on our deck. Some of her men, who no doubt chose the moment of malice aforethought, hoisted a large packing-case on to the rail and pushed it overboard. Our captain, scenting a prize, made for it, but it was only after losing an hour or so in launching the skiff that it was captured and brought on board. Now, the Italian master of a tramp steamer is hardly likely deliberately to throw anything of value overboard; and when I saw the case contained eggs I felt very doubtful as to the utility of those eggs. The next half-hour was spent by the cook and another sailor in religiously cracking the whole lot, one by one, to see if perchance one could be found worthy of the cooking-pot. The smell arising from this proceeding was evil enough, but served to vary somewhat the monotony of the odour that rose from a bale of raw hides piled up near me on the deck.

A few moments later we passed a torpedo-boat running into Sfax; the commander waved me a farewell, at the same time pointing whimsically at the sky. My attention was now called to the performance of a Sudanese nigger on the rusty old pump; and I could not help thinking that, if constant pumping was necessary to keep the ship afloat in fine weather, what would happen if a storm arose? I was quickly to find out!

I am afraid I am rather nervous at sea and see danger too soon; this is, I think, a legacy from the deep impression the stranding of the *Mona's Isle* made upon me when I was a child. We were travelling from Dublin to the Isle of Man on a gloomy, foggy day, and the captain, anxious to get his troublesome cargo ashore for the night, crashed on to the rocks at Castletown. I shall never forget how the boisterous merry-making of the trippers changed to abject terror.

Now, as the day wore on, the sky became more and more overcast, and a thin rain started to fall; the sea became choppy, and the spray began to add to our discomfort. To warm myself a little I tried to make some tea; but the rapidly-rising wind kept putting out the spirit lamp, and the kettle refused to remain on the tripod, owing to the heaving of the deck. At five o'clock the storm began in earnest, when a sudden squall struck the ship, tearing the mizzen to ribbons and bringing down part of the rigging with a crash on to the deck. Although quite near I was fortunate enough to escape serious injury, but for some time after I bore a large bruise on my left shoulder, where I had been struck. The sailors tried to get down the main-sail, but before they were able to get it properly reefed the furious wind tore it from their hands and carried it away. The waves now started to break right over the deck, and in a few minutes we were all drenched to the skin, a state of things, I may add, we were unable to remedy for the next eighteen hours. Night fell rapidly, and the darkness was intense; it was impossible to see anyone even a couple of yards off, and all passing to and fro on the deck had to be done by the sense of touch and with extreme caution. For a time I made my headquarters at the foot of the main-mast, but feeling how it quivered in its socket, and fearing that it might fall at any moment, I abandoned it for anything I could find. Then I clung on to the edge of the tarpaulin nailed over the opening of the hold, but the searching wind even found its way under

STEERSMAN OF THE "BOUDELBLOUS"

ON BOARD THE "BOUDELBLOUS"

To face p. 22

that and threatened to tear it away. It now began to thunder, and the lightning vividly illuminated the scene; St. Elmo's fire played about the mast-head, and the fierce wind moaned and whistled through the tangled rigging. The phosphorescence of the water added a weird touch to the picture, as when the waves dashed against objects on the deck they left for a moment splashes of greenish light.

Meanwhile, my position was not an enviable one. In addition to intense physical discomfort, I was in a state of maddening uncertainty as to the position of things. I could not speak a word of Arabic, and Ali, my interpreter, seemed so stunned by the course of events that he forgot his French and could not answer me coherently. I could see, of course, our position was not a secure one, but to what extent our lives were in danger I did not know. All this time the Sudanese black worked the pump heroically, and I myself was very glad to relieve him from time to time to warm myself, and also to feel that I was doing something to help.

Suddenly all doubt as to our security was banished, and our imminent danger became apparent to all. A heavy sea struck the ship, shaking her violently, and then rolled off, leaving us with such a list that it was difficult to prevent one's self sliding into the sea. The cases piled up on deck hurtled across the ship and pinned down one of the sailors. Attracted by his shrieks, I went to his help and succeeded in releasing him. The captain now shouted an order, and the men began to throw all the merchandise on the deck into the sea. The first thing I threw overboard myself was the bundle of skins whose odour had tormented me all day. The skiff, which was not slung on davits, but merely rested on the deck, was filled with water and helped to maintain the list. A sailor started to bale it out with a small bucket, and I lent a hand with an empty tomato can. But no sooner had we got it fairly empty than a fresh sea swept over us, knocking us both down, and again filling the little boat. In a frenzy the sailor seized an axe and rapidly cut a large hole in the side of the skiff; this afforded efficient drainage, but, at the same time, deprived us of our one hope of safety should the ship have foundered. But what little boat could have lived for a moment in that raging sea?

Seeing that their labours in no way assisted the condition of the ship, the Arabs appeared to abandon hope, and the wail of their prayers could be heard above the noise of the storm. The captain, having placed the tiller in the hands of an old sailor, made his way cautiously towards me and shouted something in Arabic. I shook Ali and asked, " *Qu'est-ce qu'il dit, Ali?* " and I got the answer back pat, " *Dans quelques moments nous serons au Paradis!* "

My only answer to this disconcerting piece of news was to burst out laughing, and I presume Abboussalam thought I was going mad. The fact is that I had always been terrified at the idea of getting drowned, and now I stood in imminent danger of it and found that I was enjoying the whole experience immensely, I expressed my pleasure by laughing.

At all events, I made my preparations for the last round with the elements. Piled up on the deck were some stout planks that had not been washed overboard;

to one of these I bound my revolver belt, overcoat and water-bottle, then, stripping to my underclothes, I was ready for the final plunge. Seeing that the Arabs were no longer working the pump, I seized the handle and laboured it violently, so violently in fact that the sores on my hands reminded me of the incident even after I had got safely to land.

The Arabs continued to shout their prayers, and I am not ashamed to say I joined loudly in the chorus. It seemed a relief to shout; and after all there is something very comforting about a prayer. Absurd and impertinent as it seems to expect the harmony of the celestial mechanism to be dislocated for the purpose of saving your own poor life, the words rush to the lips, "Help us, O Lord!" If the intense degree of hoarseness I suffered from the next day be a correct index of the warmth of my petitions, I must have prayed with considerable fervour the night of the storm.

As I worked the pump, a sudden flash of lightning showed me the staring faces of the Arabs as they squatted, wrapped in their blankets, round the stern of the boat, and I thought that in their glance I detected an element of contempt—contempt that fear of death should so drive a man that he should continue to struggle against the plain decree of God. Sometimes it is necessary to bow to other people's ideas of conduct, so I abandoned the pump and lay down on the sloping deck shivering with cold, for in the darkness I was quite unable to find the clothing I had discarded. I was hoping that dawn was not very far off, and I managed to get a glimpse at the watch on my wrist during the lightning. How merciless time can be! I had hoped for dawn, and the hands pointed to half-past nine!

For a time the waves gained in size, and their strength, which appeared about to destroy us, probably saved our lives. We sank into a deep valley of water, then rose on the crest of a wave. We hung on with might and main while the sea swept foaming over us. Another shudder shook the ship and—once again the brave little craft sat upright on the waters! The Arabs, who took this as a direct intervention of Providence —who knows?—sprang feverishly to work, yelling out a hymn of praise. I can safely say the sweetest music I ever heard in my life was the creaking of the rusty pump as the Sudanese got to work, for it told me that once again I might expect to walk the streets of London.

I noticed Ali's efforts at praying had been distinctly half-hearted. Perhaps he had been listening to the disputations of the missionaries in Tunisia, who had shaken his faith in the creed of his fathers, without convincing him of the truth of the new one. Now, however, his faith came back to him with a rush, and, waving a hand towards an imaginary shore, he exclaimed triumphantly, " And there are people there who say there is no God!"

Boussin, as well as being a skilful and courageous seaman, was a very religious man and placed all confidence in his creed. The next day he said to me quite simply, " God touched the ship with His Hand and pushed her straight upon the waters."

I was cold, shivering and miserable, my teeth

chattering like castanets. I emptied a small pocket-flask of rum at a gulp and managed to struggle into my overcoat, which although it was soaking afforded some protection from the piercing wind. At the commencement of the storm I had pushed a large sleeping-bag under a tarpaulin on the deck, and after a few minutes' groping I found it; to my intense joy it was still fairly dry. Dog-tired, I crawled into it and found it deliciously warm. Then, lying down by the mast, with my arm round some of the rigging, heedless of wet and cold, I fell asleep. When I woke up it was still raining; and the spray was continually washing the deck. I could hardly move my joints, so stiff were they with wet and cold; but a glance at the sky banished all thoughts of discomfort. For a space the heavy curtain of clouds had been withdrawn, and part of the oldest picture-book in the world could be seen. The Hunter after his eternal prey had swarmed high into the meridian, dragging with him Sirius, straining at the leash. When I saw the throbbing, pulsating light of the Dog-Star, well above the horizon, I knew that dawn could not be far off, and, comforted in mind, I again sank into sleep.

When I opened my eyes, the storm had quite cleared and the sun was trying to break through the clouds. The captain beckoned to me from his hutch, and with creaking joints I managed to get there. He handed me a tin mug of hot steaming coffee that he had brewed in his cabin. When in the interior of South America, we used to talk fondly of the delights of the iced whisky and soda that could be obtained on the Orinoco steamboat when on the way home, but this drink of thick, sweet, muddy coffee will ever linger in my memory as the most delicious thing I ever tasted.

There was, unfortunately, no means of getting rid of our wet clothes, as everything that had not gone overboard was soaked through; so we had to wait patiently until the sun saw fit to shine before we could get dry and warm. Meanwhile the captain told me that, considering the state of the dhow, it would be out of the question to make for Ben-Gardane, and he proposed to return to Sfax to refit. To this I cordially agreed, for it would have been folly for me to have plunged into Tripolitana without a fresh outfit and without renewing the medical stores we had been forced to throw overboard.

At last the sun blazed out and for a time we were all happy, a state of things that obtained until the sun climbed high into the sky, when we began to suffer from intense heat. Later we were able to rig up a rough awning with a portion of a sail, but this got blown down before it had been very long erected.

The danger of death from drowning having passed, I commenced to look round and see what was left of my stores. I had lost practically all my clothing with the exception of a few garments, packed in what had been sold as a watertight uniform case, but nevertheless nothing in this box had escaped the attention of the sea-water. More important, however, was the complete loss of provisions, with cooking-pots, canteen and water-jars. For the rest of the voyage I was forced to drink the dirty, muddy water out of the common cask. At first I had to be very thirsty before I drank this water, on account of the habits of my fellow-travellers. An Arab would go to the cask, take out the stopper, push a grimy hand through the hole and fish about in the water for the dipper. The dipper was then used as a drinking-cup, and any surplus not consumed was returned to the cask. The food was little better. Fortunately, there was plenty of Arab bread saved, and I lived on this for the next six days, although I could not touch it before it had been well toasted. At its best, the brown, sodden Arab bread is not appetizing, but after it has been kept for a while it becomes almost uneatable. At times the captain invited me to sit down with him and share his platter, but my appetite always vanished after I had witnessed the operations of the cook. He was accustomed to wash the wooden bowl, out of which everyone ate, in a bucket which also served as a toilet basin for anyone who wished to cleanse his hands or feet.

The last day, however, I felt tremendously hungry, and the savoury smell of the food conquered my squeamishness, and I sat down on the deck opposite Boussin and ate a hearty meal of macaroni with my fingers. Given another week on the *Boudelblous* and I could have eaten anything put before me; so soon do the demands of nature whittle away our conventional ideas.

From time to time we passed other small boats, and the captain offered to put me on to one proceeding to Sfax, as on account of our crippled condition we were making very slow headway; but I had no desire to exchange the unknown for the known, so although the discomforts were very great I determined to stick to the *Boudelblous*. It rained nearly every night, and all

on board got drenched, whilst every afternoon we
suffered from the merciless rays of the sun. A minor
annoyance was that all my papers and books had gone
overboard, and I had nothing to read except a pocket
edition of Byron's *Childe Harold*. My great-grand-
father saved Lord Byron from death by drowning, and
the poet now repaid the debt by saving me from dying
of ennui. Later Boussin fished out of his cabin a life
of Marat, which proved very interesting. It was an
old book written by a red-hot Republican, and painted
the Friend of the People as an angel of light, instead
of the ferocious butcher one is brought up to consider
him.

On the seventh day after our departure we ran into
Sfax (to quote the *Dépêche Tunisienne*) " in a most
pitiable state," and I experienced the greatest pleasure
in exchanging the heaving deck of the dhow for dry
land. My costume on landing attracted a good deal of
attention. All I had left of a fairly extensive wardrobe
was the lower part of a pyjama suit, a linen coat that
had once been white, a pair of slippers and a battered
straw hat. Fortunately, I had also saved my overcoat;
so with this covering a multitude of sins I slunk up
the back streets to the hotel. I had, however, to pass
the Café de la Régence, where all Sfax was gathered
drinking the morning *apéritif*. Although some friends
of the week before stared very hard at me, I was not
recognised, and when I stood before a glass in the hotel
I saw the reason why. I had lost greatly in weight,
and those parts of my face not covered by a week's
scrubby growth of beard were burnt brick-red by the
sun.

Thanks to the assistance of a few good friends and my own foresight in leaving a stock of clothes at the hotel, I was able to make myself presentable enough to appear for lunch. Once I had enjoyed a good meal and had a decent suit of clothes on my back, I commenced to count up the gains and losses of the week spent on the *Boudelblous.*

With the exception of the stores, that were fully insured, I had lost nothing, personally, that a month or two's work could not replace. I had lost, indeed, some superfluous flesh, and the pasty drawing-room complexion I had brought from London. I had learned that if lunch does not appear at one o'clock sharp and dinner at seven-thirty, one can very well do without them.

CHAPTER II.

On taking my seat in the café for the evening *apéritif*, it was not long before I noticed that I was an object of interest to the other clients, and I naturally supposed that the story of our adventurous cruise had got round and was exciting some interest. I was soon joined by Mr. William Leonardi, who after congratulating me on my escape told me that it was rumoured in the town that we had been chased by Italian cruisers, that we had had to make for French waters to avoid being captured, and we had deliberately thrown the cases overboard because they really contained contraband of war. Why it was not alleged that we had deliberately raised the storm also I really do not know.

It was, of course, highly amusing; but next morning, when I went to the docks to get my few remaining goods, I found that this extraordinary yarn was believed by the otherwise sane Custom House officials, and it was several days before I was allowed to take my things to the hotel, and that only after they had been probed and searched to the very bottom. So thorough was the search that a pocket spectacle case was carefully scrutinized, although as I pointed out to *M. le*

Receveur, who had presumably done his military service, it was scarcely possible to conceal any appreciable number of either rifles or cartridges in so small a compass. Taking it in all, France has no reason to complain of the zeal of her Corsican Custom officials.

While I merely suffered inconvenience and annoyance, poor Boussin was put to considerable expense by the authorities, as he had to empty his boat completely to show that he had nothing of a contraband nature on board. He seemed, however, highly satisfied that he had escaped with his life, and, looking upon the storm as a warning from above, he sold the *Boudelblous;* in any case the ship would have required extensive repairs before she would have been fit to go to sea again.

After dinner I had a long conversation with a journalist at the café, and the next day I found long articles in the press dealing with the voyage and the annoyances I had had to put up with, owing to the denunciation of the Italian agents. It seemed that the good people of Sfax and Tunis were getting very tired of the antics of these agents, and my troubles served as a text for pressmen in the Protectorate on which to base articles urging the Government to deal drastically with the nuisance. The *Courier de Tunis* came out with a striking article which was most appropriately headed " Un Coup de Balai, s.v.p." In consequence of these protests I was told that several of the more prominent of these informers received their marching orders.

For the few days I remained in Sfax I enjoyed considerable fame, and no sooner did I sit down on the terrace of the café than a small crowd of Arabs would gather in the road and gaze at me in an embarrassing fashion.

While waiting for the fresh supply of stores I passed a very happy time in Sfax. I spent the days in exploring the country round about, while in the evenings we played bridge at the café, enjoyed the open-air cinema at the *Bar Algérien*, or took a stroll round the sights of the native town.

Having received a wire from Baron de Kusel, who kindly watched the Society's interests at Tunis, that my goods would arrive by an afternoon train, I took a passage for myself and Ali on the *Tavignano*, a boat which coasted regularly between Tunis, Sfax and El Biban, from which latter port I should have to re-embark on a small boat for Ben-Gardane. The afternoon train arrived, but there was no sign of my goods, and I began to get anxious, as the boat sailed that evening at midnight. I was reassured, however, by a wire that they were coming on by a later train. This proved to be correct, and by hurrying I found that I should just have time to get them on board. I met the cases at the station, and was accompanying them to the docks, when a man jumped out of a sort of sentry-box and, informing me that he was the *octroi* authority, asked if I had any alcohol in the luggage. After all I had suffered at the hands of various officials, this was the last straw. Fortunately, my French had gained not only in fluency but also in a command of a more extensive vocabulary, so I was able to put my case before this official in forcible and appropriate language. After this outburst he let me through without further discussion.

On arrival on board I found the accommodation little better than that on the *Boudelblous*. As there were no cabins provided for the passengers, we all had to spend the night on the deck, which apparently had not been washed down for a long time. The filthy condition of the boat, the reek of the engines and the lack of comfort made the trip one of the most unpleasant I have ever undertaken.

We reached El Biban after about eighteen hours' steaming, but on account of the shallows the boat was unable to get nearer than six miles off the shore, so we were forced to tranship into a small sailing-boat. The sea was rather rough, and the boat that had come alongside to take us ashore was bobbing up and down like a cork, and in the darkness the jump from the rail of the *Tavignano* on to the deck of the dhow below was no easy task. Considerable confusion reigned during the transference of the cargo, the noisy shouting of the Arabs making the orders of the ship's officers almost inaudible.

After a wet and unpleasant sail of about two hours we reached the shore, where I was warmly greeted by the manager of the fish-canning business that is carried on there. This gentleman very kindly invited me to his house, where he gave me a good supper and made me comfortable for the night; at least the bed was soft and well sprung; but as I had to share it with an army corps of voracious bed-fellows, I soon had to abandon the position and sleep upon the floor.

Early in the morning I was prepared for another few hours' journey in a sailing-boat, but after breakfast I found my host had already given orders for his motor

launch to be got ready to take me across the lagoon
to the landing-place for Ben-Gardane. After an hour
in the motor boat we arrived and found the little quay
buzzing with life. Several sailing-boats had just arrived
with provisions for the Turkish Army, and the Arabs
were busy unloading them. It was only after much
difficulty that I was able to get a cart to take me into
the town. The vehicle provided was a primitive enough
concern, innocent of springs and awning. The sun was
very hot, and I was very pleased when the journey
came to an end in front of the Hôtel des Colonies at
Ben-Gardane. This hotel could not be called first-
class even by its warmest admirers; but the proprietor,
François Galea, and his good wife showed me every
attention and made me thoroughly comfortable during
my stay with them.

Unfortunately, the rooms swarmed with fleas and
other parasites, whilst on two occasions large scorpions
were captured under my bed. These pests, however,
were only a minor annoyance compared with the plague
of flies which was visiting Ben-Gardane at the time
of my arrival. In the bar they advanced in companies
to dispute possession of a glass of beer; in the dining-
room they descended upon the table in battalions the
moment they saw a meal about to be served. If one
endeavoured to entrap them with fly-papers, they
revenged themselves by committing suicide by myriads
in the soup and coffee. An enterprising, energetic and
painstaking tribe of bread-winners were these common
house flies of Ben-Gardane.

As typhoid fever was prevalent at this time in the
town, I took the precaution of boiling my drinking

water. I was engaged in this task one morning when a French war correspondent, just back from the front, eyed me curiously and asked me what I was doing with the kettle. I informed him, whereupon he became exceedingly anxious for my welfare. It seems he had warned the doctors of the German Red Crescent Mission against the practice of boiling water, and in consequence of their ignoring his advice they had lost a large percentage of their number from typhoid and cholera. To this cheerful news he added the fact that only a few weeks before a party of journalists had arrived in the town for the purpose of proceeding into Tripoli, and on hearing of the prevalence of disease there had speedily returned home. Not wishing to hear any more of this sort of news, I asked him how he had managed to keep so well. He informed me that he had escaped all infection by the simple plan of never drinking water until he had added a small quantity of absinthe. This reminded me at once of an American prospector whom I met some years ago in a fever-stricken town in South America. He claimed my acquaintance in the *posada*, and getting more and more confidential as the rum sank in the bottle, he at length decided to confide to me, for the benefit of suffering humanity, the secret of avoiding all sorts of tropical fevers. The formula had been bequeathed to him by an old Californian miner on his death-bed. I still have the greasy bit of paper on which the American wrote it out, and I give it here for the benefit of travellers : " Put two grains of quinine into a bottleful of Scotch whisky. Drink one wineglassful four times a day." The superstition that alcohol kills disease germs is strangely prevalent in tropical and sub-tropical countries. Considering the large amount of stimulants drunk by Europeans in these lands, surely disease would have been entirely banished had there been any truth in the belief.

Before lunch the Frenchman and I adjourned to the bar to put his theory to the test, and I had a friendly dispute with him as to who should pay. We agreed to leave it to chance, whereupon, much to my surprise, he called for two new fly-papers, which he placed before us on the table. The one who had caught the most at the sound of the luncheon bell was the winner.

After lunch I went round to the correspondent's house for coffee, and was astonished to find he had brought his young wife with him from Paris to this desolate spot, reeking as it did of all sorts of diseases and discomforts. The devotion of women at times amazes me. This lady shrugged her dainty shoulders at all sorts of inconveniences for the sake of being with her husband; yet if she cheerfully risked life in doing so, I could not help noticing she never even crossed the little courtyard without sheltering her complexion from the hot sun. Personally, I do not think it right to take young and beautiful women into the dark places of the world. Who would consider it right to hide the treasures of the National Gallery or the Louvre in a dirty hovel?

As I could not cross the frontier without a permit from the French Resident, I had to pay him a visit. He was politeness and consideration itself; he brushed all difficulties aside. I told him I had great difficulty in getting camels at a reasonable price. He touched a bell and gave a sharp order to the answering Arab. I had not brought a saddle, and found it very difficult to get comfortable in the native ones. He immediately offered to find me one. Was I very uncomfortable at the hotel? If so, he would put me up. Small wonder that during the period of the war Lieutenant Desevaux won the esteem and gratitude of all foreigners passing through Ben-Gardane, and by his sympathetic treatment of many delicate matters earned well-deserved promotion from his Government.

The few days passed pleasantly enough at Ben-Gardane, and had it not been for a desire to get to the scene of action as soon as possible I should have been well content to have remained a few days longer. Soon, however, I received news that a large caravan was starting the next day, so I arranged to have the camels at the hotel at daybreak, knowing by giving this order they would arrive some time in the morning.

Camels are the ugliest and most obstinate beasts of burden it is possible to imagine. The loading-up is usually a wearisome task. They are encouraged to kneel down by the drivers making a hoarse guttural noise; if this does not have the desired effect, obedience is enforced by blows upon the knees. They sink down grumbling and grunting, and usually continue complaining until the heavy burdens are adjusted by the Arabs. Should, however, the camel think he is being imposed upon, he is apt to jump up in the middle of the loading, and down come the heavy cases crashing to the ground, to the imminent danger of all standing around.

After the usual disputes incidental upon starting a

journey with camels, the caravan was ready to proceed;
but as the man I had engaged to look after my horse
had not turned up, I sent Ali on ahead with the camels
and remained behind to take a stirrup-cup with the
crowd who had gathered to see me off.

At length my man, Youssuf, turned up; and a fine
truculent ruffian he looked. He carried an ancient
Springfield rifle, the cartridges for which were in a
bandolier round his chest; his other arms consisted of
a French sword bayonet and a flint-lock pistol. This
cheered me up considerably, as there is always
adventure to be had in a country where the men
go armed.

After half an hour's trot we came up with the camels,
and I found to my annoyance that they had halted and
the Arabs were already taking off the packs. Through
Ali I asked the head camel-driver what he meant by
such conduct. He replied that the camels were still
tired after their last journey; that he purposed camping
there until morning, when at daybreak we would start
again, please God. As I was not disposed to waste
half a day sitting on a packing-case in the middle of
the desert, I ordered him to proceed at once; but
probably as Ali, who was no more energetic than the
rest of his race, did not interpret correctly—as he
seemed afraid of the other Arabs—no move was made
to reload the camels. I thought it would be foolish
to allow my authority to be flouted so early in the
game, so mounting again I galloped back to town and
told my woes to the French officer. He immediately
gave orders to his *chouach* (sergeant) to accompany me
and put matters right. The *chouach* proved somewhat

autocratic in manner, and rapped out orders to the camel-drivers in an offensive tone. I have rarely seen camels loaded quicker than these were, and I have never parted with a five-franc piece with greater pleasure than when I bestowed one upon this excellent *sous-officier*.

We purposed reaching the frontier post at nightfall, but experiencing great difficulty in restraining my horse to the two-mile-an-hour walk of the camels, I foolishly signed to Youssuf that he and I should ride on ahead. He was by no means unwilling, and spurring his horse with the sharp edge of his native stirrup, we started off in front at a good pace. After we had been about three hours in the saddle, the sky clouded over, and it became almost impossible to see the track across the sand. Frequently Youssuf had to dismount to see that we were still on the road.

This was my first day on the desert, and my lack of experience had led me into being deceived by the heat of the day. Consequently, for the sake of riding light, I had left my cape and blankets with the camels, so that when it began to rain in torrents I was soon soaked through. Youssuf now, I noticed, was steering entirely by the flash of the Italian searchlights that were being operated vigorously from one of their forts on the littoral. Suddenly my guide stopped and motioned me to halt. He dismounted, charged his Springfield with an enormous cartridge, and then came up to me, speaking in Arabic. The only words I could follow were "Give me." This much I had learned on the *Boudelblous*. What did he want? A sudden thought struck me that he was demanding money with menaces, and for a moment or two I felt very uneasy. Then he took my hand and made a motion of scratching something on the palm. It dawned upon me at last that he wanted matches, and I handed him a box, which fortunately had kept dry. I could not help laughing at my foolish mistake, and with the ready intelligence of his race Youssuf saw the cause of my merriment and grinned broadly. It seemed he wanted the matches to look at the ground to see if we were still on the road. After this little incident Youssuf and I became quite good friends.

Night had now fallen, and it became very cold. I was feeling miserable, and looking eagerly forward to a warm camp-fire and something hot to drink, when suddenly I found my guide had completely lost his bearing; for whereas, an hour before, the Italian search-lights had been very properly on our left, they were now sweeping the desert to our right. It was not a pleasant situation, lost on the plain with an Arab who could not speak a word of English; soaked to the skin, shivering with cold, and with little prospect of getting under shelter for the night. We stumbled along for an hour or more, when Youssuf's sharp eyes sighted a camp-fire about a mile off. We rode up to within fifty yards of it, when my guide dismounted and approached cautiously with his rifle at the ready. I must confess I also loosened my revolver in the holster. Had I known what later experience taught me I should probably have carried it in my hand.

The Arabs in the encampment invited us to approach the fire, and proved to be hospitable fellows. They made me several glasses of hot tea, and one of them cooked a sort of pancake over the cinders. Possibly because

I was unable to see clearly what I was eating or drinking I made an excellent meal.   I was then invited into the tent, but being as yet unaccustomed to the fœtid atmosphere that obtains in a low-class Arab's tent on a wet night, I preferred to remain outside, although it was still raining slightly.   Luckily, before starting I had put a large blanket under the saddle; so after Youssuf had fed and hobbled the horses, I wrapped myself in this, and with the saddle for a pillow lay down, and was soon fast asleep.   At daybreak we saddled up, and after a sharp two hours' ride caught up with the camels at the frontier post, where I found Ali had some hot coffee ready.   Breakfast disposed of, I delivered my permit to the *sous-officier* of the Spahis, and in a short time our caravan was treading the soil of Tripolitana.

CHAPTER III.

APPROACHED from the Tunisian frontier, Tripolitana does not give one the impression that it is a country worth fighting about. We marched along over hills of sand and down into valleys of sand. No vegetation could be seen, but always the same barren, sterile sand; sand, sand, and more sand. Surely no one could be quarrelling about this desert; but a loud booming sound from time to time came from the direction of the sea, where the enemy cruisers were spending the taxes wrung from an impoverished people in an endeavour to kill an alien peasantry, whose only crime was that the sand was their poor fatherland and they wished to live on it and have it administered according to their own ideas.

The morning was very hot, and I was beginning to long for some shelter from the fierce sun, when Youssuf pointed out to me a glittering speck far off on the horizon. It was the Turkish camp of El Assa, the western end of their long line of defence. Situated as it was not more than a few kilometres from the sea-coast and guarding the high road from Tunisia, I naturally expected to find a large number of well-equipped soldiers there, but I was astonished when I discovered that the garrison consisted of three officers,

A HALT ON THE ROAD

THE ROAD TO RAPTA

To face p. 44

half a dozen Turkish soldiers and perhaps fifty Arabs. The officers made me very welcome, and provided me with a tent spread with mats and carpets. As they had already taken their midday meal, they ordered the cook to send me in some food, and then, with the true hospitality and good sense that animates them, they saw that I wanted a rest, so left me to my own devices, after giving me an invitation to dine at the mess in the evening.

After lunch I had a delicious siesta in the cool tent, and then dressed to take a stroll round the camp. The news that a foreign doctor had arrived soon spread among the Arabs, and on opening the tent-flap I found about thirty men, women and children squatting down outside awaiting my assistance. With Ali's help as an interpreter I did what I could for them, and at all events sent them away satisfied.

The centre of life in this little camp was a small stone and plaster building, which was used as an office, and into which the telegraph wire from the French frontier ran. Here all the news from the outside world entered Western Tripolitana, and was then telegraphed on to the Turkish Headquarters at Azizia. Outside, piled up against the wall, was a mass of prehistoric arms left by the Arabs of the last caravan, who had gone to Ben-Gardane to bring back foodstuffs, as the French authorities did not permit the Tripolitan Arabs to enter Tunisia armed. Properly ticketed and arranged, this heap of arms would have been an ornament to any museum. Here were flint-lock pistols and guns, bell-mouthed blunderbusses and ancient shot-guns; revolvers in the first stage of their evolution and ancient, rusty rifles. These were the first samples I saw of the arms with which the Arabs had kept at bay the large army that was now endeavouring to take their country from them.

At sundown the Commandant sent an orderly to summon me to dinner, which was served in the little house. There were no chairs, and all sat down on the carpeted floor. A soldier placed on a small round table, which stood a few inches from the floor, a variety of dishes containing sardines, olives, small portions of fish and such like; a large platter with bread cut into slices was then added. My Moslem hosts then gave proof of their broadmindedness by getting out a bottle of *anisette* and another of *absinthe*, strictly, of course, for the benefit of their Christian guest. As I was very hungry, I vigorously attacked the victuals; and it was only after making an excellent meal that I discovered that these dainties were only the *hors-d'œuvres* of the dinner, which was to be served half an hour later. As I could not do proper justice to the more substantial food when it arrived, I made full confession of my ignorance of Turkish customs, and we all laughed heartily over my mistake.

My hosts, who all spoke French fluently and with some degree of correctness, were excellent fellows, and we sat up until a late hour talking over all sorts of things. As the night was wet and cold, I was invited to sleep in the house with the telegraphist, who lay down beside his instrument. I made a comfortable bed on the floor with a couple of blankets, and was soon fast asleep. My slumber, however, was not destined to be uninterrupted for long, for I was soon awakened by the loud buzz of excited conversation in the room. The three officers were grouped round the telegraphist, who was interpreting to them the oscillations of his instrument. A cold wind blew in through the open door, and by the light of the lamp I could see the faces of the Turkish soldiers pressing forward to catch the news. At length the instrument ceased work, and the operator leaned back and gazed at the officers. Some important news had evidently arrived, and taking advantage of a lull in the conversation, I ventured to ask what was the matter. Montenegro had declared war against Turkey! Seeing an opportunity in the embarrassment of Turkey in Northern Africa, the allied monarchs had fallen on their ancient enemy and commenced that atrocious orgy of butchery, rapine and plunder that was destined to devastate the Balkan States for so many weary months.

To me, of course, the news was of little moment, but to those who had so kindly entertained me it was everything. Two of them, I learned later, came from close to the Bulgarian frontier. How they must have suffered during the next few weeks! Unable to strike a blow for their loved ones; unable even to get news that they were safe. Tortured, day by day, as the newspapers came to hand, with accounts of the terrible atrocities the allied troops were committing on the Turkish villagers; their own wives and daughters perhaps in the hands of ravishers and murderers; their houses burned down and their lands laid waste by a brutal soldiery. Yet they stood it all with a noble calm, and carried out their duties with a simple devotion it was touching to witness. I had always imagined

there was some subtle and essential difference between
Turk and Christian that friendship could not bridge,
but during the months I spent in Tripoli I learned that
the Crescent floats over men similar to ourselves, and
it became more and more difficult for me to believe
that these brave, courteous and chivalrous gentlemen,
so moderate and humane in the days of victory, could
have been guilty of the acts of blind and unreasoning
cruelty which have so often been laid to their charge.
They have had in their outlying provinces a turbulent
population to discipline, professing different creeds and
animated by that bitter hatred of each other which we
so often see amongst the warring sects at home. Doubtless at times the Turks have had to suppress disorder
with a stern hand, and partisan accounts of these
measures to preserve order have been worked up by
sections of the press, ever ready to discredit the
Ottoman Empire, in such a way that they have appeared
to the world at large as acts of oppression and cruelty.
Have we not often been blinded by religious prejudice
and listened to hostile accounts and not given due
weight to the Moslem side? Allowing for the moment
that, acting under intense provocation, excesses have
been committed, have the soldiers of the Sultan ever
been guilty of worse crimes than those that the King
of Greece laid to the charge of the Bulgarians? Could
the Turks have perpetrated more hideous atrocities
than those of which Ferdinand of Bulgaria roundly
accused the Greeks and Serbians?

As the Commandant at El Assa provided me with
a gendarme, I was able to send back Youssuf, who
had not hit it off at all well with the Tripolitan Arabs.

Not to put too fine a point upon it, he seemed afraid of them, and was little disposed to back me up when there was any disagreement in the caravan.

I started the camels off at daybreak, and followed with the gendarme about an hour later, after a cordial farewell to my hosts of the previous night. We quickly overtook the camels, and after seeing that they were coming along at a good pace, my guide and I trotted on ahead. After a hot journey over the sand we arrived early in the afternoon at the camp of Accrobia. This I found was a fairly large encampment, with the tents pitched in a large hollow in the ground. On one side a Turkish sergeant had a long line of Arabs drawn up in front of him, to whom he was endeavouring to impart the elements of drill.

Seeing the Red Crescent floating over the hospital tent, I rode up and asked for the medical officer in charge. After a few minutes a gentleman in shirt sleeves appeared at the tent door, and was sufficiently introduced by the odour of iodoform that hung about him. He proved to be Dr. Husni of the Turkish Red Crescent Society, and, having ascertained that I was a *confrère*, he made me very welcome and placed a tent at my disposal. Husni, who had been in Paris, and spoke French with facility, was an interesting conversationalist, and we passed the hours before dinner chatting in his tent.

Having noted the Turkish liking for *hors-d'œuvres*, I opened my cases, and was able to add to the repast with some delicacies from Sfax. Fortified by dinner, we went into the hospital tent, and for the next two hours were busy with the sick and wounded. Several cases needed operation, so we put them on the table, and, taking turn and turn about with chloroform bottle and scalpel, the evening—for us—passed quickly and pleasantly. Then feeling tired after my long day, I intimated a desire to go to sleep. My colleague thereupon urged me to take his bed. To this, however, I would not agree, and proceeded to make myself comfortable on the floor. Before we settled off to sleep, he showed me a large bottle full of small snakes and scorpions, including a venomous horned viper. I duly admired the collection, and then idly demanded where he had killed them. His answer that he had caught them all in his tent made me sorry that I had so firmly refused his offer of the bed. Sleep, however, quickly freed me from any childish fears.

After morning coffee Dr. Husni took me for a stroll round the camp, and introduced me to the Commandant, a fine-looking Turk with a well-kept beard and a splendid set of teeth. He was unable to speak French, but conversed fluently in German, a language with which I was not then familiar, so I was forced to call upon my colleague to interpret. The Commandant paid me the usual undeserved compliments, constantly touching the border of his fez as a salute. He then asked me if I would care to go and visit the outposts with him; but, dearly as I should have liked to, I had to decline as I was expected in Zavia the next day. Husni and I then climbed to the top of a hillock, and with the help of glasses I was able to see the fort erected by the Italians on the coast. The palms of the oasis, near which this fort was erected, could easily be made out, and from time to time a puff of smoke,

followed by the booming of a gun, could be seen.
I turned to the doctor for an explanation. It seemed
that at times the Arabs would steal into the oasis to
get a handful of dates, and on being sighted from the
fort the gunners would send a shell or two after them.
As Husni put it, they were firing a £20 shell at an
Arab who was cutting a pennyworth of dates.

As we were sitting chatting, a long string of Arabs
filed past us, carrying all sorts of booty. There had
been a skirmish near the coast the day before, in which
the Arabs had been victorious, and now they were
returning with the spoil. They bore all sorts of
equipment—boots, uniforms, valises and haversacks.
Some had been fortunate enough to get hold of a rifle
or a sword; others emptied their bundles on the sand
in front of us, and showed a miscellaneous collection
of objects looted from the Italians' valises and pockets.
There were picture postcards, letters received from
wives and children who were hopefully waiting in some
Tuscan village the return of a father or a husband.
There were photographs too; one of a sweet-looking
woman with two little children. This I bought from
the Arab who owned it—I scarcely liked to see it in
unfriendly hands. I said farewell to Husni, and accompanied by my gendarme I set out for Ajilat, expecting
to reach there at sundown. My guide, however, was
not an energetic man, and, taking advantage of my lack
of knowledge of Arabic, insisted on halting frequently
by the wayside—at one time to light a cigarette, at
another to ask for a glass of tea at some Arab tent, or
to pass the time of day with wayfarers. As a consequence of these unnecessary halts, it was dark before

we reached the oasis, and the Commandant was already at dinner when I drew rein outside his residence. He got up from his meal and came out and greeted me, at the same time asking me at what time we had left Accrobia. I told him, whereupon he turned to the gendarme and asked him in Arabic what I imagined to be a query as to why we were so late in reaching the town. I caught the gendarme's reply—" *El hakim forsa mafish.*" Well, I knew that "*hakim*" meant "doctor," that "*forsa*" was similar to our English word "force," and one could not be many hours amongst the Tripolitan Arabs without finding out that "*mafish*" means "there is not any." So putting it all together I figured it out that my guide was libelling me to the Turkish officer in an expression equivalent to saying, "The doctor can't ride for nuts!" At this I must confess to having been rather annoyed, as one of the few things I venture to be proud of is a certain aptitude for covering long distances in the saddle without fatigue. However, I let it pass for the moment, and joined the Commandant and three other officers at dinner.

The news of the outbreak of war in the Balkans had evidently been telegraphed on to them, for the conversation at mess was of little else. They appeared to consider the allies much more formidable enemies than their present opponents, whose initiative and courage they held at a very low figure. However, as I wanted to be off early next morning, I did not sit up late, and I was shown into a comfortable room, which despite my protestations one of the officers insisted on vacating for me.

The pleasant evening I had spent with the Turks did not make me oblivious of the grave reflections the gendarme had cast upon my staying powers, and when he arrived in front of the barracks at daybreak I was not sorry to see him looking thoroughly out of condition; this state supervening upon an almost all-night sitting at a marriage celebration. He kindly suggested to the Commandant that to Zavia was rather a long stage for the foreign doctor, and thought it would be a good plan to pass the night at Suruman and get to Zavia the next morning. Despite this touching consideration for me, the Commandant, at my suggestion, made him thoroughly to understand that nightfall was to see me at my destination.

As I had a bundle of letters to deliver to my British colleague, who was in charge of the Blue Hospital then situated at Hadj Khalifa, and finding that this spot was only two hours' ride, we left the Zavia road at right angles and struck south. At Hadj Khalifa we made a light meal, and having admired the order and military precision in Mr. Turnbull's camp, we made across country to Suruman. Our journey was a monotonous one over the eternal sand, and a head wind that sprang up added to our discomfort. The gendarme covered up his face with his blanket, and I was glad to put on spectacles to keep the drifting particles of sand out of my eyes. About two o'clock we rode into the *bourgade* of Suruman, where I had the horses unsaddled and fed, while my guide and I took coffee with the *chaouch* in the *Gendarmerie*. A large number of sick and wounded gathered in front of the house, and as I was without an interpreter and only had a small case of medicines in my holster, I had hard work to send them all away in good humour.

At this period my Arabic consisted of a few essential words and the invaluable phrase, " Take one three times a day." I am afraid I did not enhance my reputation as a physician there, but one man certainly owes the use of his right arm to my chance visit. He had been wounded by a rifle bullet in the upper arm and had been treated by the local *hakim*, who had kept the limb immovable so long that adhesions had formed in the shoulder joint which prevented him raising his arm or even feeding himself with that hand. Before he could realise what I was about to do I manipulated the limb vigorously and freed the joint. His cries brought a large crowd together, and the last thing I saw as we trotted out of the town was my Arab patient proudly holding his erstwhile crippled limb high up in the air before an admiring audience.

From Suruman to Zavia the road lay across the desert and through scattered oases, and the journey became more pleasant after the monotony of our morning spent entirely upon the sand. Here and there we met mounted Turkish officers, who stopped me and anxiously asked for news of the situation in the Balkans, a matter of which I was as ignorant as they were. Constantly interrupted in this manner, I did not get into the market-place at Zavia until night had begun to fall. Here I had an unpleasant surprise. A Turkish officer came up and spoke to me and invited me to take coffee. I told him I did not wish to dismount, as I wanted to get to the British Hospital before it was quite dark. He then told me that, owing to the recent activity of the Italians, our hospital had been moved back into the desert to a place called Bir-Zenoba, which lay about a two hours' journey from Zavia.

I announced my intention of riding straight on, but to this the small group of Turks who had gathered round would not agree, and it ended in my going to their quarters and sharing a frugal meal with them.

We dined in European fashion with the table erected in the courtyard of the house. After the meal, despite the wishes of my hosts, who offered to put me up for the night, I sent the soldier who had waited on us to tell my gendarme to saddle up. He, however, had had sufficient exercise for one day, for I had succeeded in my plan of tiring him out, and he sent me word that he could not go on any farther, as he had found his mother lying very ill. Later on in the campaign, after I had been frequently given this excuse, I began to think that the Arabs were inclined to be rather too solicitous over the health of their relations, much as I honoured them for being such good sons; but I found out that this excuse was always given when they wanted to get out of going anywhere, and the fact that the supposed sick person was always a woman made it impossible to verify their statements. Two local gendarmes were then given me to guide me to Bir-Zenoba, one of whom had to help me to mount, as I was rather stiff after the long ride.

The night was very dark, and as soon as we got out of the oasis on to the desert it became very difficult to see the paths. My guides apparently steered by the searchlights directed from the Italian fort at Sidi Billal.

Soon after our departure from Zavia we crossed a group of hillocks of soft sand, and as my horse was making the descent of one of them he suddenly stumbled, and to my disgust I was precipitated over his head on to the ground. Fortunately, it was like falling on to a bed, and I got up none the worse for the fall, except for the fact that a pocketful of loose change was scattered over the desert. At this late hour I was foolish to have called attention to it, for the gendarmes apparently considered it a sin even to leave the humblest coin behind, and continued the search until their supply of matches was completely exhausted.

About midnight we reached the hospital, where I was greeted by Mr. Bernard Haig, the surgeon-in-charge, and Captain C. F. Dixon-Johnson, who was acting as general director to the British Red Crescent hospitals. Fatigue vanished on finding fellow-countrymen to talk to, and it was not before early morning that we retired to bed.

MUSTAPHA ON THE ROAD

MOHEDDIN BEY AT ZAN-ZUR

To face p. 56

CHAPTER IV.

THE British Hospital at Bir-Zenoba was excellently situated. The wells close at hand gave good water, while the town of Zavia was near enough for the Turkish Commander to send us daily supplies of bread and fresh meat. Our cook, who had accompanied the Mission from Tunisia, had a good knowledge of his important profession and served up satisfactory meals with commendable regularity. The camp was built on clean, firm sand, upon which it was a pleasure to go for a gallop before the morning tub. Walking was not a desirable form of exercise, as one quickly lost sight of the camp, and the dogs kept by the Arabs were very savage and rushed out threatening to attack any stranger who might approach their masters' tents. The Arabs, too, eyed with suspicion any foreigner with whom they were not personally acquainted, and flint-lock in hand would watch the direction of the intruder.

When I arrived the two large hospital tents were filled with patients, the majority of whom had been wounded by shell-fire. These wounds were often of a ghastly nature, and as unfortunately some time had elapsed before the victims had been transported to the hospital the wounds had become septic. It proved

a long task to put these poor fellows on their feet
again.

As the enemy had begun to bomb the Turkish camps
from aeroplanes, it had become necessary, for the first
time in the history of the world, to protect hospitals
from this diabolical form of warfare. With this object
in view, an immense white ground-sheet had been prepared, on which a large red crescent was painted. To
warn any airmen who might fly by night that the
collection of tents was a hospital, the crescent was
indicated after dusk by placing hurricane lamps along
it. In order to emphasize the emblem as much as
possible, a supply of red lamps had been ordered from
London. In due course they arrived, but unfortunately,
instead of the glass being red, metal parts of the lamps
had been painted that colour!

After breakfast, one of the surgical staff would go
into the tents and superintend the dressing of the
wounds, which was carried out by the male nurses and
hospital assistants. Although the dressings were very
often of a painful nature they were in most cases borne
by the Arabs with a stoical indifference. The work of
the nurses was usually performed in the presence of a
circle of curious relatives of both sexes, who looked
on callously at details of surgical procedure at which
an untrained observer at home would speedily turn sick.
It was very difficult to keep friends of the patients out
of the tents, as they were always highly suspicious as
to what the doctors were going to do; but as the women
folk made themselves useful in feeding the sick and
using the fly-whisk, we always allowed a certain number
to enter. Anyone misbehaving or disobeying orders

SHELTER FOR THE WOUNDED

COOKHOUSE AT BIR-ZENOBIA

To face p. 58

was put out, and if he did not get clear of the camp in a reasonable time he called down upon himself the attention of the Turkish soldiers, provided as a guard, who did not hesitate to use their whips as an incentive to good discipline.

The work in the tents finished, there were the out-patients to be seen. These gathered in large numbers outside the store tent, and would wait patiently, hour after hour, until the doctor was able to see them. A great difficulty was always experienced in getting to know exactly what they complained of, as, with one exception, all our Tunisian interpreters spoke French in a fragmentary manner and were often at a loss to translate correctly the patients' replies. Later on, when I got to understand Arabic fairly well, I was frequently astounded at the dangerous mistranslations of my interpreter, and no longer saw cause to wonder why a patient, who had been given a lotion for the purpose of bathing a wound, came back and complained that he had taken the draught as ordered, but instead of it making him better it had given him a severe stomach-ache. All sorts of bottles were brought to receive the medicine in, many of them in a very dirty state. Some presented large earthenware vessels and asked for a dose of castor oil, while on one occasion I remember an Arab offering with grave face an unwashed sardine tin as a suitable receptacle for an eye lotion.

It was quite useless to order a spoonful as a dose, as the majority of our patients possessed no such article, so we were forced to make up the medicine of such a strength that the small glass, used universally in Tripolitana for tea drinking, formed a suitable dose.

It was also a mistake to order the remedies to be taken "after food," as one was always met with the answer that the war had ruined everyone and they had no food in the house after which they could take the medicine. It was always inadvisable to give money to out-patients, however sorry one felt for them, as the recipients could not keep their good fortune to themselves, and for days after, when one had been tempted into doing so, we would be favoured with visits from able-bodied Arabs who first occupied our attention with long accounts of imaginary pains, and when supplied with medicine begged for alms, the latter being probably the sole object of their journey.

The blind and crippled were, of course, in a different category. These wretched individuals always looked thin and ill-fed and received with loud expressions of gratitude the small coins or the dole of flour which was handed out to them. A very large number of those seeking our help were people suffering from ophthalmia in some form or other, and in the majority of cases the disease had progressed too far to make treatment of much avail. Still, many went away relieved and cured, and the late Mr. Alan Ostler in his book on Tripoli says: "The British Mission took in out-patients from all the countryside, unlike the other hospitals, which treated military invalids only. Daily the tents were thronged with sufferers from ophthalmia and sores and old diseases serious from long neglect. Mothers came, bringing ailing children; men, who had suffered long without hope of being cured, came every morning, confident of help, and always had it. They lost their terror of the knife when, in the surgery tent,

AWAITING DISTRIBUTION OF FOOD

REFUGEE WOMAN LOOKING FOR GRAIN

To face p. 60

they saw tumours and ulcerous growths removed without a sign of pain. Against ophthalmia, the curse of all lands wherein dust and flies abound, the English doctors waged a mighty war, and many who had hardly known daylight from darkness blessed them for the gift of sight restored."

It is a curious thing that, after diseases of the eye, the commonest complaint of our Arab out-patients was some morbid condition of the tongue or mouth. As they drank no alcoholic liquors and were too poor to be suffering from abuse of tobacco, the diagnosis was not a difficult one, and we had the satisfaction of enabling a good many men to eat and enjoy as hearty a meal as they could afford, whereas before coming for treatment they had long endured acute discomfort with every mouthful of food they had taken.

We had, of course, many queer requests made to us. I well remember an Arab bringing a large earthen-ware jar and asking for medicine for a poor woman who lay sick in a far-off village. On being asked what she was suffering from, he became quite indignant and said he did not know, as he had not considered it his business to inquire. As he would have probably nursed a grudge against the whole British Empire for the rest of his life had we sent him empty away, I gave him a tin of condensed milk, with instructions to administer a prepared glass three times a day. I thought it highly probable that the woman in question was suffering from lack of food, so it is not unreasonable to hope that my prescription did her some good.

After the morning's work we were all ready for lunch, and this disposed of we went into the operating tent and put any patients who required operations on the table. The Arabs took anæsthetics well and even appeared to enjoy the sensation, although they made plenty of fuss over the subsequent nausea. We were as conservative as possible in our surgery, and it is pleasing to recall the fact that during our stay in Tripolitana we never had to perform a complete amputation. Owing, perhaps, to their non-stimulating diet and avoidance of alcoholic drinks, the wounds of our patients generally healed well. The injuries produced by the small conical bullets used by the Italians were scarcely ever severe, and if the wounds had not been infected by plugging them with dirty pieces of rag or grass, as was the Arab custom, and they came to us early for treatment, we had the satisfaction of soon sending them back to their duties in the field.

The day closed officially with a visit at nightfall to the hospital tents, to cast an eye over any patients who were dangerously ill and to make a distribution of cigarettes to those Arabs who were sufficiently well to enjoy smoking.

Occasionally, for a little relaxation, I took a ride into Zavia, accompanied by Hassan, a young Turkish soldier, who had acquired a certain amount of English from the members of the British Mission. We would tie our horses up in the large courtyard of the castle and then stroll about the market-place and price the curios exposed for sale.

Here everything could be bought, from a camel to a packet of pins. As I was fresh to the country, I spent money as freely as does a Cook's tourist when he finds himself, for the first time in his life, in an Eastern bazaar. Among other things, I purchased several flint-lock pistols, a good Sheffield sheath knife and some earrings, all at a very reasonable figure. Naturally there was a good deal of bargaining, this apparently being considered a pleasant way of whiling away time; but Hassan's method of cutting the price down by at least three-quarters and shouting his figure louder than the merchant could, his usually concluded the purchase in much shorter time than was the custom.

On several occasions I called on my Turkish col-league in charge of the Zavia Military Hospital. As the weather at this time was very hot, he usually received me clad in a long, old-fashioned nightgown. This gave him rather a ludicrous appearance; as ludicrous possibly as a man in a tall hat must appear to an unsophisticated native of Africa. Nevertheless, although his attire was peculiar, he always made me welcome, and never let me go before I had consumed several cups of coffee.

The second Sunday after my arrival I rode into town to see if the mail had arrived. On crossing the market-place I found a great commotion going on. Seeing a Turkish officer who could speak French, I rode up to him and inquired what the trouble was. He replied that a treaty of peace had been signed, but was unable to give me any idea of the terms.

The Arabs seemed greatly elated at the news, as they thought that they had won the war, after the way they had kept the enemy away from the interior. In order to keep the Arabs quiet, the Ottoman officers had doubtless told them that the country was not to be given over to the enemy, for it must be understood that the

Turks were very few in number, and they were not at all sure of the attitude the Arabs might take up towards themselves if they thought the Sultan was giving them into the hands of a hated foe. It is fortunate for the Turks that there were well-educated, capable leaders amongst the Arabs, or they would not have been allowed to evacuate the country and take away their arms and ammunition without serious trouble.

Two days later Mr. Haig, the surgeon-in-charge of the British Mission, received a letter from the Turkish Commandant in the district, to the effect that as the war was now over he would be glad if we would remove the hospital as soon as possible to Zavia. On the day appointed we were early at work, taking down the tents and folding and packing them in their covers. The camels were loaded up with all the baggage, and then came the difficult task of arranging means of transport for the wounded, many of whom were hardly in a fit state for travel. The camel stretchers, that had been brought from England, hardly proved a success owing to the eccentric behaviour of the camels, who kept on rising from their knees before their burdens were properly adjusted. The worst cases were carried on ambulance stretchers, and although these were handled as carefully as possible under the supervision of the nurses, the unavoidable jolting over the rough ground was very painful to those of the wounded who were suffering from fractures and shattered joints. As soon as all the camels had been loaded up, the straggling caravan set out for Zavia.

Previous to the battle of Zan-Zur the British Hospital had been stationed at Zavia, and as suitable

HOSPITAL TENT

HOSPITAL STAFF AT ZAVIA

To face p. 64

houses could not be found we had been given the Hammam to serve as our headquarters. Hammam is, I believe, the Arabic equivalent for Turkish bath, and the name will be familiar enough to the many who seek cleanliness at a well-known establishment in Jermyn Street. At all events, the newly-erected white-washed building, crowned with small graceful cupolas, had never been used as a bath and was admirably suited for our purpose. The cooling room made a good operating theatre, and the large hot room—with the fires out—served as a dining-room for the officers, while there remained a good place for the nurses' mess and another room for the medical stores. Behind the Hammam there was a large stretch of clean sand, where we erected the hospital and tents for the staff to sleep in.

As the tents of the Turkish Red Crescent Hospital were near at hand, we had no lack of visitors, and we spent many a pleasant evening in Zavia with our Ottoman colleagues. On one or two evenings we offered hospitality to the Turkish officers in the neighbourhood, and on these occasions, after dinner was disposed of, we held impromptu smoking concerts at which songs were rendered in all sorts of languages; while the official tongue for conversation was French. As most of the British contingent were by no means capable of fluent or correct French and our Turkish friends' knowledge was frequently confined to two or three expressions, I fancy an educated Frenchman listening to our conversation would have been shocked to hear his beautiful language so terribly mangled. Still, we could understand each other, and that was the main point, even if our genders were a trifle muddled and the subjunctive mood was treated with scanty respect.

At one of our concerts we called upon an elderly and grave Ottoman officer to oblige with a song. As he could speak neither French nor English, we expected his effort would be in Turkish; but to our great surprise he sang a verse of " Chin, Chin, Chinaman," from the " Geisha," in a most spirited fashion, accompanying it by alternately raising his index fingers in the air. We were all much too amazed to think of asking him where he had learned it.

After a few days at the Hammam, our numbers were added to by the arrival of Mr. Turnbull with the Blue Hospital from the direction of Ajilat.

The days passed pleasantly enough at Zavia. The mornings were well filled in seeing the large crowds of out-patients who gathered daily. In the afternoon the patients in the hospital tent claimed attention, and then the best part of the day, the glorious evenings, remained for a ride round the town or a good gallop along the sea-coast. The town was a never-failing source of interest to me, and I loved to wander through the Jewish quarter looking at the various types that thronged the streets. One evening we were returning through the town after a gallop by the sea, when I saw a striking-looking young Jew standing at his shop door. His features seemed strangely familiar to me, and another glance showed me why—I was gazing on the traditional face of the Man of Nazareth.

CHAPTER V.

A few days later we commenced to demobilize, and a small caravan was despatched to Tunisia. To show that service under the Red Crescent in Tripolitana was not without an element of excitement, we will follow the fortunes of this party to the French frontier, and as Mr. Wallice was in charge I give the story in his own words:—

" We left the Hammam at Zavia on 10th November, 1912, our party consisting of six Englishmen, a Tunisian interpreter with his wife, and the necessary camel-drivers. The British section comprised four male nurses, Captain X, a retired officer, who had been interested in the campaign, and myself. We had experienced much difficulty in getting Mahmoud Effendi, the Arab Governor, to give us permission to depart, as the Turkish officers, who did not trust themselves with the Arabs as freely as did the Englishmen, said that the journey would be dangerous, as banditti were holding up caravans on the high road. The Governor wished us to wait until a large caravan was proceeding to Ben-Gardane; but as we were all anxious to get home we overrode his objections, and at length he promised to provide us with four trustworthy gendarmes.

" As we were passing through the town, a well-known Arab merchant called me into his store and begged me to take a fairly large sum of money to Ben-Gardane for him, at the same time indicating a servant to whom I was to hand the receipt. I asked him, however, why he did not give the money to his fellow-countryman to carry for him, as I did not wish to undertake the responsibility. He answered that all the Arabs spoke well of the British doctors, and he thought his cash would be safer in the hands of one of our nationality. After this compliment I had to agree to take it, and he then had the imprudence to count out the gold to me over his counter, right in front of a group of Arabs, who included some of our camel - drivers. To this grave lack of judgment I attribute the dangers that overtook us on the journey, as the Arabs were wretchedly poor, and the temptation to get hold of so much gold was irresistible.

" Two gendarmes turned up after a vexatious delay of about four hours, and after waiting in vain for the other two we started along the road. After a four hours' journey, we reached Suruman, and as the sun was getting very low we determined to halt for the night. We encamped in the deserted *gendarmerie*, and set about preparing as good a meal as possible. Feeling very tired, I spread my blankets at the end of the room, and having thrown off my revolver belt, lay down for a few minutes before I was called to supper.

" The meal finished, we smoked a pipe and turned in. After I got between the blankets, I felt for my revolver, and found it was missing. It was apparent

KAIMAKAM AT ZAVIA

MR. WALLACE LEAVES ZAVIA

To face p. 68

that it had been stolen while we were having our meal. As it was now quite dark, and all the village fast asleep, I determined to wait until morning before sifting the matter. At daybreak I went with the interpreter to the head Sheikh, and laid a complaint. He asked me if I suspected anyone, and I told him that the thief must either be one of the two gendarmes or else one of the camel-drivers, as no one else had entered the room. The Sheikh then asked me to accompany him to a café, where he sat down with the interpreter and myself on either side. A large number of Arabs entered as well, squatting all round on the floor. After a great deal of talk, the Sheikh turned round to me and said that he was very much annoyed that a robbery should have taken place in his village, and especially that the victims should have been the British doctors, who had done so much good in the country. He then called for the gendarmes to come in, and as the first one entered all present exclaimed with one accord, 'That is the man!' The self-constituted jury having given their verdict, the gendarme was convicted without any defence being listened to, and the Sheikh ordered his effects to be examined. After a short search, my revolver and belt were discovered in his nose-bag under the corn. I then asked the Sheikh by what process they had so quickly discovered the guilty person, and his answer was a surprising one: 'He is a well-known thief in the district!' It was scarcely comforting to think, after all we had heard of the dangers of the road, that one of the men who had been told off to guard our lives and property should be the first to prey upon us. The fact that he was a convicted thief did not

appear to worry the gendarme in the least, and he
carried the matter off in a most brazen fashion,
swaggering about and exhibiting to his friends the
spoils of his prowess on the battlefield, in the shape
of portions of an Italian officer's uniform that he was
wearing. I then told him that I had no further need
of his services, and he could return to Zavia as quickly
as he liked. On my giving orders for the caravan to
start, the other gendarme came up and told me he
would not go on with us without his fellow. As I saw
he also was probably utterly unreliable, I was anxious
to get rid of him as well, but the other members of
the party, being consulted, pointed out that these two
men were responsible for our safety, and should the
caravan be looted in their absence the blame would
entirely rest with us for sending away the protectors
that had been furnished by the authorities in Zavia.
I went, therefore, again to the Sheikh, and asked for
his advice on the point. He advised me to take both
the gendarmes, and said that he would send a report
of the matter to Zavia. Not without many misgivings
I agreed, and gave the order for the caravan to start.
After five hours' march, we arrived at Ajilat, and halted
for a midday meal. Here we decided it would be a
good plan to leave the main road along the coast, so
we struck inwards in a south-westerly direction, and
at nightfall encamped on the desert near to some
Arab tents.

" At six o'clock next morning we struck camp and
proceeded in a direction indicated by the gendarmes,
on the understanding that at midday we should reach
some wells where good water was to be found. Our

guides, however, quickly lost themselves, and twelve o'clock found us still straggling over the desert. An hour later we struck some telegraph posts, and by following these we arrived at our destination at sunset. The place we had arrived at had evidently just been abandoned by a large body of men, for camp-fires were still smouldering, and the ground was littered with refuse. The gendarmes now became anxious for us to push on to El Assa, another five hours' march, as they said the district was notorious for thieves, and they could not be responsible for our safety if we halted there. We had, however, marched for fourteen continuous hours; the camels were very tired, and we were all anxious to get some rest, so we determined to camp for the night. The gendarmes seemed very much put out at this, and asked permission to return, which I refused to give; so, having piled the boxes round about us in case of an attack, we set a watch and lay down to sleep.

" At dawn I was awakened by the gendarmes, who said they had determined to return to Zavia, whether I gave them permission or not. Seeing the uselessness of trying to compel them to go farther and thinking that in case of attack they would probably turn their arms against us, I dismissed them and let them go without backsheesh.

" In order to prepare for eventualities, Captain X then took his Mauser carbine out of a case and put a bandolier of cartridges round his waist. No sooner was this done than four Arabs, armed with rifles, came up and asked us where the gendarmes had gone to, whereupon Captain X answered that he was the gendarme and was thoroughly proficient in the profession. They then turned to me and asked what I would be prepared to pay them as an armed escort to Ben-Gardane. I replied that we were well able to protect ourselves, and had no need of their services; upon which they then left the caravan. During this argument I could see our gendarmes watching us from the top of a hillock afar off.

" As the water at our encampment had proved very dirty and undrinkable, we did not fill our bottles before departing, but determined to do so at El Assa later on in the day. For about five hours we marched over the desert without seeing either a tent or a single Arab. The track, which appeared to be an old one, was very difficult to follow, and we were beginning to grow anxious when an Arab horseman appeared in front of us. I sent the interpreter to inquire of him if we were on the right road, and he informed us that El Assa lay due north and was about three hours' journey. As we did not think it worth while to go north to El Assa and then have to turn west again, we decided to take a north-westerly course, and guided by the sun we struck out in this direction. After a brief halt for lunch, we had continued our journey for about half an hour when we noticed a small band of Arabs coming rapidly from our left rear. That they approached in this direction seemed to me evidence that they had followed us all the morning, seeing that their line of march corresponded with the divergence of our caravan from the beaten track.

" The nature of the ground in front of us was peculiar, and played an important part in the events that subsequently developed. We passed down a gentle slope into a saucer-shaped depression in the desert, perhaps some 800 yards across, surmounted at the other end by a similar rise in the ground. We had traversed about a third of this depression when the Arabs appeared on the summit of the slope. We could see they were all armed and liberally supplied with cartridges, while all we could muster in the shape of arms was one Mauser carbine and the revolver that I was carrying. We drove the camels together in a bunch, and this proved rather a difficult task, as some of our camel-drivers had lagged behind to greet the approaching Arabs. Scenting trouble, I distributed the money I was carrying into as many hiding-places as I could find about my person. We had got half-way across the depression when one of the Arabs overtook us and offered his water-bottle to one of the nurses. As we had tasted no water for eight hours, he naturally took a good long pull, and while he was drinking the Arab passed his hand over his coat to try and find out if he was armed. He then offered his bottle to me, but as I did not at all like the look of him I refused to touch it. The cloven foot then appeared and he told me, through the interpreter, that it was the custom for strangers passing through to present a trifle to the men of the place. I answered him that members of the British Mission were naturally exempt from these extortions, since we had tended their wounded, fed their poor and clothed the women and children of those who had been fighting in the war. He then dropped his polite and conciliatory manner and demanded bluntly what we were prepared to give to be allowed to go unmolested. I told him that we would give him nothing.

"The Arab then retired a few yards and held up his hand as a signal to his six companions, who ran down the slope, took cover behind some scrub and covered us with their rifles. The spokesman then ran back to where they were, and a general palaver ensued. Meanwhile we pushed on with the camels as fast as possible, our progress being impeded, however, by our camel-drivers, who gathered round me, saying that they themselves had given up all their money and begging me to buy off the robbers. This I resolutely refused to do.

"We had got three-quarters of the way across the depression when the Arabs doubled forwards and commenced to spread out, obviously in an endeavour to surround us. One of the nurses, who was on horseback, volunteered to ride out to the left to check the flanking movement, and the Arabs on that side retired, apparently not knowing whether he was armed or not. Suddenly, without any warning, three shots were fired at him, and his horse, starting forward, threatened to unseat him. As soon as he rejoined us, two more shots rang out, one nearly killing the interpreter's wife and the other whizzing unpleasantly close to my head. As a man on a camel at 500 yards range forms an easy mark, we all dismounted.

"Seeing now that the fight had commenced in earnest, I gave over the command to Captain X and asked for orders. All the camel-drivers had now deserted the caravan, not wishing to get in the way of their co-religionists' bullets; all, that is, with the exception of one negro who remained faithful. I wish I knew his name, as I would like to chronicle it here in appreciation of his services. Captain X then told me to drive the camels forward while he and the nurse would remain behind and fight a rearguard action. Driving camels, at the best of times, is a difficult task. So long as they are allowed to wander along at a gentle two and a half miles an hour they are fairly easy to manage; but force them, and they are apt to break into a run all over the desert and throw their burdens to the four winds of heaven. Slowly we approached the edge of the depression, and here we encountered the most danger, for at first the Arabs had not hit off our range, and like all untrained men were firing over our heads as we were ascending the slope. Fortunately, however, we passed over the ridge without injury to man or beast.

" I was now in a most unenviable position. Looking back, I could see the Captain and the nurse lying down on the ground taking alternate shots at the enemy with the carbine; behind them the horse stood erect on the desert. Round the little group I could see from time to time the sand thrown up as the bullets struck the ground. I found it difficult to leave them like this, and Captain X, seeing my dilemma, sent his companion with an order that I was to move on as fast as possible and they would follow as soon as they could. Seeing all hopes of salvation rested with the rearguard, I handed my revolver to the nurse and again pushed on with the camels.

" In front of us now stretched level ground for about two miles, and we marched on over this, seeing nothing

of our friends but continually hearing the reports of
the rifles. After about twenty minutes the firing began
to slacken, and then died away altogether. I halted
and watched in an anxious frame of mind. Who had
conquered? Who would appear over the ridge? Our
two companions or a band of Arabs, flushed with victory
and ready to cut our throats? Five minutes elapsed,
and then we saw two figures coming across the sand
towards us. Another few minutes, and to our delight
we recognized Captain X riding the horse with his companion running at the stirrup. After the prolonged
anxiety it can be imagined, when at length they joined
us safe and sound, we welcomed them warmly.

"It appeared that the Arabs had made several
attempts to creep up to them, but as cover was lacking
and the fire of our men had been too deadly, they had
not succeeded. As to casualties, one at least of the
Arabs had been severely wounded, if not killed, while
on our side Captain X had been shot through a puttee,
while my coat had also been ploughed up by a bullet.
An interesting point is that one of the enemy had been
identified by a nurse as an Arab who had been cared
for in our hospital. It has been unkindly suggested
that this perhaps was the motive for the attack!

"Night had now fallen, but we had no wish to linger
in the dangerous zone, so taking the direction from the
stars we marched steadily on, and eventually halted at
about ten o'clock. We were all thoroughly worn out
and parched with thirst, as we had had no water all
day long. Some distance off we could see large fires;
but as we could not be sure that the Arabs would be
friendly we made no attempt to approach them. After

snatching a mouthful of food, we wrapped ourselves up in our blankets and had a fair night's sleep.

"At daybreak we started off again, and after a two hours' journey we struck the chain of salt lakes that forms the boundary between Tripoli and Tunisia. Another half-hour and we trod French territory, where, coming across a well, we slaked a twenty-seven hours' thirst in the muddiest water it has ever been my lot to drink. We had entered Tunisia at the very spot where we had left it five months previously; a curious coincidence, considering that we had been steering entirely by means of the sun and stars.

"Once on French soil, we congratulated ourselves on our escape, and even our camel-drivers forgot their own losses and seemed glad that we had got safely away, indicating at the same time the fate that was in store for us had we not beaten the Arabs off, by significantly drawing their hands across their throats."

There is little to add to the narrative of Mr. Wallice, but when three months later I was in this same district I often used to hear the affair spoken of by the Arabs. I learned from them that one Arab was killed outright, and another had had his forearm shattered. My Arab friends at Bechoul often used to laugh at the discomfiture of their fellow-countrymen, who, it seems, had anticipated an easy plunder.

Later on, when it came to my turn to pass through this unpleasant piece of country, I think it very probable that, at all events to some degree, I owed my safety to the prestige so firmly established in the district by these returning members of the British Mission.

CHAPTER VI.

On the 29th October, consequent upon the outbreak of hostilities in the Balkans, my colleague, Mr. Haig, in charge of the hospital at Zavia, received an urgent summons from the Committee of the Red Crescent Society in London to proceed to the seat of the new war at the earliest date possible. As Zavia is only one day's camel journey from the town of Tripoli and direct shipping could be obtained in that port, it was decided that the caravan should take this route instead of the long, tiresome and dangerous road to Ben-Gardane. A message was, therefore, sent in to the Governor of Zavia, asking him to be so good as to furnish us with the 150 camels required for the transport of the hospital stores.

As no answer was received, early on the morning of the 30th I rode into the town to see what could be done. Leaving our horses with a Turkish soldier in the roughly-paved courtyard of the Castle, I was shown up a flight of stairs into a decently-furnished room, where the Governor received me. Mahmoud Effendi, who was at this time in charge of the town, was a full-blooded Arab and a fine-looking specimen of his race. He wore his Arab dress with considerable dignity and received us courteously, seeming anxious to do all in his power to help. A difficulty, however, had arisen with regard to getting the camels we required. The camel-owners feared that if they sent their animals into Tripoli they would be detained by the Italians and not be permitted to return into the interior, where already a fresh resistance against Christian aggression was being organized.

It was easy to gather from Mahmoud Effendi's remarks that now peace had been made Turkish authority was no longer feared by the Arabs in the district, and consequently it was useless for us to look to him to enforce our requests. As, however, I felt quite sure that the Italian Commander-in-Chief would only be too glad to get rid of all foreigners from the interior and would facilitate their departure as much as possible, I offered to ride into Tripoli to see General Ragni, the Italian Generalissimo, and to ask him to give the personnel of the hospital leave to depart by that port and also to give me a guarantee that the camels would be allowed to return to Zavia without let or hindrance. To this suggestion Mahmoud Effendi cordially agreed and at once offered to provide me with two men to guide me into Tripoli. I stipulated that they should be men of good standing in the district, who would not be likely to leave me stranded should trouble arise on the road; for it must be understood that at this time the terms of the peace were little known or understood by the Arabs, and, suspicious as they are by nature, it was not improbable that they might make trouble for anyone proceeding past their guards into the Italian lines.

After lunch at the Hammam we saddled up, but my

departure was delayed by adverse criticisms on the rough way my overcoat and blanket had been rolled and strapped on to the saddle. Mr. Haig kindly came to my assistance, and the artistic effect produced by his efforts proved that he had had plenty of practice in such things during the time he had trailed a pike in the South African War. The party was completed by Mohammed, a Tunisian interpreter, who proved fairly competent in turning the bad Tripolitan Arabic into fragmentary French. He took an early opportunity of informing me that he also spoke English, but from the examples he gave me I sincerely hope he had not acquired his knowledge in the British Hospital, for it was painfully evident that his professors had frequently been provoked into using expressions of the strongest description.

It was raining slightly when we left the camp, and a Turkish soldier, seeing I had no protection against the wet, very kindly offered me the loan of a riding cape. I was about to put it on when one of my colleagues pointed out that it was an Italian uniform cape and had probably been looted from the dead body of an officer. It can be imagined I quickly dropped the garment in question, for I did not wish to be guilty of the bad taste of riding into the enemy's lines wearing the garment of one of their dead.

It was surprising, by the by, to note the number of Arabs who carried Italian rifles and wore clothing taken from the enemy. At Zavia Italian clothing, arms, haversacks, valises, and other articles could be bought at a very cheap rate in the market-place. It seems fairly obvious that the tales told by the Arabs of the hurried retreats of their enemy were in no sense exaggerated, considering the widespread dispersion of European equipment of every description.

The Arabs have been severely blamed for stripping the bodies of their dead enemies, but personally I am unable to see anything criminal in this procedure. It was certainly a lack of good taste, but it must be remembered that during the war they were miserably clad and suffered intensely at nights from cold; hence the temptation to take a warm garment, when occasion offered, must have been well-nigh irresistible. The well-clad, well-fed soldier may look scornfully upon men who are guilty of robbing the dead, but he who knows cold and hunger will be disposed to be more charitable. All soldiers who have passed a winter campaign will agree that cold and wet are to be feared more than the enemy's fire.

After half an hour's sharp ride we reached a ruined house which served as a shelter for the Arab outpost. Our arrival was signalled by loud barking of dogs, which roused the guard, and about thirty savage-looking Arabs streamed out into the road and clustered round us. They were armed with Martini-Henrys, Mausers and Springfields, whilst one or two, unable to get hold of rifles, carried muzzle-loading, flint-lock camel guns. My Arab guides were able to satisfy them after a time, and I was very glad to get away and leave them, an unkempt-looking group, on the sandy road. Coming to a level piece of road, we let the horses have a good gallop. Mohammed's style of riding did not appear especially good, although he proudly informed me he had been a professional jockey in Tunisia.

Later in the day, the uncomfortable manner in which
he sat his horse and his decided objection to proceed
at anything faster than a walk confirmed my suspicions
that he was more accustomed to sitting on the floor of
a café than in a saddle.

A couple of hours more and we rode into the village
of Lemaya, which had been abandoned by the Arabs
after the battle of Zan-Zur. The houses were fast
tumbling to ruins, grass was growing in the streets,
the gardens looked dried up and neglected, and dogs
wandered in and out of the dwellings that once had
been busy with life. Another turn of the road and
we sighted the oasis of Zan-Zur. The sun was now
hidden by clouds, a fine rain had commenced to fall,
and a slight haze overhung the country. In the distance the oasis looked dismal and mysterious. As we
approached no sound of life came from it; no cheerful
creaking of the wells; no lowing of cattle or barking
of dogs. The oasis that should have been giving
shelter and food to hundreds of poor Arabs was now
completely deserted.

It was at Zan-Zur that one of the last engagements
of the war took place. A large Italian army attacked
the Arabs, the latter being greatly outnumbered by the
enemy. The Arabs seem to have been successful in
beating off the Christians, who left many dead on the
field, whilst the Moslem slain totalled 85. Seven guns
fell into the hands of the victorious Arabs, who, however, gave way to their habit of looting instead of
trying to get away with the guns, which were eventually
retaken by the Italians. But if the Arabs in this battle
lost a fine opportunity of driving their victory home,

REFUGEES

AN ARAB PATROL

To face p. 82

the Italian General also missed a chance of making a dramatic march on to Zavia. The ammunition of the Arabs was, for the time, completely exhausted, and had the Italian attack been renewed the next day the Arabs would have had to fall back and leave the road open to Zavia and Azizia. A bold handling of cavalry at this moment would have given the invaders a crushing and decisive victory.

We rode along with the oasis on our right hand until in the distance we sighted the Italian fort, situated on a hill called Sidi Billal. As we were the first people from the interior to approach it after the declaration of peace, I thought it advisable to show some sign that we were bent on a friendly mission, so I handed a handkerchief—as white as an Arab washerwoman could make it—to the head gendarme, who hoisted it as a flag of truce on his riding-whip. As we got nearer to the fort it seemed to my unprofessional eye that a few shells would have blown the whole structure down, although it was strong enough to resist capture by an enemy unprovided with artillery. The sea formed its northern boundary; its eastern aspect was protected by the fire of the sister fortress of Sidi Abd-el-Djelil; while the other sides sloped down to the desert, giving the defenders a splendid field of fire and every chance to mow down an assailing force with their machine guns. The wire was thick and well arranged, and would have proved a formidable obstacle to an assault-ing party. Night attacks were provided against by means of powerful searchlights, which were diligently operated during the hours of darkness.

At first not a sign of life could be seen, but as we

drew nearer the fort roused up like a hive of bees, and the soldiers in large numbers came swarming down to the barbed-wire entanglements. The first man we came up with was a young officer of artillery, who at once opened fire on me and my escort with his kodak. My knowledge of Italian being confined to an abusive expression I had used with considerable success during my student days to induce organ-grinders to move into the next street, I made no attempt in this language, but hailed the lieutenant in French, in which tongue he at once replied. He led me round the base of the entanglements to the eastern aspect of the fortress, where we passed in through a gate guarded by sentries, and proceeded to find the Commandant. We passed between some hundreds of soldiers, who gathered round scrutinising us curiously, evidently under the impression that I was a Turkish officer coming in to make my submission. In a few minutes I was face to face with the General, who eyed me sternly and acknowledged my salute with a curt nod. My appearance, I must own, was far from prepossessing. It was quite impossible to get anything decently washed in Zavia, and I defy any man to look a credit to his country when he has no collar on, when his clothes are soaked with rain and his attire is finished with an Arab head-dress. At all events the Commandant's welcome could not be described as cordial, nor was his attitude such as might be qualified by the word affable, but I charitably concluded that, as the fort of Sidi Billal had only been recently constructed, and it was probably his first important command, the strain and anxiety produced by the possibility of an assault on this excellently forti-

fied position by a handful of half-naked Arabs was
weighing so heavily on his mind that he had no time
to be even decently civil to a travel-stained surgeon.
After I had informed him of my business I fell into the
hospitable hands of some of my professional brethren,
who entertained me and my Arabs to tea, which was
thoroughly appreciated after our long ride.

Night had now begun to fall, and as I was anxious
to get on, although loth to leave the pleasant company
in which I now found myself, I asked and received
permission to push on.

It was quite dark when we passed the sentry at the
gates of the fortress, and I was fortunate enough to
be accompanied by two genial officers, who volunteered
to take me as far as Sidi Abd-el-Djelil.   Both the
Italians were excellently mounted and rode with that
ease for which they are famous, and they could not
help showing polite impatience at the slow pace of my
little pony, who had already done a good day's work.
Moreover, I had Mohammed to think of, who was
doing his utmost, by rising in the stirrups and clutching
hold of the front of his saddle, to prevent further loss
of cuticle.   At this stage he wisely refrained from
boasting of his racecourse exploits in Tunisia.

A short distance along the road we were picked up
by the searchlight from the fort at Abd-el-Djelil, which
kept a glittering eye upon our party until we arrived
at the gates.   Here my kindly guides left me and
returned to their quarters.

Having been thoroughly scrutinized by the guards,
I was led into the fortress and conducted to the quarters
of the officer commanding, Major-General Clemente

Lequio, who, when my errand had been explained to him, received me cordially and asked me to dine with him and his officers. After a good wash I sat down to dinner opposite the General, who made me feel quite at home and, incidentally, gave me an excellent dinner. After the large supplies of water I had consumed at Zavia out of deference to our Moslem friends, I found the Italian wine genially stimulating, and forgetting for the while an incurable shyness, I managed to converse fairly fluently in French, while, thanks to some knowledge of Spanish, I was able to understand a good deal of the conversation in Italian that took place at the table.

I was questioned at some length as to the state of things in the interior, but I was forced to plead that my short stay in the country scarcely permitted me to speak with any authority on these matters. Other questions as to what impression the Turks had formed of their enemies I had to turn aside as diplomatically as possible, although I should like to have informed them that, although the Ottoman and Arab officers did not esteem very highly the *élan* and courage of the Italian rank and file, they all united in praising the bravery and cool leading of the officers, who always advanced to the attack well ahead of their men, regardless of the hottest fire. After all, you cannot look for a very high standard of conduct from a man reared in the slums of Naples—or, for the matter of that, London or Glasgow—nor can you expect him to lay down his life on the altar of patriotism as cheerfully as a well-educated man, who is imbued with national pride and has large interests at stake. It is amazing to me to see miners, weavers and labourers giving up their lives in quarrels that do not concern them in the least, and of the causes and objects of which they have little or no knowledge.

To illustrate a difference in national character, it was interesting to note all through the campaign in Tripolitana that the Italian press grossly exaggerated the minor successes of their soldiers, turned defeats into victories with a stroke of the pen, and minimized their losses in an astounding fashion, while during the South African War our own press seemed to take a delight in daily frightening the public with news of some disaster or other, in hopes, I presume, of rousing the sporting instinct of the race to try and give the enemy one back.

After dinner I joined the three Arabs, who were being entertained right royally by the non-commissioned officers of the medical staff. The two Zavia Arabs were sitting at one end of the table, with smiling faces protruding from the folds of their blankets; they evidently did not find their Italian enemies such bad fellows after all. Mahommed, who was evidently having the time of his life, had been entertaining the company with an Arab song, and I strongly suspected from his glittering eye and extreme volubility that he had been finding inspiration in a cup of forbidden wine. However, happy as they all seemed, we had to make an early start for Tripoli in the morning, so I was forced to break up the party and send the Arabs off to bed.

General Lequio had been good enough to put two tents at my disposal—one for the Arabs and one for myself. On getting to my own tent I was addressed by the orderly, who had been told off to look after me, in fluent American. He had been a barber for many years in New York, but had neglected to take out naturalization papers, with the result that, being at home when the war broke out, he was promptly called to the colours. He took but little interest in the war, but was ready to discuss at great length Taft's prospects for the Presidency or the question of the Panama Canal tolls. He finally completely upset my gravity by referring, with pleasing impertinence, to England as "the old country"! Having rigged me up a bed on an ambulance stretcher, he left me reading the last two numbers of the *New York American*, a paper which seems to appeal powerfully to the newly-arrived immigrant in the States. Not finding much room to turn round on the stretcher, I made a bed on the sandy floor, and was soon fast asleep.

In the morning, after coffee, I gave orders to have the horses saddled up; whereupon my American orderly informed me that as General Lequio had noted my desire to get into Tripoli as soon as possible, he had placed a motor car at my disposal. Leaving Mohammed at the fort I got into the car with the two Zavia Arabs, and we were soon on the way to Tripoli. A young officer accompanied me, and made the whole journey very interesting by pointing out to me the different places of interest we passed. It is no exaggeration to say that the country from Sidi Abd-el-Djelil to Tripoli was one vast armed camp. We met soldiers of all arms on the road, whilst the Air Service was represented by three dirigibles floating gracefully in the air, the early morning sun glittering brightly on their aluminium-

sheathed gas-bags. Italy, certainly, had left no stone
unturned to make good her conquest of Tripolitana;
yet even four months after this date, within a day's
sharp ride of the city of Tripoli, a large Arab army was
allowed to remain unmolested and even attack and
loot an important town!

My companion pointed out to me the cemetery where
the victims of the cholera epidemic lay at rest, and I
could not help thinking that water-borne diseases would
take a terrible toll of the Italian conscripts before the
flag of their country waved unchallenged over the
whole of this ancient Turkish *vilayet*.

Later we came across a few companies of Italy's
black troops from Abyssinia being drilled by a coloured
officer. They looked a smart enough body of men,
but I have been informed by a European officer, who
watched the war on the Turkish side, that they had
not distinguished themselves in the campaign; they
were unused to the country and wanted a lot of driving.

At length we arrived in Tripoli, and the car pulled
up outside the quarters of the Commander-in-Chief,
where I was handed over to the care of a young Sicilian
officer, who from his appearance and excellent English
might easily have passed for a British officer. While
waiting for an interview with General Ragni he kindly
showed me round the town, which, although bustling
with life owing to the large number of troops in the
district, did not appear very attractive. Still, as the
Italian occupation had been of so short a duration,
perhaps it would be unfair to expect them to have
smartened the place up in that time. Arriving at the
post office, I was allowed to send off a cable to London,

paying in good French gold and—significant detail—
receiving as change Italian paper money. I only had
time to make one purchase, and that was a large illus-
tration in brilliant colours of the battle of Zan-Zur,
where the Italian soldiers were depicted giving the
unfortunate Arabs an exceedingly bad time. This I
presented to some Turkish friends on my return to
Zavia, as an example of history as it is written.

I should have been very glad of a change of linen
and a general clean-up before visiting the Commander-
in-Chief, but as no opportunity occurred I was forced
to console myself with a phrase constantly used by the
Turkish officers when they apologized for the poorness
of their hospitality, *A la guerre comme à la guerre.*

After a few words with His Excellency's Chief-of-
Staff, who in faultless English asked me if I could give
him any news of the Italian prisoners in the hands of
the Turks, I was ushered into the presence of General
Ragni. One naturally feels a certain amount of diffidence in addressing a man who has been entrusted by
a great Power with the command of a vast army, and
this diffidence is not lessened when one feels dirty and
unkempt and has to speak in an unfamiliar tongue;
but General Ragni speedily put me at my ease, with
his grave courtesy and simple, unaffected manner.

Fortunately I am used to addressing Generals, for
in South America I have the honour to count among
my friends a large number of these high military
dignitaries. As a matter of fact in that country it is
a good plan to address all men mounted on horses as
"General." If the title does not prove to have been
correctly bestowed, by changing to "Doctor" you are

sure to be right five times out of six. But, of course, the mode of address that would suit these gentlemen would hardly consort with the dignity of an officer who really had an army at his back. I made a good start with " *Votre Excellence*," which as I gained confidence I changed to "*Monsieur le Général*," and finally, seduced by General Ragni's kindly manner, I lapsed into " *Mon Général*."

The General was kindness itself to me. He offered all facilities for the transport of the hospital, and even suggested that if the camels brought the goods as far as Sidi Billal, the Italian Government would undertake to bring them into Tripoli.

This business over, after the kindly way in which he had received me I thought it only right to inform His Excellency that if the Arabs in the interior should agree to carry on the war in an organized and civilized manner some of us had determined to retreat to the hills with them to look after their sick and wounded. General Ragni seemed to think that this would not be possible, as once the Turks had withdrawn any Arabs continuing the resistance against the Italian Government would be considered and treated as rebels. This was a point I was quite unable to discuss, as the question of remaining or not rested entirely with our Committee in London; but at the same time I respectfully pointed out to General Ragni that should any more Italian prisoners fall into the hands of the Arabs it would be a great source of assistance and protection to them to have the British Hospital near at hand. In the light of future events it is only fair to General Ragni to record that he warned me that if any of us remained with the Arabs and were captured we could not look for better treatment than the rebels themselves.

After the privilege of this pleasant interview, I took my leave of the General, thanking him most heartily for the kindness and consideration he had shown me. I was then conducted into another room, where an officer commenced to make out the necessary papers for me. On his asking me my name, and seeing he was unfamiliar with English, I thought he might have some difficulty with the spelling, so I handed him my passport, in order that he might copy the name. Thinking he was not looking at the right part of this important document, I ventured to look over his shoulder, and found I was being described as " We, Sir Edward Grey, Knight of the Most . . ." I was therefore compelled to interrupt, and inform him that my modest name was to be found lower down on the sheet. Having at length secured the paper duly signed and sealed, I said goodbye to various officers I had been introduced to, and started off back to Sidi Abd-el-Djelil.

We arrived at the fort at about one o'clock quite ready for lunch, to which General Lequio had had the goodness to invite me. Apparently the General is as good a sportsman as he is a soldier, for the fish and birds provided at the mess were, I was told, of his killing. In course of the meal, during which the conversation was animated, one of the officers asked me what effect the dynamite bombs dropped from the dirigibles and aeroplanes had had on the Arabs. I turned the question aside as best I could, for when being so hospitably entertained I had no wish to tell them that unfortunately the bombs had usually fallen amongst non-combatants, and had killed and mangled several women and children. It speaks volumes for the humanity of the Turkish officers that, although the Italian aircraft had violated the rules of civilized warfare—as we read them at this date—when an aeroplane fell in the Ottoman camp the aviator was hospitably entertained and afforded respectful treatment, instead of having to face a firing-party. It seems difficult to conceive that this diabolical form of destruction will be allowed in future warfare, as the airship manœuvres so high up that it is well-nigh impossible for the bomb-thrower to see on whom his shells will drop; while Red Crescent and Red Cross flags flying over hospital tents cannot be distinguished from above, nor can the ground sheets with Cross or Crescent be made of sufficient size to be of any value.[1]

While smoking a final cigarette before my departure, an amusing incident occurred. I have taken pains to point out that during my ride into Tripoli my personal appearance was far from being prepossessing, but I have not explained why I endeavoured never to remove my fez. Being a victim of incipient baldness, on the cynical advice of a colleague I had been foolish enough to submit to having my head shaved the day before we left Bir-Zenoba. At the date of my visit to Tripoli, instead of the exuberant crop I had hopefully anticipated, the hair had made but the poorest attempt to re-cover my scalp. As I stood cap in hand making my adieux, a young Italian officer entered the mess-room, and when he removed his helmet I noticed that

---

[1] I wrote these lines in June 1914, and now (1924) I see no reason to alter them.

he also had had the middle part of his scalp shaved in the vain hope that it would induce a stronger growth of hair. We looked at each other and laughed, and our merriment proved so infectious that we soon had everyone laughing at our expense.

A final handshake, a last click of the kodak, and jumping into the saddle I rode away, leaving behind as good-hearted and hospitable a lot of men as one could find in Africa. General Clemente Lequio is a fine soldier, and I was glad to hear that when the Arab resistance in the mountains was finally overcome it was he who scored the greatest successes of the whole war, afterwards treating his vanquished opponents with justice and moderation. Some people are always complaining about their fellow-men. It seems to me they must walk about with a sensitive soul and a very critical eye, for everywhere I go I only meet with nice people —people who seem anxious to help one all they can. I can only hope that Lequio and all those good fellows who sat around him at Sidi Abd-el-Djelil survived the dangers of the campaign and lived to serve their country and the world in the titanic struggle that even then was brewing—a struggle in which the chivalry of an heroic Italy found a cause worthy of their steel.

Riding along with my thoughts busy over the doings of the last two days, I did not notice I was getting out of touch with my companions, and suddenly, just before we reached the guard-house, I was awakened abruptly out of my reverie by an Arab boy springing up from the sand and presenting his Martini at my chest. As at this time I could not speak any Arabic, I was unable to proclaim my identity, and I felt devoutly thankful when my guides came up and explained that I was not an Italian. Had I been alone I have little doubt that in a few minutes the naked corpse of an English doctor would have been a conspicuous wayside object. Something, however, about this Arab sentry excited my professional curiosity. It was not that he was a young boy; for one constantly saw mere children in the Arab ranks. It was not that he was miserably clad in one torn and scanty cotton garment, which was soaked through with the rain that was now falling fast. But despite the unquenchable fire that flashed from his dark, fanatical eyes, his face looked drawn and pinched. I told Mohammed to ask him if he felt unwell. No, he was not unwell, but during the last four days they had received no money or provisions at their post, and during that period no food had passed his lips.

My thoughts flashed back to the vast armed camp I had just visited, with its thousands of well-fed, well-clad men; with its aeroplanes, its motor cars and its guns. And here, barring the passage of that great modern army, stood a half-starved Arab boy, grasping in his hand an antiquated weapon. Surely the Sultan did not lose Tripolitana for lack of valour on the part of his Moslem levies!

The sergeant in charge of the guard-house corroborated the statement of the sentry as to the non-arrival of rations, so I handed over the few shillings I had in my pocket in order that they might send into Zavia for food.

Pushing on as quickly as possible, we drew rein outside the Hammam at nightfall, after as varied a couple of days as one can reasonably expect in this workaday world.

CHAPTER VII.

AFTER the departure of Mr. Haig and the nurses to the coast, the small party remaining at the Hammam awaited with great anxiety the coming of orders from London. The Arabs by no means considered themselves beaten, and at a great council of Sheikhs and notables held in the hills they had decided to make a determined effort not to lose their independence. The inhabitants of Tripolitana are accustomed to the coming and going of conquerors. Phœnicians, Romans and Turks had all swept victoriously over their deserts, yet they had had their day and had disappeared. Surely the new invader in his turn would at length be forced to pack up and go, and leave the Arab to pursue peacefully his mode of life and to wander at will over the burning sands with his camel.

The leading spirit of the movement for Arab independence was Sheikh Suliman Bahrouni, who previous to the outbreak of war had been a Senator for Western Tripolitana in the Ottoman Parliament. He was a man of great influence, and it was largely owing to his efforts that the tribes had rallied so loyally to the Turkish flag when the invader appeared off Tripoli. As well as being a well-educated man, with considerable organizing powers, he was never averse to exposing

BAHROUNI BEY

BAHROUNI BEY ON HORSEBACK

To face p. 96

himself to hostile fire, and in this way made a reputation for himself amongst the Arabs as a soldier.

When the Arabs heard that peace had been signed and that the Sultan had abandoned them to the Italians, they became infuriated with the Turks, and I feel sure that it was entirely due to Bahrouni that the handful of Ottoman troops was allowed to leave the country. Moreover, he brought all his influence to bear to enable the Turkish commander loyally to fulfil the Treaty of Ouchy, although by so doing he was endangering the success of the Arab efforts.

Despite the great value of arms and munitions to the Arab troops, he allowed the Turks to withdraw their scattered garrisons and to march to the coast with their guns and equipment complete. It was Bahrouni who sent the Italian prisoners down to Tripoli under the guard of his most trusted men. When I think of the smiling faces and well-nourished forms of these captives of the Mussulmans, in comparison with the thin, wasted victims of a European nation's hate and spleen, I wonder again if we are right in trying to crush out of existence one of the few remaining Moslem States.

Bahrouni was obviously anxious not to embarrass in any way the Ottoman Government by giving Italy the slightest excuse for not carrying out the terms of the Treaty. With this object in view he even refused to ask the departing Turks to leave a military surgeon and some hospital necessaries behind, so that his sick and wounded could have been properly attended to. He therefore turned to the Red Crescent Mission and begged us, as an international organisation, to remain behind and share the fortunes of the Arabs. As we

had all made good friends amongst the people and had
no wish to desert the hosts of patients who still flocked
to us for medical advice, we felt it hard to refuse
Bahrouni's request, although we had plenty of warnings
that it would not be safe to remain alone with the
Arabs.   However, in Captain Dixon-Johnson the Arabs
had a sturdy champion and a loyal friend.   Deeply
read in all the intricacies of the Eastern Question, he
devoted all his leisure to cementing the friendship that
had existed, since the reign of the great Elizabeth,
between our country and the Ottoman Empire.   During
the war in Tripolitana he seemed to have a premonition
that we were witnessing the portents of a great storm,
and he saw the vital need of having the Moslem world
on our side when at length it broke.   In this hour of
the Arabs' need he made the strongest appeals to the
Society in London to allow a hospital unit to remain
with Bahrouni's forces.   Meanwhile, in anticipation of
a favourable answer, we made all preparations for a
journey into the mountains; for the Arabs, not possessing a single piece of artillery, and seeing the
impossibility of defending the coast towns, determined
to abandon them to the enemy and make the hills their
line of defence.

Personally I was very sorry to leave Zavia, as the
oasis was most attractive and the nearness of the coast
gave all facilities for sea-bathing.   The evenings were
always cool and beautiful and I used every night to
stroll on to the desert to watch the setting of the sun.
I remember especially the evening of November 11th.

The afternoon, spent in the operating-room, had been
hot and stifling, and it was with a distinct feeling of

relief that we saw the sun sink behind the oasis, leaving
the western sky ablaze with colour. Low down, the
graceful shapes of the date palms were silhouetted
against a crimson background—a burning sheet which
streamed upwards from the horizon, first hiding, and
then blending with the blue of the sky. In a few
minutes the heavens began to display their choicest
treasures. The moon, in slender crescent, touched with
her gentle light every aspect of the scene. Under her
soft touch the squalor of the East vanished and nothing
was left but the romance. The broken houses of Zavia
became palaces and the roofs of the Hammam seemed
to be the domes and minarets of some mighty mosque.
In striking contrast to the pearly light of the moon
was the lamplight flame of Venus and the steady shine
of Jupiter. To the south, where the desert sweeps down
to the Sahara, the sky was darker, and one by one the
lesser lights of heaven peeped out.

Here and there could be seen the forms of shrouded
women, driving home their cattle from the pastures.
As they passed me veils were carefully drawn to avoid
the gaze of the stranger. The only sound that broke
the silence was the lowing of the cattle and the creaking
of the wells as the Arabs drew their evening supply of
water. A more peaceful scene could not have been
imagined, but soon the figure of War appeared. A band
of savage tribesmen from far-off Fezzan came shuffling
over the sand. Relieved from their duty of keeping
watch and ward over the coast - line, they were now
making their way back to the mountains. Fierce-
looking, swarthy warriors were these, wrapped round
with strange clothing, and in some cases adding to their

barbaric appearance by wearing masks over their faces. As well as the rifles slung over their shoulders, they retained the weapons of their forefathers, carrying as each one did a spear or sword. Many a strange tale could these swords have told, some of them bearing traces of ancient make and wrought perhaps for one of the Crusaders of old. Tough-looking soldiers were these Fezzanese, and I could quite believe that they made themselves thoroughly respected by the enemy. Their camels gave another picturesque touch to the scene. On their backs were the carefully-screened litters in which the women and children of the tribesmen travelled. At length the desert swallowed them up, and I was turning to go home along the sandy road, which was now lit up by the moonlight, when my companion touched me on the arm and pointed. A shadow was creeping towards us along the road, blotting out as it advanced the glint of the sand. As it swept past us, we saw the forms of soldiers marching, with here and there the figure of a mounted officer. Like a phantom army, weird, stealthy and silent, they padded softly over the sand. No noisy chattering or cheerful murmurs came from the ranks; no snatches of song as one would expect from soldiers who near their bivouacs and scent the cooking-pots on the camp fires. Nothing was heard but the occasional jingle of a bit or the rattle of an accoutrement to tell us that it was not the ghost of a regiment that passed. But stay! It *was* a ghost; it was the wraith of a past that marched by. It was one of Turkey's scanty but gallant regiments making its way to the concentration camp, preparatory to evacuating the country, for which they had fought so bravely, so victoriously, but alas! so unavailingly. Now and again the moonlight glittered on a polished, well-kept arm, but left one to imagine the tattered, war-worn uniforms, the valises empty of little comforts that soldiers love. We could imagine the efforts of the officers to look smart and tidy, and the piteous shoeless condition of the men. These were the men who, scantily equipped, had carried on for months a desperate warfare against a huge army, amply supplied with all the dread machinery of war. They had passed through a campaign where rifle alone, shouldered by brave hearts, had held its own against howitzer, machine-gun and airship. They had proved themselves worthy successors of their fathers, who in 1877 had hurled back the Russian hordes from the wretched defences of Plevna. The British Mission had gathered their wounded from the battlefield, had nursed and tended them in the hospital, and we had learned to admire their simple courage and stalwart bravery. We had rejoiced with them in victory, and now could do no more than sorrow for them in the hour of misfortune.

It is hard to fight and lose, even when victory would have been a miracle; but to have fought victoriously, to have passed through a hard campaign with untarnished banners, and then to be robbed of the fruits of victory by the scratch of a pen, surely that is heartbreaking.

The light of the moon lent an indescribable touch of melancholy to the picture that unrolled itself before us, and my companion turned away to hide the emotion that overwhelmed him as he saw the remnants of the Ottoman Army passing from Tripolitana.

.   .   .   .   .   .

On the 12th November we received a cable from London authorizing us to stay with the Arab forces and to accompany them to the hills. This was exactly what we were hoping for, since, alluring as was the prospect of the new campaign in the Balkans, the interior of Tripolitana seemed mysterious and romantic, and I, personally, looked forward with great pleasure to exploring the mountains and the places behind them.

The morning of the 13th saw us all early afoot, dressing the wounds of our patients and applying new and clean splints. As we were about to transfer them to our colleagues of the Turkish Red Crescent, we were anxious to sustain our reputation as *alumni* of British hospitals and to hand over our charges looking as respectable as possible.

Towards midday all our patients were clean and tidy, the whole business reminding me of the feverish preparations that are made at home when Royalty makes an inspection of a hospital.

The tiresome proceeding of loading up the camels was going on meanwhile, and an hour later saw the caravan crawling out of Zavia. The party consisted of myself, Captain Dixon-Johnson, Mr. Turnbull, two nurses (Messrs. Davie and M'Kenzie), Mustapha, a well-educated Arab from Tunisia, Mohammed the Algerian cook, and Muktah, who acted as a personal attendant. We had 120 camels carrying the luggage and hospital kit, with the customary number of barbarous-looking drivers, who all carried flint-locks of prehistoric appearance. To keep them in order and also for the sake of protection, Bahrouni had kindly

furnished us with a guard of twenty-four gendarmes
under the command of Hamid Effendi, the stout and
elderly lieutenant of the Arab police.

After a pleasant day's journey, we encamped for the
night in the open desert. It was a cold, clear night,
and as we had been used to the warm rooms of the
Hammam most of us found the air of the desert rather
chilly, so the gendarmes scoured the plains and soon
brought in sufficient brushwood to make a large, blazing
fire. After a glass of hot rum and water and a last
pipe, we rolled ourselves in our blankets and enjoyed
a thoroughly good night's sleep.

We had already saddled up in the morning, when
the local Sheikh sent us a message inviting us to go
to his tent and drink tea with him. As we were anxious
to see as much of the local people as possible and to
get to know their mode of life, we all went, and I was
able for the first time to observe closely how the ceremony of tea-drinking is carried out. Previous to my
arrival in Tripolitana, I was always under the impression
that coffee was the national drink of the Arabs, but I
soon found out my mistake, for although I was given
some thousands of cups of tea it was almost impossible
to obtain coffee anywhere.

To satisfy Arab taste, the beverage must be prepared
in a special manner. Whilst the much-blackened teapot
is being boiled outside the tent, a row of small, thick
glasses is placed on a low table inside. As soon as the
pot boils the requisite amount of tea is put in. A large
white sugar cone is then produced, from which large
chunks are knocked, the instrument for this usually
being the butt-end of a rifle or a stone picked up off

the desert. These lumps of sugar are then placed in
the pot and allowed to dissolve. The tea-maker then
fills all the glasses on the table but promptly pours
them all back into the pot, leaving, however, one half-
filled; this he drinks with a critical air, to make sure
that the brew is satisfactory. The teapot is then placed
on the fire again until it boils. The tea is now ready
and served to the company in the small glasses. It is
considered polite to ejaculate piously, " *Bismillah*,"
before drinking, and should you wish to intimate to
your host that you find the tea good, a loud " *Ouallah* "
after the first sip will greatly please him. As the sweet,
syrupy liquor is usually very hot it is as well to drink
cautiously at first, and as Oriental politeness does not
demand noiseless drinking, if a slight sucking noise be
made no offence will be caused to the assembled
company.

I always enjoyed the Arab tea, finding it pleasant and
stimulating, but my enjoyment was at first very much
marred by the fact that when the glasses were filled for
the second and subsequent times one could never be
sure of getting the same glass back again. I was
always particularly unfortunate in this respect, for,
should there have been amongst the company some
particularly villainous-looking ruffian with a crop of
sores on his lips, I always seemed to get the glass that
he had used. When asked to tea in Tripolitana it
should be remembered that it is considered polite to
drink as many as six glasses, but foreigners can usually
escape with three, if when the next round appears the
guest lays his right hand on the epigastric region, as
much as to say that he can find no further space.

MUKTAH, MUSTAPHA AND FRIENDS

MUKTAH

To face p. 104

I soon found it wise never to judge the social position and rank of an Arab by his dress or appearance, for amongst those who are still untouched by contact with Europeans, life remains in the patriarchal stage, and master, servant and slave look very much alike. On the occasion that I write about, I thought the distinguished-looking coloured man who prepared the tea was my host, and on leaving the tent I warmly wrung him by the hand, to his evident astonishment. Mustapha told me afterwards that this man was a domestic servant and that the host, who could have put five hundred riflemen in the field, was the insignificant-looking old man wrapped up in a blanket!

The second day of the journey passed uneventfully, with the exception of the fact that Muktah, who had been dozing on his camel, fell off and sustained a severe fracture of the left arm. Our caravan was also augmented by the addition of two soldiers we picked up on the way; they had both been wounded in the battle of Zan-Zur and were, obviously, dying for lack of proper attention. It is gratifying to be able to record here that both these men were restored to health and strength after a long stay in hospital.

Having arrived at a suitable camping ground, we had already unloaded the camels and Mohammed was just about to prepare supper when a soldier came up and presented the compliments of a Turkish colonel, who begged us to go and dine with a party of Ottoman officers, who were encamped for the night in the neighbourhood. They had just evacuated El Yefren and were marching to the concentration camp near Zavia. We walked over to join them and were soon

made at home. Having done ample justice to the
dinner, we lit our pipes and passed an interesting couple
of hours chatting over world politics. It was pleasant
to note how intensely they admired our nation and all
things British, and while regretting that our diplomatists
were now neglecting the traditional friendship that had
existed so long between the two great Moslem Powers,
they spoke with gratitude of all that Palmerston and
Beaconsfield had done for their country. I have always
found Turkish officers courteous, well-behaved and
kind-hearted gentlemen, and since my experience in
Tripolitana I have seen no cause to modify my belief;
indeed, during the Great War it has only been
strengthened by the statements of Australian and other
officers who have fought the Turk in Gallipoli and
elsewhere. It is, of course, lamentable that our Kut
prisoners should have had to endure such terrible hardships, and I make no attempt to minimize their sufferings or to excuse those at fault; but it must be
remembered that the standard of life obtaining in the
Ottoman Army is very much below that of ours, and
a ration that would be considered luxury by a Turkish
soldier would spell almost starvation to an Englishman.
It is fairly obvious that the real culprit in the matter of
the treatment of the Kut prisoners was General Liman
von Sanders, who, aware of the fact that the town was
about to fall, and knowing the constitution and needs
of European soldiers, did not insist on proper accommodation and food being prepared for them.

Having said goodbye to our Turkish friends, we
went to our own bivouac and prepared our beds on
the ground. Unfortunately, I was little accustomed at

this time to sleeping on the floor, having passed my nights for the previous four years swinging in a hammock, and now, having unluckily chosen a stony place on the desert, I spent most of the night rolling from side to side trying to get comfortable. Towards morning, however, I fell asleep, and did not wake until the sun was well above the horizon and Mohammed's cooking-pots were calling alluringly.

After breakfast the caravan started, and in a short time we were able to distinguish the main features of the hills. This historic barrier got nearer and nearer, and I thought, as I rode along, that the scene must have changed very little since the dawn of civilization. Up this path had toiled the Phœnicians, the Romans, the Arabs and the Turks, all probably imagining that rich treasures and booty would be found at the end of the road. Here had passed the great explorer Clapperton, who a hundred years before had boasted that the road from Tripoli to Fezzan was safer by far than the road from London to Edinburgh. Now it was our turn, and I think we all wondered in a light-hearted way what experiences we were going to meet.

The ascent from the plains was fairly arduous; here and there we crossed small streams, and at times the rocky path was so steep that we had to dismount and lead our horses, although all sorts of road, rocky or sandy, seemed alike to the camels, who trudged stolidly along. Although an ugly beast, the camel is an admirable product of evolution. Fitted perhaps more especially for use in hot countries, where food and water are scarce, it is, nevertheless, able to hold its own in the colder zones. It can support, for instance, the hardships of a Siberian winter, its coat becoming thicker and longer to enable it to resist the cold. To the Arab wandering over the desert the camel is indispensable. Owing to the peculiar formation of its stomach, it is able to store up water, and is thus able to travel several days without drinking. Its diet is also of the most frugal nature, cropping as it does the coarsest and spikiest growths of the plains; moreover, should there come a time of special privation, it is able to support itself without eating by absorption of the reserve supply of fat in its hump. The callous soles of the foot uniting the toes admirably fits the beast for walking on sand, while the large callosities on the knees and breast enable it to kneel down on the hardest rocks with impunity. The long fringing lashes protect the eye in a sandstorm, while the closable nostrils prevent the air passages becoming choked in a like case.

But, apart from its use as a beast of burden, it is invaluable as a domestic animal. The flesh can be eaten, the milk is made into butter and cheese and the hair woven into fabrics of all sorts. The skin can be tanned and makes a leather of excellent quality. The dung is used as fuel, and this was in ancient times the principal source of sal-ammoniac.

The caves and hidden crevices of the hills were well known to harbour bad characters, and whenever I lingered behind to get a specimen of a rock or to take a closer look at some formation, Hamid Effendi would send back one of the gendarmes to hurry me on. These men were a bright, cheerful lot of fellows and always ready to give one more or less accurate details about the country; but as at the time I still understood

THE ROAD TO EL YEFREN

MAIN STREET AT EL YEFREN

To face p. 108

very little Arabic I was not able to reap much benefit from their conversation. However, I always encouraged them to talk, as it is only by hearing the spoken language that the ear can be trained. How often in my life I have repented the priceless hours of youth utterly wasted in learning such ridiculous rubbish as Greek irregular verbs, when a beautiful language like Spanish can be mastered in a few months! We have been rightly called a nation of shopkeepers, and yet the boys of our country who, in their adult years, are to have the management of our enormous foreign trade, are turned out of our grammar schools with a scrappy knowledge of Latin and Greek and utterly unable to speak even the most-used of all foreign languages with any degree of fluency.

The first sight of El Yefren was satisfying in the extreme, especially to one who loves mountains and dreams of the mysteries that they seem to hide. The town was most romantically situated. The huge towering cliffs frowned down upon us, and on their apparently inaccessible edges the battlements of the castle and other ancient fortifications could be seen. It seemed, to quote old Ritson of Wastdale, that "naught but a flying thing could get up there." But still round and round, and up and up, the path wound, now seemingly cut out of the solid rock by the tools of man, now cleft by the Hand that shaped the mountains. Sharp turns were often protected by small fortresses, so cunningly blended with the natural features of the cliffs that it would have been difficult for an artillery observer to have picked them out. But even if these had been destroyed by high explosive shells, a few hundred marksmen concealed behind the rocks could have held up an army corps. Perhaps some of our own troops, trained in the hard school of the Indian frontier, could have won their way to the summit, but against soldiers only experienced in European manœuvres I judged the approach absolutely impregnable. The Turks, of course, had utterly failed to make any sort of preparation against attack; there was not the sign of a trench anywhere, nor was there a single strand of barbed wire put out for us to tear our clothes upon. Although the Ottoman Empire has been fighting defensive wars for the last fifty years, the Turks have never learned the lesson of always being ready for war. Caught unprepared by the enemy they have been flung back from their natural defences and then have saved the honour of their army by some heroic stand. Thus when the Russians pushed them from the Danube, one of the finest natural boundaries a nation could possess, they fell back on the miserable earthworks of Plevna, where Osman Pasha astonished the world by the magnificent defence he made.

Once we had gained the plateau, the country displayed a totally different aspect. Olive trees were growing on all sides and the ground showed signs of having been cultivated in an industrious manner. As we neared the town and were approaching a small group of wooden huts, we were invited by Hamid Effendi to put our cigarettes out, as these huts were used for the manufacture of powder. We promptly obeyed, and ever afterwards stopped smoking when within fifty yards of the place. I noted, however, that some of the shacks had been injured by fire, and it looked very much

as if an explosion had occurred within recent times.
I ceased to wonder at this later, when I was allowed
one day to watch the progress of manufacture, for one
of the Arab workmen, who was mixing some black
substance suspiciously like gunpowder, was meanwhile
smoking furiously with the cigarette hanging negligently
from his lips!

On arriving in the town we were invited into a large
house to meet Bahrouni and the notables. All showed
the greatest delight at our coming, and an hour or so
passed very pleasantly. Afterwards we walked through
the ill-paved streets to our quarters, and I must confess
I opened my eyes wide at much I saw. I never felt
quite sure before that men really did walk about in
real life with large, elegantly-chased flint-lock pistols in
their sashes; nor was I aware that, except in panto-
mimes, men paraded Eastern streets with curved scimi-
tars at their side. But here I saw it all before my eyes.
For the first time, too, I began to understand the Bible.
Here were the camels waiting to pass through the city
gate; here, too, were the blind beggars squatting at the
roadside asking for alms. We passed the women
drawing water at the well, some sitting on the coping-
stone awaiting their turn, while others were carrying
away the filled jars to their homes. We walked down
the "street that was called straight," and here we saw
signs of Western civilization in the large iron telegraph
posts of British manufacture which stood outside the
post office. Then we heard the blare of a gramophone
grinding out an operatic selection in the Turkish
coffee-house.

Bahrouni had placed at our disposal the old Turkish

military hospital. Little complaint could be found with
these quarters as far as aspect and view were concerned,
for, situated as it was on the very edge of the precipice,
we could see spread out in front the brown and vast
expanse of desert. Unfortunately, however, the building was an old one, and swarmed with those Oriental
pests which the Crusaders brought home with them,
and which have been known ever since by their Arabic
name. Still, we philosophically made the best of things,
and were busy sweeping out the rooms when one of
Bahrouni's men turned up with a sheep that had been
sent as a present. The animal was accompanied by a
Jewish slaughterer, who speedily killed it, to the accom-
paniment of the prayers proper to such occasions.

We all camped for the night on the floor of the
consulting-room, but this term must not be taken to
convey that it was one of those large, airy apartments
that we usually associate with the word. It resembled
much more an English cellar, or a dungeon in a German
" strafe " camp. Still, after Mahommed had ministered
to our excellent appetites and we had taken our rum
ration, when we sat over the large brazier with our
pipes alight, we did not feel that there was much
wrong with the world.

Next morning we all set out house-hunting. The
keys of all the largest dwellings were handed to us,
and we were courteously invited to choose the one that
suited us best. An intelligent young Arab escorted us
and pointed out the advantage of each one, with the
affable volubility of a London house-agent. After going
over a good many we chose a well-built, compact house
quite near the hospital, which had been used as a court-

VIEW OF EL YEFREN

HOSPITAL AT EL YEFREN

To face p. 112

house during the Turkish occupation. It was a one-storey house, constructed, like most Moorish dwellings, with a big courtyard in the middle, and with the rooms round it. The windows were made to open and shut and were paned with glass, but the greatest attraction, perhaps, was that it seemed perfectly clean and was free from vermin.

In a short time we had it swept and garnished, and when we had installed our camp furniture the whole place looked very cosy and even home-like. During the stormy winter we spent in El Yefren we often congratulated ourselves that we had chosen so good a house. As there was no water laid on, we employed women to supply us. They usually fetched it from a spring in the valley, and for this charged so much for each load they brought up. As far as possible we employed for this duty women who had lost their husbands in the war, thus relieving to some extent the great distress that prevailed.

Before our arrival in the town the Arab farmers had been complaining bitterly of the lack of rain. Several crops had been lost for this reason, and everyone said that unless rain fell soon there would be little chance of getting any harvest at all during the coming year. While conversation on this subject was going on during our ceremonial visit to Bahrouni's house, I piously expressed the hope, through the interpreter, that the coming of the British Mission would bring them better fortune. This was put into Arabic by Mustapha, who translated it with Oriental effusion, not forgetting to embroider it with religious quotations. It would ill become me to boast that I was responsible, but the fact remains that the day after our arrival the rain began to fall in a regular deluge. No such beneficial rain had fallen for years, and the members of the Mission gained considerably in prestige and popularity, at least amongst the more ignorant portion of the community, who superstitiously saw some connection between our arrival and the coming of the rain. To us, however, it did not prove an unmixed blessing. During the night the storm raged furiously, and the howling of the wind and the beating of the rain against the windows made sleep almost impossible. From time to time came a loud roaring noise from the valley, just like the burst of a large shell, when some gigantic slab of rock, loosened by the rain, went crashing on to the screes below. When the rain ceased for a while we could hear the gushing of the water running in rivulets near the house, and we often feared we should get flooded out. In the morning, however, we found the house had stood the strain well and had proved absolutely watertight. Unfortunately, the hospital had not escaped as well. We found the patients in the ward in a miserable condition, for the wind had blown out the windows and the roof had leaked badly. Water had flooded in through the door, and the cement floor was covered with 3 or 4 inches of water. As the beds and blankets were soaked through, we all had a good morning's work trying to dry them, and also attempting to mend the leaks in the roof. At first we were favoured by a few hours' sunshine, but in the afternoon the rain started again, and as we had not been able to make a very good job of the roof, we erected tarpaulin shelters over each of the beds, in hopes of keeping the patients dry.

Farmers are proverbially difficult people to satisfy, but I should think the most confirmed grumbler must have been silenced by this rain-storm. Several inches must have fallen during the forty-eight hours it lasted, for the insignificant little cascade at the apex of the Ein Romiya valley became transformed into a powerful waterfall that dashed furiously from the precipice on to the rocks below.

Meanwhile we heard from Hamid Effendi that the Italians had reached Zavia and had pushed out a force to Azizia, where the Headquarters of the Ottoman Army had previously been situated. Considering that Bahrouni now disposed of several thousand well-armed Arabs, we naturally supposed he would take advantage of the inclement weather, and profiting by his local knowledge would have tried to cut the Italian lines of communication, or at all events would have made some attempt to harass the enemy. But I was told that Bahrouni was away at a place called Fessato, where he had gone to spend a feast day with his father. Touching as it was to note the filial devotion he displayed towards his father, it rather reminded me, at the time, of the historical performance of Nero on the fiddle. As it turned out, his irresolution at this moment practically sealed his fate. Still, these matters of politics worried us little; we were there to attend to the wounded and relieve distress, and whatever the inactivity of the Government may have been, we always had plenty of work on hand.

Towards the end of November the weather became very cold. Icy winds whistled round the draughty old hospital, and it was difficult to get warm anywhere.

The only thing to do was to go for a good sharp walk, or failing this to crouch over a brazier. These braziers were the only means we had of getting the rooms warm, but they certainly had their disadvantages, for if the room became inviting on account of the heat engendered, the smoke and highly-unpleasant fumes given off tended to drive one out again.

Personally, I was ill prepared for this sort of weather. I had only brought out with me sub-tropical kit, that proved utterly inefficient to keep out the cold in the hills. By the expedient, however, of wearing two suits of pyjamas under my outer clothing I managed to keep fairly warm, even if the figure I presented was not a very elegant one.

The rainy season soon passed, but with the cold came fogs and mists, the latter making it very difficult to move about the countryside, so well did it hide all landmarks. The fogs also brought to the out-patient department large numbers of Arabs suffering from bronchitis and other chest troubles.

I thought the climate of El Yefren greatly resembled that of the Island of Skye. Many a time have I stood on the edge of the precipice in front of the old castle and imagined myself again on the crags above Loch Coruisk. Looking down from the hospital terrace, all one saw was the thick, blanket-like mist, concealing completely the countryside. At the back of one would be the walls of the fortress, but although it was only a few yards off it was completely hidden. Then something would seem to stir the depths of the fog, and in a flash, suddenly and dramatically, the curtain would be raised. In a few moments the whirling mists and vapours would vanish and the sun-lit desert appear. Villages, towers and palms showed up clearly on the sandy background, and the pools of water round the trees glittered like diamonds. In Tripolitana it is quite useless to seek protection from the rain under a tree, as the Arabs dig little canals to guide the water to the roots, so that after a heavy shower a large pool gathers round the trunk, making approach impossible.

The 7th of December was the day appointed for the remnant of the Turkish garrison to march out, so on the night before we invited all the officers to dinner. It was a bitterly cold night, and we all sat round the table huddled up in our greatcoats; but fortunately Mohammed, who was really capable of great things in the culinary line, served up a magnificent dinner. In fact the Turkish Commander showed his knowledge of the classics by saying that it was a feast worthy of Lucullus, and also delighted the cook by avowing that he had had no idea that so excellent a meal could have been obtained in the country.

With the notable exception of one, whose fluent French betrayed the fact that he had been in close touch with Western culture, all our guests were teetotallers, so we served them with Vichy water, in the lack of anything more palatable. Under the perhaps mistaken idea that a little alcohol would enable us to combat the effects of the harsh weather and make us more efficient in the exercise of our duties, we had provided for ourselves a quantity of *bukha*, which is a strong white spirit brewed locally by the Jews. In order not to offend the religious prejudices of our guests, this fiery liquid had been placed in an empty Vichy bottle.

Most unfortunately this bottle got mixed up with those containing the more innocent drink, and one of the Mussulmans present, again unfortunately the most strict as to religious observances, poured out a large glass of the *bukha* and took a long drink before he discovered his mistake. . . . It was some time before the serenity of the evening was restored.

The next day the Turks marched out, and at last we were alone with the Arabs.

TURKISH SOLDIERS

THE LAST TURK LEAVES EL YEFREN

To face p. 118

CHAPTER VIII.

THE range of hills known to the Arabs as Djebel-i-Gharbi, on which El Yefren is situated, runs almost parallel to the seacoast, and forms part of the natural barrier to the interior about which Rohlfs, the German traveller, spoke. On top the plateau is extensive, and is covered with fairly fertile soil, of which the Arabs, with their primitive agricultural implements, have taken full advantage. Although in the dry season the tops of the hills look brown and barren, after the rains grass springs up, affording ample pasturage for cattle. Olive trees are not cultivated to any great extent, so it is obvious that things have changed in this respect since the time of Pliny the Younger, who informs us, perhaps with some exaggeration, that he rode from Carthage to Alexandria without seeing the sun, so thick were the olive trees on the road.

The mountains appeared to me to be largely composed of eruptive rocks, although here and there I thought I recognized formations of the Cretaceous Age. Some of the rocks were highly mineralized, and I often picked up rich specimens of various ores. The Arabs showed me places where the Italian prospectors had been most active, and they—the Arabs—were under the impression that the presence of these minerals was one of the determining factors in bringing about the hostile invasion. At all events it would not have been the first time in the history of the world that mines have produced international disagreements; and I have often wondered how long the opulent goldfields south of the Orinoco river would have remained in the hands of the natives had they been, like the Turks, under the tutelage of the Great Powers, instead of under the protection of the Monroe Doctrine.

During the course of long ages the action of the elements has carved the hills of Tripolitana into fantastic shapes. Looking at the range from the north it is as though a giant, many-fingered hand had been laid upon the desert, the digits representing mountain spurs running down on to the sand. Between these spurs the valleys are filled up with silt carried down by the mountain streams. During the rainy season great gullies, with high, towering walls, are cut by the swollen rivers. In some places the silt forms a fertile soil, and I have often seen crops of various kinds growing profusely on it.

When travelling over the desert near to the range, one saw signs that strongly reminded one of the geology of countries where, in ancient times, glaciers had been at work. The sand was littered with vast blocks of stone, many of the larger boulders appearing to be striated. Large moraine-like heaps of debris could be seen, as well as rocks having the characteristic appearance of *roches moutonnées*. But as I can find no evidence that the Great Ice Age influenced these latitudes, I suppose the phenomena must be attributed to other agencies.

Standing on one of the higher eminences and sweeping the landscape with field-glasses, one could see that the tops of many of the hills were capped by small towns of typical Moorish build—perched in these positions, I suppose, to make their defence as easy a task as possible. An enemy attempting to take them by assault without adequate artillery preparation would doubtless suffer heavy casualties from the riflemen concealed in the houses.

In my wanderings round El Yefren I was usually accompanied by Mustapha, who could be relied upon to pull me out of any difficulty I got into through my lack of knowledge of Arabic. Sometimes we were joined by Djemel Effendi, Bahrouni's postmaster-general. This official, who was still quite young for so important a charge, had come out to Tripolitana as a civilian telegraph operator. After the signing of peace he had volunteered to stay behind and help to organize the post and telegraph service of the Arab State. After a few weeks' work he had succeeded in getting his lines into excellent order. We could, for example, send a telegram to London one day and receive the answer the next, such a message passing through the French station at Dehibat, on the Tunisian frontier. In addition to his other activities he instructed several young Arabs in the art of telegraphy, and the rapidity with which they learned gives some index as to the natural ability inherent in this interesting race.

The post office worked well, and we received our mail from England with commendable punctuality, always being warned of its approaching arrival by telegraph. Djemel also had great ambitions to extend the

scope of his labours into the interior, and prevailed
upon Bahrouni to let him have some fast-trotting camels
to keep up connection with Fezzan. His great trouble,
however, was the fact that he had no local postage
stamps to cancel, so he asked me to write to London
for designs and an estimate as to cost of a collection
of stamps for the new Arab State.

Apart from business, the postmaster was an amusing
enough fellow. He had been for some years stationed
at Mecca, and would keep us interested for hours with
tales of these little-known regions. For our expeditions
amongst the hills he adopted a strange mixture of
Eastern and Western attire. He usually wore a morning coat and trousers of black broadcloth, his nether
garments, in default of leggings, being pushed into
the tops of a pair of thick socks, supplied by the
Mission. A Turkish fez and a highly-embroidered pair
of slippers finished his attire.

Another of my best friends was Sheikh Sassi-ben-
Selim-Khezam, a distinguished-looking Arab of about
forty-eight years of age. He had taken considerable
part in the fighting along the coast, and had now been
appointed by Bahrouni as Governor of El Yefren. He
was a grave, serious-minded man, who spoke very little,
but his views in council were always listened to with
respectful attention. He was well educated, speaking
fluently Arabic, Turkish and Djebelli, the latter being
the difficult language used by many of the inhabitants
in the hills.

Sheikh Sassi seemed very bitterly opposed to the
Italian invaders. He apparently placed the fullest belief
in the truth of the accounts of the great massacres of

SHEIKH SELIM, SHEIKH SASSI AND DJEMEL

HADJ DJEMEL INSTRUCTING ARABS

To face p. 122

Arabs that the French and English war correspondents had reported, and moreover he said that not only did he fear the loss of independence and freedom, but also the competition of Italian labour. He told me in Tunis, for example, that the Italian was content to work for less than the Arab, and that once the Arabs in Tripolitana were conquered the native would be displaced by the invader and the standard of life obtaining there would be lowered. Personally, having seen the squalor in which the poorer Arabs lived, I very much doubted this statement. On asking him what his opinion was as to the chances of the Arabs maintaining their independence, he answered quietly and proudly that if only the next harvests turned out well and they had a good supply of cartridges, his tribe alone could hold the hills.

It was interesting to see Sheikh Sassi dispensing justice. Sitting on a sofa covered with red plush, with a large English colour-print of a Turkish man-of-war behind him, he disposed of the cases brought before him with the tact and celerity of a London stipendiary. The penalties he inflicted eminently suited the crimes. On one occasion I saw a man brought before him for stealing a sack of ' flour, and after a skilful cross-examination the culprit confessed. After a moderate infliction of corporal punishment, the criminal was forced to parade the streets and market-place with a miniature sack of flour hung round his neck. Naturally this exhibition afforded great pleasure to the small boys of the town, who followed him in troops, shouting out opprobrious remarks.

Conscious of his responsibilities as a magistrate, he spared no one who offended against the law. I well remember a case that illustrates this. There was a picturesque figure in the Arab camp in the person of one El Khani, who acted as standard-bearer to Bahrouni's forces. He had apparently wandered all over Asia as well as the Moslem parts of Africa, during which time he had acquired a fragmentary knowledge of many languages. When he conversed with me he used a sort of Esperanto, in which German, English, French and Arabic predominated. How we managed it I scarcely know, but we frequently had long talks together, and never failed to understand each other. He was a very religious man, and was most particular as to what he ate, as well as being punctilious in praying at the proper hours of the day. The odour of sanctity in which he lived seemed to give him a high position amongst the Arabs.

One day El Khani was exhibiting to me an Italian carbine he had bought in the market-place, and wishing to show that it was in good order he fired a round into the air. Sassi, hearing the shot, at once sent down gendarmes to arrest the offender, and much to the disgust of the high and mighty Khani he was hauled up before the Governor and sharply reprimanded for endangering the life of the populace, as well as for wasting much-needed ammunition.

The only case of murder that occurred during my stay at El Yefren was investigated by the Governor as carefully as a similar matter would be looked into by our coroners at home. A few miles out of the town a merchant had been shot dead from ambush, and his murderer had then rifled the body and stolen the victim's horse. Sassi asked me to go and make a post-

EL KHANI, BAHROUNI BEY, HAMID EFFENDI AND SHEIKH SASSI

EL KHANI

To face p. 124

mortem examination of the body, which was lying in one of the surrounding hamlets. There was no doubt that the man had been well and truly killed, and as a handful of buckshot had entered his chest death must have been fairly instantaneous. After much probing I brought to light the collection of rubbish which forms the usual charge of a flint-lock. The local Sheikh opened the wads, and appeared to gather some information from the crumpled paper. At all events he told the gendarmes whom to arrest, but before hands could be laid on the murderer he decamped, finding his way, it was said, into the Italian lines.

Before leaving the village for El Yefren, the Sheikh entertained me to tea, but he kept me standing a long time at the door of his one-roomed house before he admitted me, until, in fact, he had hidden his wife and daughters in a sort of attic, which was approached by a primitive ladder. I was unable to find out whether this was to be attributed to any attractive qualities I may possess or to the fact that he read a lack of moral principles on my face. He need not have worried, as the evil countenance of his wife, constantly protruded out of the opening in the roof, would, I should think, have frightened away any prospective suitors for the hands of the daughters.

At night time El Yefren was fairly well lighted with paraffin lamps, but the streets, which were kept clean and tidy, were not even enough to make walking after sunset a pleasure. The police patrolled the town after dusk, and, judging from the shrill whistling which went on at all hours of the night, I should imagine they carried out their duty in an efficient if noisy manner.

AT–E*

Bahrouni had now sworn in a hundred fresh gendarmes. They were dressed in neat khaki uniforms and were armed with old Martinis. Every day they could be seen on a bare patch of ground, being drilled by Hamid Effendi, who barked at them with the ferocity of a German *Feldwebel*. I watched them long enough to see the awkward village louts turned into smart policemen.

I frequently came in contact with these new gendarmes, for by Sheikh Sassi's orders we were not allowed to leave the precincts of the town without an escort, as, although we soon became known to the people round, he was afraid that strangers to the district might take us for Italians and open fire. Regardless of these instructions, however, Mustapha and I often managed to escape their attentions and get out for a walk alone, although if Sassi got to hear of it he would send a couple of gendarmes after us and give us a good scolding on our return.

The evenings passed very pleasantly at the house. After supper we nearly always had visitors, who came in to smoke a cigarette and chat over the news of the day. On the evening after the mail had arrived our room was generally closely packed, for the notables of the town were always anxious to hear the news which appeared in the French papers as to the progress of the Balkan War. Unfortunately, the news we were able to give them was not very encouraging.

When Djemel Effendi called he was usually accompanied by a gentleman called Abdulla. The name suggests an Arab, but in reality he was a very typical Frenchman. Apparently he had had some disagreement with his country on the subject of compulsory military service, which necessitated his living abroad. However, much as he detested drill, he had no objection to a little voluntary warfare, and here he was in El Yefren serving Bahrouni as armourer and expert in explosives. I never heard what his original trade was, but he certainly had the knack of quickly repairing the most badly-used rifle.

Abdulla was the only convert from Christianity to Islam that I came across in Tripolitana. Although one naturally looks with scorn on a man who changes from the religion of his fathers, I must say that I think it was sheer conviction that drove him to embrace the creed of the Holy Prophet of Arabia; for Abdulla was a pleasure-loving man, and the rigid moral code, the sobriety and abstinence that the Koran exacts, must have been very irksome to him. My colleague, however, took rather a cynical view of Abdulla's conversion and attributed it to a Frenchman's incurable dislike for celibacy and a desire to further his matrimonial projects.

As winter advanced it became very cold and bleak, and we had the greatest difficulty in keeping the house warm. The poor of the town must have suffered terribly, as their only garment often consisted of one ragged piece. On Fridays, the Mussulmans' Sabbath, we usually made a careful distribution of warm clothing in the name of the Mission, and many of the poor Arabs must have blessed the name of their co-religionists in India and elsewhere who had provided funds to help them. All distributions, however, had to be carried out most cautiously, for as soon as the news went round that clothing was being given out, we were literally besieged by hundreds of supplicants, who swarmed round the house.

Beggars wandered about asking for alms at the doors of the well-to-do, and called on us with great regularity. As we had some reputation as alms-givers, a small crowd of lame and blind beggars usually gathered round our door and wailed monotonously. Despite rain, snow and cold, they squatted there for hours until someone went out and distributed a few coins. Even then, the disappointed ones refused to disperse, and would continue howling until Mohammed rushed out with the rolling-pin and sent them off with a loud " *Imshi!* " (Be off!).

One day, when the chorus of beggars was in full swing, I asked Mustapha what they were calling out, and he translated it thus: " God bless the masters of the house and incline their hearts to be charitable." Looking upon this as a distinctly polite way of demanding alms, I sent little Sambo, a black boy of perhaps ten years of age, to give them a few pence. Whether he was guilty of favouritism I do not know, but at all events, instead of the howling stopping as it usually did, the storm increased in intensity and shrillness. I then told Sambo to go out and move them on. In a few minutes a terrific hubbub arose outside, and rushing out I saw little Sambo busily engaged in beating half a dozen able-bodied beggars about the head with a thick stick, without them making the slightest resistance. To compensate for this Oriental proceeding, I was forced to make another distribution of small change.

With the approach of Christmas the days became very short, and the sun sinking low in the sky illuminated

less and less the cold, dank courtyards of the town.
We eagerly waited for the shortest day to come and
go, so that we could look for the coming of spring.
Small wonder that the winter solstice is everywhere
celebrated as a great festival, giving promise, as it does,
of more light, more warmth, and more life.

One morning I was awakened by loud calls from
Mohammed, who was shouting in an excited fashion
in the courtyard. On going out I found that the whole
courtyard was thickly covered with snow. This was
the first time our cook had ever seen snow, and I fully
expected to hear him complain bitterly of the cold,
standing as he was bare-footed, but instead of that he
was smiling all over his black, good-humoured face,
and seemed highly pleased with the state of things.

The weather was distinctly changeable, however, and
some days were quite warm. I remember on one
occasion starting out for a long walk with a gendarme,
very thickly wrapped up, as there was a thick coating
of ice on the water; but before I had gone very far
the sun shone brilliantly and I began to wish I had left
my overcoat at home. On the way back we had to
make our way through a heavy hail-storm, and then
were almost unable to find the path leading to the town
on account of the fall of a dense fog.

However, the days passed quickly and pleasantly
enough, despite the worst that the weather could do.
The hospital was always full and provided ample work
for those who cared about it; moreover, out-patients
gathered in large numbers every morning, and it
required a good deal of tact and patience to send them
away satisfied. Having disposed of the out-patients,

we went inside to attend to the more serious cases. These, however, were the peculiar province of my colleague, who took extraordinary pains with his dressings, and in a good-natured sort of way rather resented than welcomed assistance; so it usually ended in me looking after the outdoor department while Mr. Turnbull performed feats of surgical skill inside worthy indeed of Edinburgh Royal Infirmary. This arrangement suited me splendidly, and I stood outside in a greatcoat and practised my kitchen Arabic on the long-suffering out-patients.

Having finished with this duty, I used to go with Mustapha or Mohammed up to the market-place and do our shopping. Most of the traders were Jews, and we soon found they could drive a bargain in full accordance with the traditions of their race. Meat, vegetables and other table necessities were rather dear, nor was there a large variety to select from, but as we had plenty of canned goods in our store there was little fault to be found with the meals that Mohammed served up.

After lunch my colleague usually went up to the hospital again, and having seen that the beds were dressed with military precision and that the patients were behaving themselves, he would take a dignified walk down the Bond Street of El Yefren. As he was an expert at laundry work and could iron and " get up " collars and shirts better than a Chinaman, I have little doubt he was the best-dressed man in Tripolitana. His faultless attire certainly did much to enhance the prestige of the Mission.

As for myself, with great difficulty I was breaking

with the siesta habit that I had acquired in the tropics, so after lunch I would put on an old pair of climbing-boots and go for a scramble on the rocks, if time did not permit of a longer expedition.

In these days I was giving a rather unwilling Mustapha some elementary instruction in the art of rock-climbing, and the crags in the Ein Romiya valley formed our practice ground. One day, when scrambling about on the screes at the foot of the precipice, I heard voices at the top of the cliff, and Mustapha started running away, shouting out to me that a bomb was about to be thrown down. This infernal machine was an invention of Abdulla, and he was as proud of it as I presume Mr. Mills must be of his own deadly con-trivance. At all events, I had no desire to allow the bomb to prove its efficiency on me, and as I had no time to get away into the valley I looked for a suitable place to hide. I found a narrow rift in the cliff, splitting it from top to bottom, blocked at the top, however, by a large chockstone. The walls of this "chimney" were beautifully rough and uneven, and the rift as a whole presented an irresistible attraction to the climber; so with my feet against one wall and back against the other, I commenced to make my way upwards in the orthodox manner of the cragsman. In a short time Abdulla's bomb went off with a concussion that was probably highly satisfying to himself, but which nearly shook me to the bottom of the "chimney." As I got nearer the top, I began to find that my climbing muscles were sorely out of practice, and by the time I had reached the chockstone I was nearly exhausted. Judge then my consternation when I tried to wriggle between

the stone and the cliff and found there was scarcely
sufficient space for me to pass; the most I could do was
to get my head and one arm through the hole. It was
now too late for me to think of going down again, as
my legs were trembling with the strain, so the only
thing to do was to trust to the strength of my arms
and so pull myself over the chockstone. Suddenly I
made a dash for it and scrambled over, landing on the
top in a panting but thankful condition. The amusing
part of the whole thing was that I landed right in the
middle of a group of Arabs, who saw with amazement
my head suddenly appear over their inviolable cliffs.

I had one very favourite walk, and that was to the
Jewish village of Shgana, which lay at about half an
hour's sharp walk from El Yefren. It was delightfully
situated, standing as it were piled up on a spur of the
mountains. Dividing it from the main block of hills
was a deep valley cut clean out of the solid rock by the
action of water. Approaching Shgana from Yefren one
was brought to a standstill by this formidable gorge,
and here a magnificent view could be obtained. The
eye travelled down the precipice, then across the valley
that formed the old bed of the torrent and up the cliffs
opposite. On the top of these heights the town was
built, the houses being erected right on the very edge.
Then they rose tier by tier, until the crest of the hill
was reached. Although we were still fairly far from it,
noises from the village could be plainly heard, owing
to the acoustic properties of the deep valley. To the
left the gorge opened out widely, but a direct view on
to the desert was blocked by a mountain called Tamalilt.
This eminence was beautifully shaped, rising to a lofty

SUMMIT OF TAMMALILT

SUMMER HATS

To face p. 132

graceful cone, and from the way it was anchored to the ground the whole picture strongly reminded me of our own mountain Snowdon.

Between Tamalilt and the higher part of the gorge the valley had been filled up with the fertile silt from the plateau above, and this ground was in a state of high cultivation. In fact, the scene beneath gave the lie to the assertion that the Arabs are an idle race. Infinite pains had been taken to use even the smallest fall of rain by the construction of conduits to lead the water into every little patch of garden. Standing on our eyrie we could see clumps of palm trees and the figures of women, looking as small as ants, washing round the wells. Herds of goats stood out like specks on the yellow ground, and groups of small, sturdy cattle were being driven.home from the pastures.

Some days, when we had plenty of time, we clambered down a steep, rocky staircase, crossed the valley, and then ascended the path into the village. Here the Jewish houses were better built than those of the Arabs, and the girls and women, who sat in the sun carding wool, looked much more attractive than their sisters at El Yefren.

One day, when sight-seeing in Shgana, I was politely accosted by the Jewish rabbi, who offered to show me the synagogue. He conducted me into a neat little building, which although poorly fitted up was clean and well looked after. It was apparently used as a school during the week, as I saw a large class of boys busily engaged in acquiring the elements of the Hebrew language. I was then shown the Scrolls of the Law and the other sacred objects necessary for the due

observance of this venerable creed. Looking round,
I thought what an amazing hold his faith has on the
Jew; how through centuries of persecution and affront
he has never thought of abandoning the creed of his
fathers.

The Jew seems to have met with fairer treatment
from the Mussulman than from the Christian. For
one thing, the Moslem, although he venerates Jesus
Christ as a prophet, does not believe that He perished
on the Cross, and so harbours no hatred against the
whole of the Jewish people because one of their number
betrayed Him. Moreover, in the days of the Holy
Inquisition, Mussulman and Jew were sent equally to
the torture chair and perished, side by side, in the fires
of the *auto-da-fé*. The large Spanish-speaking Jewish
population in the Balkans is a tribute to the hospitality
and broad-mindedness of the Turk, in that he received
them and protected them from the fanatical fury of the
rest of Europe.

The rabbi at Shgana had no complaints to make
against the Moslem population, with whom they all
lived on terms of friendship. They were allowed the
fullest religious liberty and their homes were respected.

As I was on the point of going, he begged me to
call and see a member of the community who was lying
sick. I accompanied him through the town, and was
finally shown into a house where a middle-aged Jew
was lying on a palliasse. I was making a careful and
impressive examination of his condition, when a shadow
cut off the bright sunlight that was pouring through
the door. Before I could look up, I heard the excited
voice of Mustapha saying, "*Mon docteur, regardez*

MARKET TOWN NEAR EL YEFREN

MARKET PLACE AT EL YEFREN

To face p. 134

donc la jolie juive!" I glanced at the figure in the doorway, and, ignorant as I am in these matters, I at once saw that during his stay in Paris my interpreter had by no means neglected the most important of all studies, for the young Jewess was indeed beautiful. A mass of black, glossy hair crowned a head poised proudly on a slender, graceful neck. Dark eyes, veiled modestly under curving lashes, looked out from a delicately - chiselled face. Surprised at the sight of foreigners, whom she now beheld for the first time in her life, and who did not spare her an admiring scrutiny, a rich blush drove the pallor from her cheeks. The colour sped in a wave down her neck, fired the whiteness of her bosom, and tinged the rounded arms that escaped from her scanty robe. Her half-parted red lips revealed a perfect row of teeth, and her eyes falling gently to the ground invited a glance to her arched feet and slender ankles.

Sometimes one is apt to forget that sedate middle age has chilled the blood of youth, and I must confess that, for the moment, my attention was singularly diverted from the woes of my patient. I patted the mat invitingly and asked the damsel to sit down, but she preferred the standing position, evidently fearing to approach too nearly the strange *hakim*. She was, however, answering my questions in an animated and intelligent fashion when the sick man interrupted us. He not only disliked his pains and aches being neglected, but apparently took exception to the admiring glances that Mustapha was throwing upon his daughter. Wishing to continue the conversation for a while, I put a clinical thermometer in the Jew's mouth and told him not to open his lips until I took it out. I had just elicited the fact that the girl was going to marry one Yakob by name, when an agonized look of suffering and suspicion on the father's face made me take compassion on him, and I removed the thermometer from his mouth. He then got up from the floor and announced that the medicine had done him a great deal of good and he already felt able to walk.

A few days later a desire to see that the old Jew was doing well induced me to pay him another visit, choosing a time when I thought that domestic duties would permit of the daughter explaining to me the progress of the case. I found the patient quite alone, a state of things that not only appeared to give him satisfaction but also enabled me to give undivided attention to professional matters. He expressed himself so much better that he thought if he could have one more suck of the tube the cure would be complete. As it threw no heavy expense on the Mission I allowed him the full use of the thermometer for five minutes. To an outsider, we should have looked an interesting group sitting there on the floor—the bearded Jew, with the magic tube held solemnly between pursed lips; the grave-faced *hakim*, with a Mayfair bedside manner, watching the patient attentively; Mustapha, with the longing of youth, regarding the door hopefully.

Having once again relieved suffering humanity, we were lingering for a while for the purpose of enjoying the laconic conversation of the Jew, when suddenly the door was pushed open and in walked the fair daughter.

Although it was miserably cold and a little snow was falling, she was without any shoes or stockings and as lightly clad as a London maiden in a dance frock. Before I left I handed her a few shillings from my own pocket to buy another wrap with, for much as one appreciates beauty unadorned, it is not pleasant to see a pretty girl shivering with cold.

I have noticed everywhere that the Jews are a home-loving race and have great affection for their wives and children, and in Tripolitana they proved to be no exception to the rule. Fathers, having children in need of medical treatment, would carry them for many miles in order to get advice from the Mission. On several occasions children were brought who obviously were very ill and needed the most careful attention. As they went from bad to worse in the hands of their parents, our two British nurses were very anxious to take them in and tend them in the hospital. Unfortunately we could never get the consent of the parents, or it would have been interesting to watch a little baby being looked after by two stalwart ex-soldiers.

The Jewish population, as well as the Mussulmans, were all very exact in their religious observances. I well remember an old Jewess being brought to the hospital in a very weak condition. It was obvious she was suffering more from lack of nutrition than disease, so I offered her a trifling sum in order that she might buy some food. To my surprise she wearily refused the gift. I looked at Mustapha for an explanation, and he told me that as it was the Sabbath it was not lawful for her to receive money.

With another Jewish patient I had a very interesting

experience. He was old and wizened, but although he complained of all sorts of maladies, careful examination failed to reveal any disease. Nevertheless, as I was anxious if possible to help him, I filled up his bottle regularly, and as he looked wretchedly poor I occasionally gave him a few coins to buy food with.

One day, however, Mustapha, our official interpreter, was away, and I had summoned Mohammed the cook to assist me. Apparently the old Jew trusted the latter more than the more polished product of French culture, for he came up very near and then whispered something to Mohammed. On this being interpreted to me I understood that the old man had in his house something very valuable he wished to show me. As to the nature of the object he refused to say a word, and then, frightened at the questioning of Mohammed, he added that it was really nothing and probably would be of no interest to a foreigner.

As the village where he lived was some distance off, I thought no more of the matter, until one day, returning from a visit to some Roman ruins in company with the postmaster of El Yefren, we passed through a little hamlet. Suddenly the incident came back to me, for I saw the Jew standing at the door of a dwelling. I pulled up and asked him how he was, and to my astonishment he at first pretended not to know me. However, at last he condescended to recognize me, and asked me into his house. Judging from the energetic manner with which his wife was working at some sort of a mill, I thought it possible that she might be the valuable object referred to; or it might even have been the soft-eyed daughter, a tall

Jewess of about twenty-five who scrutinized us long
and gravely, as though in some doubt as to our
respectability.

After we had drunk tea and eaten a few dates, seeing
that the subject of the treasure had not been broached,
I ventured to refresh his memory with regard to his
conversation with me at El Yefren. At first he flatly
denied having anything of value in his miserable house,
but when the postmaster had spoken to him in rather
a hectoring fashion he became abject and promised to
produce it. First he locked and bolted the outside
door, and then trustfully leaving the Turk and myself
with his wife, he went into the inside room with his
daughter. I heard a noise of heavy stones being moved
and boxes being pushed about. After about a quarter
of an hour he came into our room and invited me to
enter alone. I went into a sort of musty, smelling
cellar, lit dimly by an old-fashioned oil-lamp. Then the
old man locked the door and put the key in his pocket.
After this he lifted up the lid of an iron-bound chest
and produced several highly-odorous pieces of old
clothing, followed by a bundle of rags, about the size
of a baby in arms. I felt quite excited as to what was
going to happen. The Jew commenced to unwrap the
bundle, the daughter meanwhile holding the lamp quite
near and never taking her eyes off me for a moment,
as much as to say, "Can we trust you?"

Occasionally my own eyes wandered for a moment
from the uninviting bundle of rags to the woman's
face, only to meet a steady, disconcerting stare. Slowly
the wrappings were taken off, and the bundle assumed
quite small proportions. Then a last fold of silk was

undone, and the old Jew placed carefully in my hands the most beautiful weapon I have ever seen. It was a large flint-lock pistol of Arab or Persian manufacture. Made by a patient master-hand that loved the art, it was richly inlaid with gold, while the stock was incrusted with seed pearls and amethysts. The hammer was fashioned into the shape of a wolf's head, the opened jaws grasping the wedge of flint. The grip terminated in an ivory ball, exquisitely carved into figures that had a curious Chinese appearance. Although Arabic characters were spread over the whole weapon, I was astonished to find a gold band, running round the barrel, apparently hammered on to it, that bore a few words in the Latin tongue: *Pro gloria et patr* . . .

Altogether I can give no adequate description of this beautiful pistol, but I can truthfully say that in all the museums I have visited I have never seen a weapon to approach it for elegance of workmanship or symmetry of line.

To see it was to desire it, so I asked the old Jew how much he wanted for it. In answer he showed me a piece of paper with Arabic figures on it, but as I was quite unable to decipher them, I proposed that I should call in Djemel to assist. To this proposition both the man and his daughter vehemently objected, and the latter taking the lead said they would come over to El Yefren if I would get Mohammed to interpret.

The next day the old Jew arrived, not forgetting to bring the woman with him to see fair play, and again to disconcert me with her steady, persistent gaze. At first a hundred and fifty Turkish pounds were demanded, but after an hour's bargaining he came down to one

hundred. I firmly believe that the pistol was worth
the sum asked, and I ardently desired to possess it, but
I hardly cared to spend so large a sum on a curio; in
any case I should have had to send to Tunisia for the
money. After we had been arguing nearly all afternoon
about it and I was unable to beat him down, I presented
him with a few shillings for his trouble and let him
go.

How fascinating it is to ponder over the inscrutable
history of things like this! I can see this pistol in
the sash of some Oriental potentate, whose child climbs
on his parent's knee and plays with the golden barrel.
Years pass and it slips from the quivering hand of age,
to be picked up by the son, now grown a man. He in
turn hands it to his son. . . .

Perhaps, some day, I shall see it in a museum, where
I may go to look at it from time to time, each period
of time told off and measured by a little increase in
dimness of sight, a little stiffening of the joints, a little
more difficulty in catching the words around me—and
lastly, when all that remains of me is a box of moulder-
ing bones, the pistol will still glitter provokingly in the
case.

.   .   .   .   .   .

Early in the new year urgent private affairs called
Captain Dixon-Johnson home, and accompanied by
Muktar he made an uneventful journey to Ben-
Gardane. He was hoping to return fairly soon, but
the collapse of Bahrouni's resistance caused him to
alter his plans.

CHAPTER IX.

MEANWHILE, it may be asked, what was Bahrouni doing during these critical months? He had several thousand well-armed men in the camps of Rapta, Lossaba and Bechoul, men who were anxious to fight and itching to seize hold of any booty that might come to hand. Loot of any description has the greatest possible attraction for the Tripolitan Arabs, and like the ragged veterans of Lee and Jackson they would charge through Hell to get a grip on a well-filled haversack.

But day after day and week after week passed without Bahrouni making any sign, a state of things which produced great discontent amongst his lieutenants. When I met him, I was always careful to refrain from talking about politics, and only conversed with him on general topics. The one great interest we had in common was astronomy, and unsatisfactory as a conversation always must be when carried on through an interpreter, I formed a high opinion of his intelligence, for he had a deep knowledge of this fascinating science. Certainly he was not up-to-date, for he still placed great faith in the teaching of Albategnius, the "Ptolemy of the Arabs." He had great dreams of a revival of scientific knowledge amongst his people, and hoped that the time would come when the Moslem would

again be in a position to give Christian Europe instruction in science.

Bahrouni had with him at El Yefren an excellent
astronomical telescope, and as Saturn was at that time
conveniently situated for observation, we had the glass
pretty constantly on it.

In a democratic community such as the Arab it is
difficult to get much privacy, as all around wish to
share in the pleasures of the more highly placed. Thus
the manipulator of the telescope always had a large
queue pressing up behind him anxious to get a look
through the magic tube. Personally, I rather enjoyed
seeing the Arabs take an interest in the science that
they had done so much to preserve when the rest of
Europe was plunged in the darkness of the Middle
Ages; but at the same time it was disconcerting in the
extreme to see some of the diseased and inflamed eyes
that were pressed against the lens.

But, if Bahrouni did take an interest in the stars,
he showed little inclination to get on with the war.
To me it appeared he had formed the idea that, providing he committed no act of aggression against the
Italians, they in turn would leave him and his range
of hills in peace; but obviously a waiting game was
the only one for the enemy to play, just as it was
Bahrouni's to irritate the Italians with a guerilla warfare
and keep them in a state of nervousness. Meanwhile,
the enemy had ample time to dig in and put out their
wire, whilst the Arabs were eating up their stores of
flour and emptying their war-chest. The scarcity exist-
ing in the Moslem camp began to undermine the morale
of the soldiers, and reports of the good living to be

had on the other side of the line, as well as the high wages alleged to be paid to deserters, were daily causing defections in Bahrouni's ranks.

To add to the general discontent obtaining in the district, a serious item of news now arrived; the enemy, following a policy of peaceful penetration, had succeeded in persuading the Arab Governor of Gahrian to receive an Italian force, his scruples having been overcome, it was alleged, by means of a bribe. As the town of Gahrian is situated only a few miles off, to the westward of El Yefren, and stands on the same range of hills, it was apparent that Bahrouni's chances were dwindling. Later news showed that Gahrian had been occupied by a large Italian force and that the railway from Tripoli to Zavia and Azizia was rapidly being constructed. Although this work could have been impeded, and lines of communication threatened by a handful of courageous snipers, the Arab chief took no action; in fact, he did what was worse—he made a present to the enemy of the whole of his dispositions, in allowing his three police officers to proceed to Gahrian to offer their services to the enemy!

Although my personal inclination was to stay and see the finish of an extraordinary situation, at the same time I felt that we were rather wasting charitable people's money, so I wrote to Bahrouni, who was away at the time, saying that as hostilities had now apparently ceased, I felt I must ask him to supply me with camels and a couple of gendarmes, so that I might leave the country. I intended first, however, to visit the interesting city of Ghadarmes, on the caravan route to Ghat.

ARAB POLICE OFFICERS

ARAB SCOUTS

To face p. 144

A few days later I received a message from Sheikh
Sassi begging me to call on him at the *Gendarmerie*.
He told me that Bahrouni had received my letter, and
that he requested me to stay a little longer, as the war
was going to recommence in a very short time. He
added that he thought I was a little tired of El Yefren,
and that, as there was a good deal of sickness at Rapta,
he would be glad if I would go down and see if
anything could be done. Needless to say, I was
delighted with the prospect of this journey, and
accordingly early in January I set out from El Yefren
on my way to the Arab camp. I was accompanied
by two gendarmes and a young Arab lieutenant, who
fortunately spoke a little French.

I had already seen some of the more desolate parts
of the world, but never had I travelled through a
bleaker, wilder, or more inhospitable countryside than
this portion of Tripolitana. Rough, rugged and barren
hills, covered with sharp stones painful to the horses'
hoofs, alternated with deep valleys, into which huge
blocks of stone had fallen from the precipices, making
the winding road difficult to traverse. Here and there
we passed sad and lifeless villages perched on the tops
of the highest and most inaccessible peaks.

In the larger valleys there were some signs of
cultivation, small green patches standing out on the
yellowish soil, often overshadowed by a clump of palm
or olive trees. Each little group of gardens was
dominated by a tall, white watch-tower, and although
no sign of human life could be seen elsewhere, a foot
of rifle barrel jutting out from the top of the towers
showed that there, at all events, was a vigilant eye bent

upon resisting the predatory tendencies of the neighbours. These towers were miniature fortresses, built strongly of stone, with doors of sheet iron, over which could be seen a little window, conveniently placed for pouring hot water or oil on whosoever might attempt to beat down the door. These watch-towers must have existed from the earliest times, and it is not difficult to understand how the Arabs became interested in the stars. Here the guard would stand all night with little else to absorb him but the movements of the celestial bodies. The sky was his theatre, and the constant movements of the stars gave him a nightly change of programme. Given an intelligent man and he would notice the swift changes of the moon, the crawling of the planets over the sphere, and the relations of different stars to the rising of the sun. Little by little it would dawn upon him how he could predict an eclipse of the moon, and then, perhaps, one day his brain would grasp the fact that even the awful darkening of the sun in daytime could be robbed of its terrors by foretelling the hour of its arrival.

My companions and I were now moving through a country filled with suspicion and distrust. Women and children fled at our approach, while men engaged in ploughing with camel or ox left their primitive implements and picked up rifle or pistol, that lay ready at hand. Travellers on the road halted and primed their flint-locks, and refused to pass us until they had scrutinized us carefully.

Early in the afternoon we ran into a little adventure, and as it was the first time I came under fire in that country, it left a marked impression on my mind. We

AN ARAB WATCH TOWER

A WAYSIDE HALT

To face p. 146

were just rounding the corner of a valley when we heard the sound of rifle shots, apparently fired at no great distance from us. In a few moments we spied an Arab, kneeling down and firing with his Martini at a mark. Now, as cartridges were very scarce in the district, Bahrouni had given orders that there should be no waste of ammunition, and that offenders against this rule should be punished by forfeiture of the rifle. Khalifa, the Arab lieutenant, questioned the culprit, and finding that he could give no adequate excuse, told him that he would have to give up the rifle. As it is the height of an Arab's ambition to possess a modern weapon, the man refused, saying that he would die before he surrendered it. The gendarmes were lingering behind, and neither the lieutenant nor I was carrying a rifle, so the Arab saw a chance to escape and darted off down the valley. Khalifa, who had dismounted to interrogate the man, drew a revolver and ran after the fleeing Arab, firing as he ran. One of the shots took effect, for the fugitive suddenly whipped round, showing an ugly, bleeding gash on the side of his face. He then brought his rifle up to the hip and fired at Khalifa, but the shot missed, and the big leaden bullet spat viciously on the rock behind me. I felt rather glad at the time that M. Martini's invention did not include the provision of a magazine to the rifle which bears his name. After his wasted shot the Arab threw down the weapon and disappeared amongst the rocks.

An hour afterwards we rode into the little town of Kikla, situated about half-way between Yefren and Rapta. Here we intended to rest the horses for an hour or so, and then to push on to the camp. To this programme, however, the aged Sheikh of the town would by no means consent. He would not hear of us going any farther that day, and conducting us into the castle said that dinner was already on the fire and would soon be served up. While waiting for the meal I had a look round the town. With the exception of the schoolhouse, erected by the ex-Sultan Abdul Hamid, there was not a decent building in the place, nor is there ever likely to be, as the town stands isolated on the bleak, forlorn hills. What a country to spill blood over when the fertile lands of the world call for labourers! One wondered more and more what there was in this poor province to tempt the cupidity of an invader. It seemed a pity that these poor mountain Arabs, who were happy and contented enough, despite their poverty, should be dragged into the whirl of our fussy, grasping, Western civilization.

The Arabs of the hills, devoid of some virtues, possess to the full that love of independence and that dislike of unsympathetic control which seems to distinguish mountaineers all the world over. Their bold character has been developed through many ages by the hardness of their life and their struggle with an infertile soil. The barrier of hills has prevented the development of commerce, prohibited the accumulation of wealth, and fostered a democratic spirit.

After seeing all the sights of the town, I returned to the castle, and having satisfied myself that my pony was enjoying a good feed, I was ready to attend to the large crowd of patients who had gathered in the courtyard. Diagnosis proved rather difficult, as Khalifa's French was bad, my Arabic was worse, and the English of an Egyptian who officiously pushed himself forward as an interpreter was execrable. Still, we managed all right, although it was rather disconcerting to see an aged woman, to whom I had given a few grains of calomel, swallow it together with the piece of the *Daily Mail* in which it was wrapped. She evidently attributed therapeutic powers to the cabalistic letters printed on it, and as there is undoubted efficacy in the process of auto-suggestion, I feel quite sure she still lives to bless the name of the foreign doctor.

On this occasion, however, I relieved one patient who afterwards followed me about for some time, increasing my prestige by loudly shouting my praises in every market-place. Being of a simple and believing nature, I always attributed this activity on his part to gratitude, but there were not lacking those who pointed out that the fact that he lived on me, and was clothed by me, was the real reason for his attachment to my person. At all events, when I saw him at Kikla, he had a large sort of polypus on the inside of the upper eyelid that hung over the pupil and made him almost completely blind, as his other eye had been ruined by trachoma in childhood. On examination, I found that the growth hung by a slender stalk and that its removal would be the simplest of surgical tasks. He lay down on the flags of the courtyard in a mass of mud and filth, while I cocainized the eye, but before this could be done his struggles were such that the gendarmes had to hold an arm apiece, while some willing spectators, in order to get a good view of the proceeding, controlled his feet. A rapid snip of the scissors and the operation was complete. The patient, despite a film of blood, could now see clearly, and he gave thanks to God in a loud voice and called down blessings on my head. Amid his vociferous shouts I frequently heard my own name, and Khalifa told me that he was explaining to the crowd that I was the cleverest doctor in the world. The exuberance of his compliment and the slight degree of exaggeration therein may perhaps be pardoned in one who has just had his sight restored.

Having finished ministering to suffering humanity, Khalifa and I went into the justices' room, where the notables of the town had gathered to welcome us. It was a large, bare, draughty apartment, without any sort of furniture, except in so far that there was a concrete bench covered with a piece of carpet to sit on.

The day was now ending, and it was becoming miserably cold. Seeing me shiver, the Sheikh had a large wood fire made in the centre of the floor, the smoke of which wandered about the room until it found its outlet in the hole knocked for that purpose in the ceiling. In a few minutes my eyes were smarting badly, and I was almost choking with the fumes; so I abandoned the concrete bench for the floor, where the smoke was not so dense.

By this time both Khalifa and myself were desperately hungry, and yet there was no sign of the promised food; the dreaded quarter of an hour before dinner was being prolonged to more than two hours. To me waiting was specially boring, as I was unable to join freely in the conversation, so I searched in my saddle-bags for Whitaker's Almanack, without which I never travel on account of the interesting reading in it, and to my annoyance I found that Mohammed had packed the

Nautical Almanack instead. Anyone who knows this latter publication will understand that I was much relieved when finally, after a wait of four hours, the dish of *cous-cous* was put before the company. We all sat on the floor round the large bowl, and after the necessary ablutions and customary prayer, we began to enjoy our meal. I sat next to the Sheikh, and had many little compliments paid to me by him. For instance, he raked deeply in the dish with his hand to find me the choicest pieces of meat, and then enhanced the favour by stripping the muscle off the bone with his fingers. I was not, at the time, very used to Arab table manners, and at first felt a little squeamish, but the old man's fingers were so beautifully clean and well-kept that my appetite was in no way affected.

After dinner, several more of the leading men in the district came in, and we all settled down to an evening's tea-drinking. Conversation turned on the war in general and what was going to happen when and if the Arab resistance collapsed. The Sheikh greatly lamented the departure of the Turks, saying that the rule of the Sultan had been benevolent and sympathetic, and that all around felt very lonely and depressed without the Ottoman officials. Although I tried to keep out of the discussion, deeming it unwise and no part of my duty to counsel a hopeless struggle, I was repeatedly asked my opinion of the Italians and how I thought they would govern. I replied that in Somaliland they had proved themselves good administrators and that I felt sure they would respect life and property. One of the company thereupon got rather excited, and Khalifa explained that his family had been *killed* in the fighting round Tripoli. The word used was apparently " massacred," but custom has ordained that this word is only appropriate when the killing has been done by the Turk.

As best I could, through Khalifa, I gave them a brief description of the benefits of civilization. How advantageous it would be to be able to run into Tripoli for the day on a good railway; how a factory would spring up or a mine be developed, where good money could be earned to buy bowler hats, gramophones, cramping boots and bicycles, and—incidentally—to pay the Royal taxes. Even work would be found for the women, and doubtless the younger and more attractive ones would find employment in that mode of life that the West prefers to the polygamy of the East. Moreover, instead of sitting drinking a poor sort of tea in a cold, miserable room, they would be able to have boisterous evenings with proper stimulating liquors in a good café. But, alas! the prospect seemed to please them even less than it did me.

At a late hour we settled off to sleep. Whilst Khalifa and the sheikhs, wrapped in their robes, lay down on the concrete bench, a large flock bed was brought in and laid down for my benefit. The benefit, however, proved entirely on the side of its voracious occupants, and I was soon glad to slide off it and get on to the ground.

Waking in the morning after a very inferior night's sleep, I proposed to Khalifa that we should make an early start. He interpreted this to the Sheikh, who immediately said he could not let us go so soon, as it was the custom that anyone making a visit such as this

should "sit down" for at least three days. I had no
wish not to observe the proper etiquette, especially
in dealing with a venerable old man, but I felt that to
sit on a concrete bench for three days with nothing but
the Nautical Almanack to read would drive me to idiocy,
so I begged Khalifa to explain that Sheikh Sassi had
requested me to proceed to Rapta as quickly as possible. This apparently weighed with the Sheikh, who
said he would order the horses to be saddled as soon
as we had had the morning meal. I ventured to ask
how long this would be. He replied that it was already
"on the fire," from which reply I gathered that some
considerable time would elapse before we should see it.
I largely attribute my patience in public restaurants,
when the waiters are slow, to the admirable training
I received in Tripolitana.

Having seen and treated a number of patients in the
courtyard, I went back into the room to warm my hands
over the fire, where I found a number of guests had
arrived to scrutinize politely the foreign doctor. I was
unable to converse very much with them, as Khalifa
had gone out to visit a relation, so when conversation
languished I made an attempt to entertain them. I have
some skill in making objects out of paper, and I find
this art invaluable in amusing children—as well as
myself. I tore some leaves off my writing pad, and
after the usual manipulations the Arabs were astonished
to see water boil in a paper kettle over a fire that burst
into flame when blown by a pair of paper bellows.
There was a purse, too, into which a coin was dropped
and then disappeared, only to be found again on opening
it a second time.

The show proved a great success, and I was just getting to the end of my repertoire when dinner was announced; unfortunately it was so highly spiced that I had to follow each mouthful with a gulp from the goblet. After the meal we took our leave of the company, but the Sheikh, who seemed highly pleased with my visit, insisted on accompanying the party for a distance, so as to set us safely on the road.

Fortunately it had turned out a fine morning, and the sun, shining brilliantly, had chased away the morning mists. The shattered rocks and peaks stood up sharp and clear, the whole scene looking much more attractive than it had the night before.

For the first part of the journey our road wound along the top of a precipice, which formed one side of a valley. It was a good example of a natural roadway but it was difficult to say to what extent the natural conformation of the rock had been aided by the hand of man. At all events, if there had been any artificial help, it must have been very long ago, for only one of the great nations of the old world would have undertaken such a piece of engineering. The strata of the hill were placed on top of one another like a pile of muffins, the top layer being cut away round part of its circumference, leaving a broad shelf, sufficiently large to enable a small car to be driven along it. As we rode on its smooth, hard surface, we had the precipice on our left hand and a rocky wall on our right— a pleasant enough path for a fine day, but I should imagine rather dangerous on a dark night. However, with my fondness for mountains and wild scenery, I enjoyed every inch of it, and only longed for a companion, who spoke my language, to share in the pleasure.

We said goodbye to the Sheikh at a place where the road turned down the hillside, and so sharp was this descent that we had to get off and lead our horses. Once in the valley we journeyed over large mounds of silt, into which the mountain streams had cut deep ravines. In one of these we were held up by an Arab, who said he had been waiting for some hours for the *hakim*. On asking him what was the matter, he pointed to a much-decayed molar and requested me to pull it out. Fortunately I never travel without some dental forceps, so I sat down with his head in my lap and, after a little exertion, extracted the offending tooth. The man was so pleased with this operation that he followed me into the camp, and at the first consultation asked me to oblige him with an emetic. As he was well over forty, and from the confidence he reposed in me I imagined him no fool, I acted on the old proverb and allowed him to be his own physician. His subsequent contortions in front of my tent afforded great satisfaction to a large crowd of Arabs, who collected to see the doctor at work.

Early in the evening the palm trees in the oasis of Rapta loomed up, and we spurred our horses so as to get in as early as possible. Soon after we had got on to the sand of the desert we crossed the deep bed of a river in which large pools of water still lingered. As my horse drank I noticed that the floor of the stream was composed of conglomerate, pebbles of all sorts and all colours being imbedded in a matrix, which had the appearance of limestone. This conglomerate

was cut into fantastic shapes by the action of the river.
I should imagine that the first geologists who go into
the petrology of Tripolitana will have a most interesting time, so varied and intriguing are the formations
of the rocks.

Half an hour's brisk ride brought us to the oasis,
where we drew rein outside the tent of the Arab
General Staff. The soldiers gathered round in large
crowds to have a look at me, but Bahrouni's gendarmes
on duty proved themselves as efficient as London
policemen in the art of dispersing a crowd.

As soon as it was dark the stars shone brilliantly,
and I thought that we were in for a cold night; but,
as it turned out, in a short space of time the inside
of the bell-tent allotted to Khalifa and myself resembled
the hot room of a Turkish bath. A large brazier was
first brought in, and very soon after the whole of the floor
space was filled by the various notables who came in
to greet me. The smoke resulting from the burning
of green wood was thick and suffocating, but as it
appeared to be in accordance with local custom, I made
no demur. I could not help feeling somewhat nervous,
however, when all our guests hung their bandoliers,
well stocked with Martini cartridges, on the tent pole,
just over the brazier. When the servant threw a fresh
handful of twigs on the fire, the flames seemed actually
to lick the cartridges, but as I was the only Englishman
present I thought it hardly dignified to point out the
danger.

The conversation again turned on the war, but fortunately everyone was interested in the Balkan campaign, so with the help of the French papers he had

brought from El Yefren, Khalifa was able to keep our guests entertained.

Turning to matters nearer home, one Arab, who looked as if he had a sense of humour, propounded a brilliant scheme. In order to disarm the natives the Italians were buying rifles from deserters at a fairly high figure. Now, could I not help him to buy a camel-load of obsolete rifles in Tunisia so that he could send trusted men into the Italian lines to sell them? As he did not seem annoyed when I merely laughed by way of answer, I did not imagine he took the proposal very seriously himself.

As the stony state of the ground was not conducive to sleep, I got up at dawn, and calling a gendarme started for a walk round the camp. It was situated on the fringe of a beautiful little oasis, an oasis that stood out like an emerald in the golden sand of the desert. In the centre a large spring welled up, filling a round pond with a clear and sparkling water, from which a brook ran babbling through the numerous little gardens, giving to each one a trickle of the precious fluid. Graceful palm trees overhung the pool, round which the women were gathering to draw their supply of water.

The morning was delightfully fresh, and the early sun shone gently through the palms, stimulating with its soft warmth the birds, who twittered joyously in the trees. As I sauntered along the mossy paths I thought of the wonderful passage in *Don Quixote* where the master hand of Cervantes depicts the charms of a summer morning. I seemed to be riding with the knight to some extraordinary adventure, and I was

not disappointed, for a little later I was destined to
see a sight that it is not given to many Englishmen to
behold.

Returning to the tent, I found that the servants had
prepared a light breakfast, which consisted of Fezzanese
dates largely adulterated with sand and a skin of buttermilk. I knew the fruit came from Fezzan because
Khalifa, on seeing the stones, at once named the oasis
in which they had been gathered. He did not pretend
to a deep knowledge of this science, but he told me
that he knew an Arab scout employed by Bahrouni who
could without fail deduce from the refuse round a
deserted bivouac fire exactly where its recent occupants
had come from.

As soon as we had breakfasted Khalifa, who had
made himself smart in a new khaki uniform with a
large cavalry sword and an Italian officer's riding-cape,
asked me to stay in the tent until he came for me;
then he went out, closing the flap carefully after him.
Something was evidently afoot in the camp, for I heard
the throbbing of a big drum and a hurrying of footsteps
over the pebbles.

After about half an hour he returned with a mounted
group of local notables, to whom I was introduced in
turn. Then my horse was brought up and I was invited
to mount. We trotted off through the trees and broke
cover on the north side of the oasis, and there, drawn
up in battle array, stood the Rapta Division of the
Arab Army. It was difficult to estimate their number,
but a cursory, untutored glance inclined me to believe
that about 3000 men were on parade.

Standing before that armed assembly, so silent and

still, in the setting of palm trees and sandy wastes, I seemed to be transported to a scene in the Middle Ages, when a Saracen host stood ready to wage war for the Holy Sepulchre against the stalwart blows of Richard Cœur de Lion. In a dream I rode forward into the square, preceded by a cloud of horsemen, who manœuvred their steeds with the traditional skill of the Arab. Behind us swung a dozen swift-trotting camels, each bearing a rifleman perched on a high saddle.

With Khalifa on one side and the Arab Commander on the other, we trotted close to the ranks, accompanied by a strange group of musicians. Some blew an instrument similar to the bagpipes, others played native flutes, while two huge negroes furiously belaboured drums. At first the music sounded barbaric and harsh, but as the ear became accustomed to it one was conscious that the exhilarating and exciting notes were not without a species of weird and strange beauty.

Oh, the faces of the soldiers! I stood before an ethnological museum of all the races of North and Central Africa. The full-blooded negro stood side by side with the pale, aristocratic-looking Arab of the coast; a slit-eyed Asiatic, adrift perhaps from Zanzibar, covered a fuzzy-haired fanatic from the East Soudan. All ages were there too, from the lad of fourteen to the aged greybeard leaning on his staff. The greatest force that lures the heart of man—a love of freedom—had called them from their homes to strike a blow.

And the arms they carried! What would collectors of swords and ancient firearms have given to see the weapons these Moslems bore! There was every stage in the evolution of the rifle, from the simple tube

discharged with tinder to the death-dealing magic of
the Winchester repeater. I saw an ancient Peabody,
a Remington, a Springfield, piled perhaps by veterans
of the Confederacy, after their hopes died at the Court-
house of Appomattox. I saw a Gras, once the hope
of France, then discarded to the Greeks, and flung
away by them in their panic flight to Larissa, with the
victorious Turk hard on them. I saw Martinis, filched
perhaps from some sleeping sentry in the Soudan, or
maybe relics of the disastrous expedition of Hicks
Pasha or telling of the fate of Chinese Gordon. Pistols
of all sorts were thrust into sash or belt; from the
bell-mouthed flint-lock to the first efforts of Colt, from
the finished product of Smith & Wesson to the furious
Browning.

As well as firearms many of the Arabs wore swords
at their sides—great two-handed swords, curved tul-
wars, and rapiers thin and pointed. With these blades
there kept company knives of all descriptions—daggers,
houghing knives and lance heads; while here and there
a spear jutted up from the ranks.

At the sight of one soldier I drew up in amazement.
His head was decorated with a steel-helmet of ancient
make, from which a curtain of chain hung down to
protect his neck. His chest was covered with a breast-
plate, and in his hand he carried the family heirloom
—a flint-lock gun richly inlaid with mother-of-pearl,
with the butt decorated with amethysts.

The clothing of these troops was as varied as their
armament. Some wore khaki, others the usual Arab
blanket, whilst many carried pieces of Italian equipment
in the shape of capes, trousers, valises or haversacks.

As we rode along the line the Arabs stirred into life, brandishing their weapons in the air and yelling a fierce greeting. Then I noticed that I was riding a few paces ahead, while Khalifa and the rest lingered behind, so I pulled up and waited for the lieutenant to come abreast. Thereupon he told me to take the salutes, as the review was being held in my honour. Unfortunately, owing to his imperfect French, I was unable to intimate to him, at that moment, that it was no part of the duty of an English doctor to pass an Arab army in review, and moreover, if the matter leaked out, I stood in grave danger of being crossed off the Medical Register. Nevertheless I succeeded in getting him and the others up into line with me.

We made the tour of that astounding square for the first time at a walk, and then, warmed up by the shouting and fanatical enthusiasm of the soldiers, we tore round it at full gallop. Not being too good a horseman, I had several narrow escapes of getting thrown, but fortunately passed through the ordeal in safety.

At an order shouted down the line, the formation now changed, and the men fell into two long ranks, with a space of forty yards between. Up and down this course thundered the best horsemen in the Arab Army, giving a splendid exhibition of fantasia.

Rifles were unslung, loaded, pointed and discharged, while at full gallop. Two Arabs rode abreast, one managing the horses, whilst his fellow aimed at imaginary pursuers. Then suddenly a bugle sounded and the soldiers broke their ranks. An aged man with a long white beard led a furious gallop to the top of a large eminence in the vicinity. Those on foot followed at a run, shrieking and shouting, while from the tents at hand came the scream-like cheering of the women-folk. On the crest of the hill the old man made a long and passionate appeal to God to help them in their efforts to maintain their independence. I was not unmoved at the sight, and with the rest I let the reins fall on Darkey's neck and held out my hands, with palms upturned in supplication, for it was a venerable old man who prayed and they were fearless men who listened.

When the excitement had cooled down I returned to my legitimate sphere and made a tour of those tents which harboured sick people. At first, I was viewed with suspicion, but this I disarmed with a smile and a careful compliance with etiquette, so that after visiting the first patient or two I was made quite welcome. The diseases I saw were chiefly of a water-born character, so I took a good look at the lie of the land and made careful inquiry as to where and how they got their drinking water. Having ascertained these facts, I was able to explain to the local authorities how the number of their sick could be largely decreased. I pointed out that all slops and swills were thrown into a ravine, from whence they were washed by the first shower of rain into the pond in the oasis. Moreover, I pointed out that a string of filthy rags, used for lowering buckets into wells, contaminated the water and spread disease.

I noticed regretfully that even some of the better educated Arabs looked upon sickness as an affliction to be borne patiently as sent by God, very much in

CROSSING THE DESERT

A SAND STORM

To face p. 162

the same way as does the Book of Common Prayer.
I reminded them, however, of the words of the Holy
Prophet: "Trust in God but keep your camel tied!"
and they all grasped the point. Show a man the best
in his religion and he values it the more; show him
the worst and try to prove that it is false and you make
ten agnostics to every convert. However, my advice
was taken and proved good, and I was glad to learn
later that the number of men reporting sick at Rapta
became very small.

When I returned to my tent, I found a stalwart,
fierce-looking Arab waiting for me, holding his little
daughter by the hand. She was suffering from a mild
affection of the eyes, which I hope cleared up quickly
under the simple remedy I prescribed. She was a
bonny little thing, and the gift of a few biscuits soon
won her confidence. As I held her in my arms she
caught hold of the rather gaudy silk scarf I was wearing
to keep the sun from my neck, and seemed reluctant
to let it go. It ended, of course, in my taking it off
and tying it round her own neck; whereupon, to my
great delight, she put her chubby arms round me and
kissed me.

As the Arab was turning to go I noticed he was
wearing a large and handsome sword. I asked him
how much he would take for it. With fond, fatherly
pride he looked at his little girl, beaming with the joy
of her possession of my scarf; he looked thoughtfully
at the bottle of eye lotion in his hand; his whole
attitude expressed gratitude, but he shook his head
and replied, "Nay, Doctor Bey, is this the time for a
man to sell his sword?"

During the rest of my stay I had a thoroughly enjoyable and interesting time, becoming familiar with many sides of Arab life. In the morning I would squat on the sand with the magistrate and see how he dealt with the cases which were brought up. At these trials one thing that amused me was the great latitude allowed; for example, a small boy, with the quick intelligence of youth, seeing some point that had escaped the judge, would, quite unrebuked, put a question to the prisoner. Frequently, as a compliment I presume, I would be asked my opinion as to the guilt or innocence of the accused.

In the afternoon I usually went for a ride with two cultured and interesting Arabs, Abdulla Effendi and his cousin Ali. Once well out on the desert they took me in hand and gave me instruction in the trick horsemanship of the country. Many a tumble I had on the soft sand of the desert and many a blow I got on the back of my head with the butt of the camel gun while trying to unsling and point it while riding at a gallop. The Arabs tried their best to smother their laughter politely when I took the first fall, but when I laughed loudly myself they joined in freely, seeing that I considered it a legitimate cause for merriment.

On some days we scoured the desert for gazelle, taking with us a light lunch of dates and buttermilk, to be eaten under the shade of rock or tree. Unfortunately, however, the sport was poor, as there were so many hungry men in the district on the lookout for game. The Arab soldier only drew a few handfuls of flour a day for pay and rations, so he naturally tried to supplement this poor fare with anything that might fall to his shot-gun.

Some evenings we spent over the teacups with the Arab notables, and other nights, especially when it was moonlight, we would ride out on to the desert, where one of the sheikhs had erected tents in which to entertain us. Here I was first introduced to the favourite dish of the country called *bazine*. It was made, I believe, chiefly of flour and water with a good mixture of spices. Having been well cooked in a basin it set fairly hard, and was now turned out into a big wooden bowl. Then hot olive oil was poured over it and pieces of meat and hard-boiled eggs laid round. After having washed, all hands go into the bowl, mixing up the flour with the oil, the loud resulting squishing noise not being greatly relished by the European novice. At first, one has to be very careful, as the oil is piping hot and it is easy to burn one's fingers. In order to cool the food before placing it in the mouth, small round balls may be made and these stuck along the rim of the bowl; as soon as they are cold enough they can be picked off at leisure. The giver of the feast sometimes does not sit down with the company but walks about directing the servants and seeing to the comfort of his guests. It is polite, however, to hand up to him any choice piece of meat, while a like compliment may be paid to any of the guests.

Everyone having eaten his fill, the bowl and litter are cleared away and a servant comes round with a pitcher of water and a piece of soap. Hands are washed over a bowl on the floor, while the servant pours a steady trickle of water from above. The lips

and moustache are then cleansed, and finally the hands
are filled with clean water which is taken into the mouth.
This is then expectorated into the bowl underneath, the
mouth being carefully screened by the hands, so as to
give no offence to the company. Another little point
of etiquette to remember is that when the soap is
handed to your neighbour it should always be offered
on the back of the hand and not in the palm. As this
careful washing is carried out even by the poorest Arabs
before and after each meal, it is not surprising that one
scarcely ever sees one with dirty hands. Their excellent
teeth, lasting into old age, prove the wisdom of
Mohammed's command when he ordered that they
should be cleaned regularly. If this simple sanitary
precaution were taught and enforced in our own schools
we should not see the decayed, rotting teeth and septic
mouths that too often confront the doctor and dentist.

One morning I gathered up scraps of conversation
that rather disturbed me, to the effect that some of
the Arabs at Rapta were not at all satisfied with certain
doings of Bahrouni at El Yefren. As I was uncertain
as to what was going to happen I thought it best to
get back to the hospital, so I asked Khalifa to send a
gendarme to ride back with me.

It was with a distinct feeling of regret that I said
goodbye to the notables at Rapta, for they had proved
themselves the best of good fellows and had entertained
me right royally. Moreover, I had been learning. I was
beginning to respect their religion, to admire their
simple mode of life and to understand how people can
be happy without the luxuries that wealth and civilization bring. An Arab camp may not be the acme of

comfort to a European and many little things jar on
him at first, but the Arab gentleman is naturally
endowed with refined feelings and a ready intelligence,
and is quick to see the likes and dislikes of his guest,
and despite his poor surroundings will do his best to
give his visitor a good time.

The Arab, despite his faults—and they are many—
is ever true to the bonds of hospitality. Once eat with
him and a knot of friendship is tied which cannot be
easily loosened.

At Khalifa's request we were to make the journey
back to El Yefren as quickly as possible, as he was
anxious we should not linger on the road. On the
previous day some shots had been fired by banditti at
a flour caravan, and the escort of gendarmes had been
unable to discover the aggressors. Local opinion had
it that these men were in the pay of the enemy, who
desired to interfere with the supply of foodstuffs to
the Arab army; but in my opinion the would-be robbers
were simply common thieves, as it was obviously not
the policy of the Italians to provoke hostilities until
their preparations were complete.

We rode swiftly all morning, and only drew rein
at midday in order to rest the horses and eat our dates.
In the afternoon the gendarme was foolish enough to
try a short cut, which in the end proved very much
longer than the ordinary road. Late in the afternoon
the condition of the horses demanded a rest, so we
agreed to halt for half an hour on the plateau. Here
in the mountains the heat of the desert gave place to
a raw chilliness, which was accentuated by a piercing
wind that bit through one's clothing. I was very glad

to take shelter for a few moments in a stone hut that stood by the roadside. When the gendarme gave the signal to start I lifted my blanket from the large block of sandstone on which I had been sitting and was surprised to find it cut square and clean, as well as being beautifully carved on one side. Looking closer at the hut, I saw that it had been built of large oblong blocks, which certainly had never been fashioned by Arab hands, so I made a note of the place and determined to return another day for further investigation, as it was obvious that some Roman ruin was near at hand.

The gendarme was now anxious to press on to El Yefren as quickly as possible, so we spurred our horses, and about a couple of hours later we rode down the streets of Bahrouni's stronghold.

CHAPTER X.

ALTHOUGH I had had so enjoyable a time at Rapta, I was not sorry to get back home; that is to say, to the only home I have had for years—the place where I keep my luggage. During my absence the mail had arrived and I found a good budget of letters awaiting me, as well as all the latest London, Paris and Caracas papers, so I was able to settle down to the most satisfactory of all debauches—a debauch of reading.

The next morning, while I was arranging with Mohammed about the marketing, I was sent for to go up to the hospital. On arriving there, I found one of the nurses wished to put a question to an old woman who was having a sore on her foot dressed. I translated to Mustapha, who put the question in Arabic; but apparently she did not understand this language, so our interpreter turned to El Khani, who was standing near, and asked him to try the patient in Turkish. But the woman again shook her head. Khani now called up a Turkish-speaking Arab and asked him to see if he could understand the woman. He questioned her in Djebelli, the language of the hills, and she at once replied. One can imagine, however, the difficulties of diagnosis when questions as to symptoms had to run the gamut of English, French, Arabic, Turkish and Djebelli.

As my colleague at El Yefren seemed willing, if not anxious, to continue practically the whole of the work of the hospital during the next few weeks, I was free to ride out to the neighbouring camps and villages. This was exactly what I wanted, as it enabled me to give attention to the outlying sick and wounded who were not able to come into town. I did not forget, however, the Roman stones I had seen on the road from Rapta, so one day with Djemel Effendi and a couple of gendarmes I rode out to see if we could find any ruins. On questioning one of the gendarmes, he looked around for a moment and then pointed to what appeared to be a tree stump on a hill far away. I picked the object up with field-glasses and saw that it was some sort of a building. It was certainly most beautifully situated, perched as it was on the highest hill-top in the range. From all sides it would serve as a landmark to people travelling to and from the mountains. As we approached it, I saw many signs of Roman occupation. A broad, well-cut road, overgrown with moss and grass, was pointed out to me by Djemel, while the coping-stones of a well at the wayside had evidently been cut and carved by these wonderful old masons.

At length we came to the elegant little ruin. The upper part had either fallen or been thrown down, for it presented a shattered appearance, and many large, squared blocks lay round about on the ground. But the whole structure was so solidly and strongly built that after a brief examination little doubt existed in my mind that it had been attacked with explosives. In their everlasting search for loot the Arabs had blown a passage into the plinth, and the resulting concussion had probably brought down the upper courses of stone. Bending down, I crawled through the hole into the chamber, where, by the light of a candle, I made a careful examination of the interior. The large blocks of stone were beautifully adjusted, scarcely leaving room for a knife blade to be thrust between them. In the walls the masons had cut niches, perhaps for the purpose of placing therein lamps, vessels, or statues of their deities.

It was interesting to speculate for what purpose this graceful and imposing monument had been built. Was it to commemorate some victory or other, or did the column at one time shelter the remains of some noble Roman soldier?

Leaving Djemel and one of the gendarmes to have a rest—why do some people always want to rest?— I rode off with the other man in search of anything else of interest to be seen in the neighbourhood. We had not gone very far, however, when I was startled to hear the crack of a rifle, coming from the direction of the monument. Imagining the postmaster attacked by a body of bandits, we rode back at full gallop, our pace being greatly accelerated by the sound of rapid firing. On getting near I saw Djemel and his companion lying down on the grass and, regardless of the reverence due to ancient structures, directing shots against the ancient tower. Curiously enough the postmaster utterly failed to understand the cause of my heated and angry expostulation, and seemed rather offended when I censured his vandalism. However, I soon smoothed things over by posing him, rifle in hand, on the plinth and then taking his photograph.

On returning to the town I was saying goodbye to Djemel at the post office when a boy came out and asked me to go up into the telegraph-room, as Bahrouni Bey wished to speak to me. Having ascended the rickety stairs I found the Arab chief in company with some of his officers. He did not, however, introduce the subject about which he wished to ask me until we had drunk a cup of coffee. Then he told me that he wished to send M. Poincaré a telegram of congratulation on his election as President of the French Republic, and also one to King George of England, imploring his protection. Would I be so good as to write these messages for him in French? I answered that I would do my best, but it would take me a little time, as they would have to be drawn up in proper diplomatic language.

Not being accustomed to this class of work, as governments up to that time seemed to have got on very well without my help, I was fortunate enough to find at the house a copy of the *Matin*, in which there were many congratulatory telegrams to the new President from rulers all over the world; so, after studying them closely, I succeeded in drafting a message in passable French, observing due deference to the customs of diplomacy. The telegram to our own splendid King took me less time; a few concise, respectful words, tinged with a sense of humour—how could I resist it? I have no doubt that if it ever reached his hands, which is very unlikely, he must have scratched his head—if kings do these things—and exclaimed to his consort, "I have had such an extraordinary telegram from Africa to-day, my dear! ..."

This is the first and last time I ever dabbled in diplomacy, although since then I have had the good fortune to converse with both the exalted personages I thus addressed from the heights of El Yefren in the name of the Arab State.

At all events Bahrouni seemed highly gratified with my efforts, and emboldened by this I ventured to impress upon him the urgent question of sanitary reform in the town, which question he promised should be looked into at an early date.

About this time I was confined to the house for a few days, owing to the return of a chronic malarial fever. As soon as I was able to get about, in default of more violent exercise I strolled about the town and paid a few visits. In this way I got to know a good many children, and being very fond of youngsters I asked several of them to come to our house for tea. At first they were very shy, but, encouraged by the example of Sheikh Sassi's little daughter, who walked freely in and out, they soon began to come in increasing numbers.

I have never seen children better behaved or with more perfect manners. As they entered the house they would salaam, uttering the usual words of greeting, then seizing my fingers in their chubby little hands they would raise them to their breast, lips and forehead. There was about them none of that awkward shyness that so often affects Western children when they go, for example, to a juvenile party.

In the reception-room blankets were spread on the floor, on which they sat down after they had removed their shoes. Mohammed then would put fruits, cakes and other little delicacies before them, but although they eyed the eatables with interest they would touch nothing until their hands had been washed. After this ceremony they all sat there, as good as gold, with hands raised, so as to touch nothing unclean, until I gave them the signal to start. Then, after a brief prayer, they would commence to eat with the good appetite of childhood.

Mohammed, who doubtless thought of his own children at home, waited on them hand and foot, and would keep on bringing up more food or pouring out fresh glasses of tea, until sometimes I was forced to expostulate on medical grounds. Still, they never seemed the worse for what they ate, and as they came back time after time I suppose they enjoyed themselves.

Walking about the town I frequently met the Arab doctor, who used to come to the hospital to see what was going on. I once had an amusing experience with one of his clients.

One morning I was consulted by an Arab, who complained that he was losing the sight of his right eye. A cursory glance showed that he was suffering from a growth of a fleshy nature that was gradually encroaching on the sight—a complaint common enough in tropical countries. I at once offered to relieve him of the trouble, and he consented to undergo the operation, but unfortunately the sight of the knives frightened him, and he insisted on getting off the operating table, saying he would come back another day. A few days after this the Arab *hakim* came round to the hospital and begged me to go to his house, as a friend of his was about to perform an operation and they wanted me to put something in the patient's eye to make it insensible.

On my arrival I was introduced to a very seedy-looking Arab who had come from Socna, where he enjoyed considerable fame as an ophthalmic surgeon. The patient was lying on the floor, and I was somewhat astonished to find that he was the very man who had consulted me for his eye trouble a few days previously. Apparently he placed more faith in his fellow-countryman than he did in a stranger, and I am sure few will grumble at him, for there is nothing more unpleasant than to be treated by a foreign doctor who cannot speak your own language. As it would have been a poor exhibition of professional jealousy to have refused to assist, I adopted the humble rôle of anæsthetist and cocainized the eye, while my colleague from Socna prepared his instruments. He produced a leather bag, very similar to the sort that a shoeing smith carries, and shook a few pieces of old iron on to the dusty floor. He then threaded two large needles with cotton and laid them on a piece of sacking. He was now ready for the operation, and having refreshed himself with an enormous pinch of snuff, he knelt over the patient. Hardened as I am to the roughest sort of surgery, I must confess I shuddered as I watched the proceeding. The eye of the poorest or most depraved is a priceless, delicate object, and it seemed almost sacrilege to see it attacked by those dirty and mediæval instruments. Still, he made quite a satisfactory job of it, and even if he was unnecessarily violent, it was evident he had had plenty of experience.

The operation finished, I warmly congratulated him

on his success, and I was taking my leave when the patient intruded in the conversation, purse in hand. He asked how much he was to pay, and on my Arab colleague fixing his fee at one shilling and threepence, the patient became quite indignant and offered fourpence as the maximum he was prepared to give. As the discussion became acrimonious and heated I took my leave, reflecting on the fact that ours is a poorly-paid profession. Still, the *hakim* doubtless felt a degree of moral satisfaction, even if his fee was not sufficient to procure him a dinner.

This was the last time I saw the practitioner from Socna, but I frequently came into contact with the El Yefren doctor. He often complained to me that the free consultations at the hospital had ruined his practice, and that he and his family were starving in consequence. This was, of course, an obvious hint, and as there was probably a good deal of truth in what he told me, I usually gave him a few shillings a week by way of compensation, during the rest of my stay in the town.

I did my best to encourage him to learn a little of modern surgical routine, but he did not prove a very apt pupil, probably thinking he knew more about the subject than I did. He pinned his faith almost entirely on " firing," and it was astonishing to see how popular this method of treatment was amongst his patients. He would listen gravely to the symptoms of the case and then place a sort of branding-iron in a brazier. When this was red hot it was pressed on the flesh in the vicinity of the trouble. The loud, sizzling noise, the smell and the pain thus produced all had their effect on the patient, who would go away firmly convinced that he was on the high road to a cure.

Sometimes he would write a few signs on a piece of paper, which would be swallowed by the patient with a gulp of water—an unorthodox method of treatment, but as efficacious, perhaps, as some of the nauseating mixtures taken in good faith by people nearer home.

I am always chary of criticizing too harshly the methods of native doctors, as I have seen many excellent cures made by them; and, after all, the test of a good doctor is, Can he cure? I once had a patient in the person of a young man who was suffering from epileptic fits. I treated him carefully for many months by means of those drugs and hygienic measures that are considered efficacious by the profession, without ameliorating his condition in the slightest. I told him frankly that I could do nothing more for him, and he drifted into the hands of a negro bush doctor. The latter hung thirteen assafœtida seeds round the patient's neck and wrote a prayer on his chest with the green juice of a herb. Whatever the explanation may be, the young man had no more fits during the next year!

As I came away from my colleague's house I met Djemel, who had just finished moving operations. He told me that he was giving a house-warming that night and he hoped that I would go in to dinner with him. At the hour appointed I made my way along the uneven streets and after some difficulty found his new house. The table was already laid with a bountiful supply of the usual *hors d'œuvres*, with a couple of bottles of *bukha* to take the place of cocktails and whisky. I noticed with some amusement that as we were dining in European fashion the resources of Djemel's pantry were not sufficient for the occasion, so his servant had been round and borrowed plates and cutlery from our own cook. We were served with a variety of dishes that proved most appetizing, but which I should not like to attempt to name.

Djemel as usual proved an entertaining companion, and told us many interesting stories of his stay in Mecca. He had roamed the Balkans too, and after the cloth was drawn volunteered an Albanian love song. He accompanied himself very effectively on a sort of guitar, the notes of which blended very well with the somewhat nasal voice of the performer. Suddenly I noticed that I understood what he was singing, as most of the words had a Spanish or Italian flavour, so when the song was over I asked what language it was written in. This Djemel could not tell me, as he had never seen it in print, but had learnt it in his childhood from an old nurse. I asked him kindly to write down the words for me, and when he had done this I at once saw it was in a debased form of Spanish. It is fairly obvious, then, that the song had originated from one of the large settlements of Spanish Jews in Macedonia, and not from the mountains of Albania.

Djemel, although conversant with written Arabic, spoke it very badly, and often when speaking with anyone of importance would call in his assistant to turn his Turkish into the language of the Koran. The fact that Djemel was not very fluent enabled me to learn a good deal of Arabic from him, and in return I gave him a few lessons in English. It is amazing

how simple English is and how easily it is acquired
by foreigners when they are taught in the right way.
I have helped men of all nationalities to learn our
language, and it has always amused me to see how
they look for difficulties and how astonished they are
to find it so easy. The simplicity of the grammar,
the absence of gender and the paucity of inflections
render speaking it a task within the reach of everyone.
Once simplify our archaic spelling and English is the
true Esperanto of the world.

In this manner the days passed pleasantly enough,
and despite many rumours the war seemed as far off
as ever. From time to time, however, we had reminders
that the enemy were gradually infiltrating the country.
Strange Arabs wandered in and out of the town, giving
information as to the movements of the Italians, and
doubtless returned to Tripoli giving equally reliable
reports as to what was going on in Bahrouni's camp.
Naturally, we were always interested to hear what was
happening in Zavia, as during our stay there we had
all got to like it. One day an Arab came round to
the hospital and said he had a beautiful horse for sale
if anyone wished to buy it. Mustapha asked to see
the animal, and the Arab replied that it was on the
plains, but he would go down and bring it back in a
few days.

In about a week he returned riding a magnificent grey
horse. It was obvious that it had neither been clipped
nor shod by an Arab, as the hair where the saddle rests
had been left and the shoes were of European manufacture. I asked him where he had bought it and he
replied, with a grin, that it had belonged to the Italian

Commandant at Zavia and that he (the Arab) had gone into the town one night and brought it away. I should very much have liked to have purchased the horse, but although there was a war on it seemed rather like receiving stolen goods.

CHAPTER XI.

GOING about the country as I did and conversing with all kinds of people, I soon began to understand the causes for the disaffection that prevailed among the Arab soldiers at Rapta. They did not understand why they received no orders to move and were beginning to think that Bahrouni was playing a double game. An incident that now occurred strengthened their belief in the latter idea.

A certain sheikh, by name Af-Khini, who lived in the hills on the left of Bahrouni's line, was reported to have accepted a bribe from the enemy. If this were to be followed by an Italian occupation, it was clear to everyone that with the enemy in force on both flanks the position at El Yefren was in great jeopardy.

As soon as this report reached Bahrouni's ears he sent for the sheikh to come and explain matters. However, Af-Khini seemed little disposed to obey this summons, in this way rather confirming the rumours, and it was only after Bahrouni had despatched a large force of gendarmes to enforce his orders that the sheikh condescended to come to El Yefren.

Although watched by a guard, he did not seem to be under any sort of arrest, for he was allowed to wander

AT–G

about the town as he pleased and to converse with anyone. On one occasion he paid us a visit and proved a pleasant enough fellow, although I thought his solitary eye did not look upon us in too friendly a fashion. However, he and Bahrouni seemed to get on very well together, and if gossip were to be trusted the two of them spent long hours together, talking earnestly and seeming to be in thorough agreement.

The news of these interviews fanned into flame the discontent at Rapta, which had already been fired by Bahrouni's inactivity in face of the fact that the enemy were making themselves secure at Azizia and Gharian. Accordingly on January 25th a body of about a hundred Arabs, chosen from the wilder spirits in the camp, marched from Rapta to El Yefren, openly avowing their intention of killing Af-Khini.

They reckoned, however, without Sheikh Sassi, who, dearly as he would have liked to deal with the culprit in a drastic but legal fashion, was far too wise a ruler to allow the mob to have its own way.

I happened to be in his office when a travel-stained gendarme rushed in and announced that the armed rabble from Rapta was within a mile of the town. Sassi calmly took a few whiffs at his cigarette, stroked his beard, and gave a few concise words of command to his sergeant. In a few minutes the whole of the Yefren police were on the tops of the houses in the main street, where Af-Khini resided, ready to pour a hot fire into the crowd should it get out of hand.

Despite Sheikh Sassi's protests, curiosity drove me to the door of the *gendarmerie* to see the mutineers pass, and when I beheld them streaming by, excited and angry, I thought we were in for a hot time. To me, however, they were very polite; I was saluted by several of them, and one old patient fell out to beg for a cigarette. As Sassi had only got two gendarmes to protect him at his office, it is a good thing they did not decide to fall upon him. As it was he had his revolver on the table and saw that the action of his rifle was in good order, for Sassi was not the sort of man to be killed without first taking heavy toll of his assailants.

As a violent row now started in the streets, and Sassi had ordered his horse so that he could go and super-intend operations, I had no wish to be left alone at the *gendarmerie*, so I slipped down the deserted side streets and at length gained our house. Here I found everything quiet.

Later I learned that the mob had been quite over-awed by the gendarmes, and, finding that they were not to be allowed to kill Af-Khini, started quarrelling amongst themselves. Sheikh Sassi was wise enough not to interfere in this, as he judged a little blood-letting would do them no harm. In the evening a dozen or more Arabs were led up to the hospital in the custody of Hamid Effendi to be treated for sword and knife wounds, so I should imagine that the opposing factions had had an enjoyable little scrap together.

The excitement, however, did not die down, and there seemed to be every possibility of further civil disturb-ance, unless the Rapta Arabs were assured that Bahrouni was quite loyal to their cause.

Fortunately, at this time there was a very important sheikh from Fezzan staying in the town, a man who enjoyed great reputation as a religious leader. Accom-

panied by Sheikh Sassi, he rode down the streets
haranguing the crowd and ordering them to gather
in front of the Mosque.   Here he delivered a long
address to his audience, and then, taking his seat in
front of the door, the whole crowd passed in procession
in front of him, salaaming and kissing his hand.   After
this ceremony everyone went home, apparently quite
satisfied.   To this sheikh and to Sassi we owed it that the
streets of El Yefren did not run with blood that day.

During the latter days of January we had many
interesting visitors calling at our house.   One of them,
Aboubaker Effendi, became a very good friend of mine.
He had been an official under the Turkish Government
in the walled town of Socna, and was now making his
way to Constantinople; for although by birth a Tripolitan, he did not care to stop in the country now
that the Turks had abandoned it.

Aboubaker Effendi was a good specimen of an Arab
gentleman.   He ate dinner with us in European fashion,
and no complaint could be made of his table manners.
He gave me the impression of being used to good
society, and carried himself with a simple and unaffected
dignity.   His clothing was of Western cut, and he wore
what appeared to be an English-made overcoat.   He
was thoroughly conversant with world politics, and
proved himself an interesting conversationalist.   One
thing he told us interested me greatly—that in his
youth his grandfather had related to him a story of
the coming of some English travellers to their town
in the interior, and how they had rested in his house.
I have been unable to find the reference, but I believe
that Captain Clapperton in one of his travels speaks

AN ARAB OUTPOST

AN ARAB SHELTER

To face p. 184

of an Arab of this name who entertained him. At all events, in return we did our best to make an agreeable impression on the grandson.

One sometimes finds among Arabs and Turks, mingled with their natural astuteness and intelligence, a certain degree of trustful simplicity. This quality was shown by our guest from Socna. While Aboubaker deplored the loss of the *vilayet*, the reason of which he could not understand, he wondered why the question had not been submitted to the arbitration of the Hague Tribunal!

At this naïve statement I could hardly suppress a smile. I explained to him as gently as I could that this excellent institution was not regarded seriously in Europe, that useful as it might be to decide minor quarrels between great Powers, who feared the economic derangement of war, it was not to be expected to step in and stop a big nation robbing and bullying a little one. I was further explaining to Aboubaker Effendi that Britain was the only nation that gave the smaller peoples a fair chance, when I was greatly shocked to see our guest solemnly winking across the table to Mustapha!

Aboubaker said that he hoped the present war would prove a good lesson to Turkey, and that she would completely reorganize her Army and Navy, so that in future she would be able to bargain better with her many enemies. He said that Anatolia produced some of the finest soldiers in the world, who, if they were only well led and backed up by efficient artillery, would be more than a match for their Balkan opponents. He seemed to think that it was well for a nation to have a

keen sword to throw into the balance when the scales
of justice were quivering.

Aboubaker appeared to take a great interest in our
welfare, and before he left he spoke rapidly in Arabic
to Mustapha, who turned slightly pale at his words.
I asked the interpreter what our guest had said and
felt somewhat perturbed at the reply—that the country
was in a very disturbed state and he would advise us
to get home as fast as we could. Moreover, report had
it that we had large sums of money in the house, and
on that account it would be advisable to keep our
eyes open.

Personally, I did not worry much over this. The
Turks and Ottomanized Arabs seemed rather afraid of
the ordinary natives, and did not care to move about
the country unattended as we were accustomed to do.
And as for danger—it is to be found everywhere, often
in the place where one feels most secure. How often
has the man in the dug-out been killed and his comrade
in the trench spared! How often have the occupants
of cellars been sealed up by the bomb, while their more
trustful neighbours have slept peacefully in their beds!
If we trust our immortal souls to the Almighty for all
eternity, surely we can trust Him with our bodies for
a space.

To me the desert had whispered a mighty secret, a
secret that cradles and soothes the fretful heart of man,
and enables one to walk serenely through the dangers
of both peace and war—that which is written will come
to pass!

Another interesting visitor was Sheikh Sauf-ben-
Nassur, the leader of the Arabs on the plains to the

north-west of El Yefren. He was an oldish man with
a lined face, tanned by the sun to a darker shade than
the colour of his native sands. He sat down wearily
and looked very tired and worried. After the first
customary compliments, he remained grave, pensive and
silent, his eyes looking steadily ahead, as those of a
man who is accustomed to gaze over vast wastes of
land or sea. Hard on his heels came his son, clad in
a smart new uniform, rattling his spurs and clanking
a large Italian sword on our flagstones. Young, full of
health and strength, he was enthusiastic about the Arab
prospects, and his mind evidently harboured none of
the cares and doubts that weighed so heavily on his
father.

And so the different types streamed through our
little reception-room. Military chiefs, religious leaders,
and traders; men from the desert and men from the
hills. I listened eagerly to tales of Misda, with its
Roman ruins; of the vast rocky plateau called Hamada
El Homra, until I almost felt inclined to abandon my
duties and, despite Bahrouni's prohibition to travel far,
to set out with the first straggling caravan that left the
hills for the interior. Still, I had to have patience,
hoping that the Arab Government would establish itself
so firmly that I should be able to see more of the country
later on. Alas! these desires were not destined to be
satisfied.

CHAPTER XII.

AT the end of January Bahrouni seemed to have made up his mind that he must do something aggressive, and in this he was probably not uninfluenced by the suspicions of the troops at Rapta. At all events, as a preliminary step, he determined to connect the camps at Rapta and Lossaba to El Yefren by telephone.

With this end in view he ordered Djemel Effendi to divert the old telegraph line that ran from El Yefren to Gahrian into the camp at Lossaba. Being a sociable soul, Djemel had no wish to go alone, so begged me to go with him. Naturally, I was only too pleased to get out of the town and see a little more of the country, while my colleague was delighted to stay and carry on at the hospital, as he viewed with some repugnance any departure from the Capuan delights of El Yefren. Rejoicing over the utter lack of friction and complete unanimity that prevailed amongst the personnel of the Mission, I packed my saddle-bags for a fortnight's leave of absence.

The party consisted of Djemel and myself, two gendarmes, and an Arab called Doghman Chaouch, who had some knowledge of telegraphic constructional work. He proved to be a willing and obliging fellow, and in

addition to his professional work undertook the duties
of cook, valet and interpreter. It was only with his
help I was able to get to know exactly what a patient
complained of. I spoke to the postmaster in French,
Djemel handed it on to Doghman in Turkish, and the
latter translated it into Arabic or Djebelli. Our caravan
was to be completed with a couple of camels and the
necessary—though utterly unreliable—drivers.

At the hour fixed by Djemel I was quite ready, with
Darkey saddled up waiting at the door; but at the last
moment the resources of the Arab Government broke
down. They were quite unable to furnish their postmaster-general with a horse! So Djemel was forced
to follow the example of all the Arabs in El Yefren,
who when they wanted anything at all out of the ordinary came round to see if they could get it from the
Mission.

A few months previously Mustapha had bought a
big, fine horse from Mr. Alan Osler, the war correspondent, and it was the dream of our interpreter's life
to ride this animal back in triumph to Tunisia, saddled
and bedecked with the silver trappings so dear to the
Arab's heart. This was the animal that Djemel now
wished to borrow. Naturally, Mustapha rather objected
to lending it, knowing perfectly well that a horse's life
was rather a hard one in the camps, and that probably
it would not be well looked after. In vain I urged
Djemel to borrow the Italian horse that now belonged
to one of the leading men in Yefren, but nothing but
Mustapha's mount would suit him, so in the end our
interpreter was obliged to lend it.

The animal was brought to the door and saddled,

just as Mohammed was taking the saddle off mine;
for as neither the gendarmes nor the camels had turned
up, and I knew from experience they would not come
for at least a couple of hours, I did not see why I should
put Darkey to the inconvenience of standing for this
period with a load on his back.

After a delay of about two hours the little caravan
was ready, and we moved out of the town with the
sun in our faces.

Now, it was quite impossible in these days to travel
any distance in Tripolitana without several unauthorized
persons attaching themselves to the party. For one
thing they were glad of the protection afforded by the
rifles of the gendarmes, and in the case of the Mission
they knew they could always pick up a few scraps of
food, when the time came to put on the cooking-pots.
As well as men, there was nearly always a small boy
who, quite unasked, would officiously help with loading
the camels, gathering wood for the fire, or grooming
the horses. It was impossible to drive them away, as
any attempt to do so was met with the reply that they
were doing no harm and merely " walking with the
camels." It is only fair to add that they usually made
themselves so useful that it would have been unfair
to refuse them a dip into the food-bowl at nights or
a small backsheesh on our return to town.

We had not gone very far before I had to dismount
to shorten my stirrup leathers, and no sooner had I
touched the ground than the inevitable boy doubled
up, salaamed respectfully and seized the reins. Although
not more than twelve years of age, he carried one of
the heaviest pieces of ordnance I have ever seen outside

a museum. It looked like a musketoon—not that I have any clear conception as to what sort of a gun this term is applied to, but the name seemed to suit the boy's weapon better than any other. When we got well into the country and out of the range of Sheikh Sassi's keen ears, I asked Ali—for this was the boy's name—if it would really go off. Although a trifle hurt at my scepticism, Ali offered to fire a shot. He wound up some mechanism near the lock, primed the piece with powder from a leather flask, and with due solemnity pulled the trigger. A wheel whizzed round with a loud scraping sound, the powder fizzed in the pan, and the gun went off with a report that caused Ali great satisfaction. The boy immediately reloaded the gun, while the caravan halted to watch the process.

After this delay we hurried up the camels, and arrived at the gates of Kikla about one o'clock. Not wishing to put my aged friend the sheikh to the trouble of entertaining me, nor myself to the pain of sitting for several hours on a concrete bench, we agreed not to halt at Kikla, but to have a light meal at the foot of the hills and then to push on to Misga, a little hamlet that the gendarmes promised we should reach in a couple of hours. As usual, however, it turned out that they were entirely wrong in their calculations, and by the time we had crossed the Rapta Valley and entered the ravine in which Misga is situated, daylight had begun to fail.

As we approached the opening in the cliff I could just see by the failing light that a mountain stream had cut through the solid rock as cleanly as a piece of string divides a bar of soap, forming a gorge that

was beautiful enough no doubt in the daytime, but
which now looked wild and forbidding. We entered
it in single file, keeping to a path that ran through an
area of irrigated gardens, where the abundance of olive
and date trees spoke well for the industry of the local
Arabs. As we mounted, the track became difficult, if
not dangerous, situated as it was on the rocky side of
the ravine. It had become smooth with the passing
of many feet, and the snow that was now falling made
it slippery in the extreme, so much so that the horses
found it almost impossible to get a foothold.

Here the camel-men refused to go any further, urging
that their beasts were very tired and they did not care
to risk them on the path. Argument proving of no
avail, I was quite ready to bivouac and settle down
for the night, preferring to stop in the inclement weather
rather than lose sight of my instruments and dressings.
The gendarmes, however, probably thinking of their
own comfort, gave Djemel to understand that excellent
accommodation was to be found in the village, and as
he then wished to proceed I was forced to agree; so
we started on the road again, leaving the camels and
their owners behind. As we mounted, the road got
steeper and more difficult; it seemed to me in the darkness that a false step would precipitate one into the
abyss that yawned on our left, from which we heard
the noise of the mountain torrent rushing over its stony
bed. The gendarme in front of me had now dismounted
and was driving his horse in front of him, and I was
only too glad to follow his example. Proceeding on
foot, however, proved little easier than riding, for the
snow was now falling heavily, hiding the track and

making it very treacherous. In addition to this trouble
I kept on losing sight of the gendarme, who was going
ahead at a rapid pace owing to the fact that his native
shoes gave him a good grip on the rock. However,
Darkey's eyes were sharper than mine, and by following
him I succeeded in keeping to the path.

Suddenly I heard in the rear loud cries from Djemel,
imploring help. He was calling out in a medley of
languages; Turkish to Doghman, Arabic to the gendarmes, and French to me. Leaving my pony to his
fate I made my way back, and found the unfortunate
postmaster lying on his stomach on the path, with his
legs hanging over the cliff. His horse was nowhere
to be seen, but I noticed that Djemel still had the reins
clutched tightly in one hand. First I helped him on
to his feet, and he stood up, shaking all over; then
taking the reins from him, I found the horse was just
over the edge of the gorge, having fortunately found
a foothold on a mossy shelf. With the help of the
gendarmes I scrambled down, and after considerable
difficulty succeeded in forcing the animal to get back
on to the track again. Mustapha would not have slept
very easily that night had he seen the state of his horse,
cut about on the knees, bleeding from the mouth and
quivering like an aspen leaf. It seemed that Djemel
had not noticed that I and the gendarmes had dismounted, and continuing to ride had taken a fall with
nearly disastrous results.

After this little excitement we continued the ascent,
and in a few minutes were greeted by the raucous chal-
lenge of a man seated on top of a watch-tower. After
a long wait outside a large gate set in a wall, an Arab

came out and spoke to us. He proved to be the head-man of the village, or, as Djemel termed him, the president. This, however, appeared to me rather a pretentious title for the poor, half-starved, miserably-clad wretch who addressed us.

He opened the gate and invited us to enter the courtyard, which was common to the whole of the inhabitants of the village; Misga consisting of only a few tumble-down houses, surrounded by a wall and surmounted by a watch-tower.

As we were all nearly soaked through and very tired after our day's journey, I did not appreciate very much the long wait we were having in the courtyard while the president was inquiring about the state of things in El Yefren, so I urged Djemel to find out at once what accommodation could be found. After some hesi-tation the Arab agreed to lodge us for the night, and leaving us to kick our heels in the snow, he went off to see where he could put us.

After about half an hour he returned, and gratified us by saying he was giving us the best room in the village. After inspecting it one could not help speculat-ing as to what the worst would have been like, for the most miserable stable in England would have been more comfortable than the place he found us. The low roof of palm boards was leaking badly, and the constant stream of water that came through it had converted the earth floor into a mass of sticky mud. The walls, as well as the roof, were blackened with smoke, so that the water which kept dropping from above dirtied everything it touched. As we entered, a woman was kindling a fire on the floor, and the choking fumes

wandered about the room until they found their way
out through the hole in the roof. It was a poor sort
of a place, but the most comfortable the Arabs could
give us, so we made the best of it—and a very good
best too. The fire was soon blazing merrily, and sitting
on our blankets we lit our pipes and stretched out our
hands to the blaze.

As we were all very hungry, the question of food
became paramount. Unfortunately all our provisions
were on the camels, and the village president could not
even give us a handful of flour to make some cakes
with. Not wishing to go supperless to bed, Djemel
asked the Arab to find some men to go down to the
foot of the pass to bring up the ration boxes, at the
same time offering a liberal backsheesh. Hearing this,
four Arabs, who were lounging about, at once volunteered to go. In order to stimulate them to hurry I
handed them half a franc apiece, offering to double
it if they were back within the hour. The president
shook his head rather doubtfully as they disappeared
with their flint-locks into the darkness, and Djemel
asked him what was the matter. He replied that these
four men were very savage fellows, and would beat
the camel-drivers if they refused to load up and bring
the boxes themselves. I was rather distressed at this,
as I thought we had agreed with the village Arabs that
they should do the carrying.

However, the hour was nearly up when we heard
the grunting of camels in the court and the cursing of
the drivers as they unpacked the goods. The president
proved right; his fellow-villagers, seeing no chance of
earning the backsheesh by carrying the boxes them-

selves, had made the Yefren men bring up the camels.

We now set about preparing dinner. I superintended boiling the kettle, Doghman toasted bread and fried the eggs, while Djemel busied himself skinning some herrings, which when they had been anointed with oil and vinegar made excellent *hors-d'œuvres*. Fortunately, too, I had a large flask of rum, which I shared with the postmaster, who wisely set aside religious scruples for the time in order to obey medical orders.

We made an excellent supper, but our enjoyment was rather marred by the fact that a group of hungry-looking villagers watched wolfishly every mouthful we ate. Luckily we had sufficient left over from the feast to give everyone a fair meal.

The room we were in was a very small one, and, owing to the crowd of Arabs that came in to look at us, there was not a square inch of floor left unoccupied. After supper Djemel asked the president to clear the room, which he did none too gently; but no sooner had the villagers gone than the gendarmes and camel-drivers came in, saying they could get no place to sleep in, and begging us to allow them to lie down on our floor. We could not refuse, but when we came to allot floor space it was very difficult to find a place for everyone. As a coil of telegraph wire was lying where my body was going to rest, I begged Djemel to remove it. He picked it up and threw it into a recess that formed a dark corner to the room. The fall of the wire drew loud groans from someone occupying the recess, and the president explained matters by saying that his wife was lying there, suffering from a severe form of

fever. I asked a few questions and had a good look
at the woman by the light of a candle, and quickly came
to the conclusion that she was suffering from enteric,
rare as is this interesting disease amongst the Arabs.
Hearing her call for a drink, her husband came up and,
to my consternation, gave her some water from the
very same earthenware jar that Djemel and I had drunk
out of on our arrival. Still, it would have been a poor
compliment to my colleagues who had given me three
injections of anti-typhoid serum before I left London
had I fretted over the fear of infection. Moreover, if
one is going to worry about all one eats and drinks,
not to speak of washing cups and plates after each meal
in permanganate solution, it is better to stop enjoying
foreign travel and to get run over by a motor car in the
streets of London, Paris or New York.

Djemel, however, did not take the matter so philosophically; he begged me to give him something to
obviate the risk of infection. As I had no wish to open
the medicine chest at this late hour, I gave him a couple
of potash pellets I happened to have in my pocket.
The satisfaction with which he swallowed them and the
effusive terms in which he thanked me made me a trifle
ashamed of my prescription.

Finally we settled off to sleep—Djemel, myself and
Doghman on the floor with the camel-men and gendarmes, the president vigilantly chaperoning his wife
in the corner. In addition to the usual night attacks by
the commoner parasite, we were subjected to raids on the
part of bugs, which crawled out of the old walls to take
their toll of the strangers. Nevertheless, we were all so
physically tired that we enjoyed an excellent night's sleep.

The next morning we were early afoot, and on putting my head out of the fœtid atmosphere of the room to get a breath of fresh air, I was not surprised to see that a fair number of sick had gathered to consult me. After a cup of tea, with the assistance of Djemel and Doghman I began to treat them. The first glance showed that the trouble most of them suffered from was a lack of good food, so having given them a little physic apiece in rather a perfunctory manner, I opened the food boxes to see what we could spare. As I noticed the postmaster looked somewhat concerned at this proceeding, I quoted an Arabic phrase that I had picked up from El Khani, to the effect that God would provide. Judging from Djemel's looks as a pair of his beloved dried herrings disappeared into an old woman's bag, I began to fear that his faith was weak.

Bathed in the rays of the early morning sun, the gorge looked charming, and I should dearly have loved to spend an hour or two exploring it, but Djemel had orders from Bahrouni to get on with the work as soon as possible, so we were obliged to set off. Having climbed another hill we came to a large, bare plateau, where we soon picked up the telegraph posts running across to Gharian.

My companion was now anxious to make sure that the line was in working order, so, taking advantage of a place where the wire had fallen to the ground, he connected it with his travelling telephone set and called up El Yefren. He got through far quicker than the average subscriber gets his number in London, and the Arabs stared at him with amazement as he carried on an animated conversation with an unseen person. After speaking to Bahrouni, Djemel facetiously gave the Italians at Gharian a ring, but was unable to get any reply. When he had disconnected his instrument, one of the Arabs, who had been closely watching the proceedings, put the cut end of the wire into his ear and looked very disappointed when he heard nothing!

Arabi Effendi, one of my best friends amongst the Arabs, told me that when the telegraph wires were first laid into the interior, the less-educated natives asked anxiously what they were for. A Turkish officer, anxious to increase the prestige of his sovereign, replied that the posts were being erected for the purpose of talking to the Sultan. This idea seemed to take root, for on several occasions afterwards petitions to the Emperor, together with a present of fruit or eggs, were to be found left at the bases of the telegraph posts by the less-educated natives.

Early in the afternoon we rode into the Arab encampment of Lossaba. It was quite near to the mountains of Gharian and only separated from them by a broad valley. Little as I knew about the effects of modern artillery fire at this moment, the Arab position appeared to me to be very insecure, as they could have been shelled out of it any moment the Italian gunners liked to open fire.

Sheikh Ali, who was in command here, was a thin, gaunt, ascetic-looking man, full of religious enthusiasm, and ruled his flock with a rod of iron. I suppose that some orthodox people would have described the Arabs in this camp as "perishing heathen," but at the same time the religious tone prevailing reminded me personally very strongly of the spirit that history tells us

animated Cromwell's Ironsides. First of all, alcohol in
any form was strictly tabooed, and much to Djemel's
disgust even smoking was frowned upon. No shouting,
singing or unseemly noises were allowed, but the
consequent quietness was amply made up for by the
constant intoning of prayers. In the next tent to the
one set aside for Djemel and myself a religious teacher
had taken up his abode, and he passed the day reciting passages from the Koran to a large audience, who
repeated the entire fragment over and over again until
they were word perfect.

But as well as this outward show of religion a good
moral tone seemed to obtain in the camp. Petty theft,
a thing that one had constantly to guard against elsewhere, was quite unknown; even valuable articles could
be left about without their being touched. The horses
were fed punctually, and no attempt was made to pilfer
their corn, while the Arabs were polite, civil and
obliging.

As I watched the Arabs constantly bowing reverently
in prayer on the sand, and saw them offer up thanks
in their tents over their humble food, I began to wonder
more and more if we are justified in devoting large
sums of money for the upkeep of missions against the
Moslem faith. It is difficult to conceive what good
we can do by trying—for it is only trying—to turn
Mohammedans from their ancient faith. Most of them
are sober, frugal and hard-working, while the standard
of morality set up by the Prophet of Arabia is certainly
a high one. As Professor Margoliouth says: "Humility,
patience, gentleness, refinement of speech, giving good
for evil, truthfulness, fidelity, sympathy, respect for

poverty and misfortune, care for orphans, attention to the sick, condolence with the bereaved, the suppression of such passions as envy, malice, the desire to defame, are all eloquently and earnestly commended " (by the Prophet Mohammed). It is certainly unfortunate that very often these principles are unobserved by Moslems, very much in the same way as the teaching of Jesus Christ is neglected by Christians. As to the effects of the adoption of Islam by native races, Sir H. H. Johnston, in *The Opening Up of Africa*, says : " But to Negro Africa, and no doubt to parts of India and Malaya, it [Islam] came as a great blessing, raising up savages to a state, at any rate, of semi-civilisation, making them God-fearing, self-respecting, temperate, courageous and picturesque."

No doubt slavery and polygamy are taught in the Koran, but equally are these ancient institutions upheld in our own Bible, and it is within the memory of living men that the holding of slaves in the United States of America was fiercely justified by a Christian clergy by means of quotations from Holy Writ.

CHAPTER XIII.

I THOROUGHLY enjoyed my stay at Lossaba. For one thing, I was very much freer than at Rapta, and was allowed to wander about where I liked without a guard. Religious as were the Arabs, they seemed to be without any fanaticism, for although I was well known to be a Christian, I met with the greatest courtesy everywhere and was well received by all classes.

The members of the medical profession enjoy a great advantage in winning their way into the hearts of people. A man relieved of a tumour or even of an aching tooth is thankful for the relief, and is nearly always anxious to show his gratitude. I found the Arabs no exception to this rule, and as soon as my patients knew that I took an interest in old ruins and curiosities of all descriptions, I had no difficulty in finding guides to many interesting places. All sorts of things were brought for my inspection, including ancient arms of all kinds, old pottery and Roman coins, one of the latter being a gold piece of the Emperor Vespasian in mint condition.

The only thing we had to complain of was an excessive hospitality on the part of the notables. We were nearly always asked out to lunch or dinner. Many a time Djemel and I, longing for a good European meal, were just preparing the food when an orderly would come along and tell us that Sheikh Ali was expecting us to eat in his tent. Naturally, we had to invite them back, and in order not to offend their religious prejudices I engaged a Jewish youth to see that only the right sort of meat was bought, and also to superintend the slaughtering and cooking.

On the first day of my stay I had the misfortune to earn the gratitude of an elderly black Arab. I say the "misfortune" advisedly, because his thankfulness took the form of bringing me presents of various sorts of food. In vain I told him that we had ample food in the tent; in vain also did Djemel tell him that my religion forced me to fast on certain days, but nothing would stop him bringing his dirty old sack containing a handful of dates, Arab cakes or a few grilled camel's ribs. These he would lay down with a benevolent air and request me to fall to. The meat he looked upon as a special delicacy, and before offering it to me he would pull the muscle off the bone with his clean but black fingers. Well, I used to swallow it, for who would be base enough to dry up the springs of gratitude coming from a poor man's heart?

One day, to our great joy, we heard that Sheikh Ali and his staff were going out to inspect the outposts, so the postmaster and I prepared to have a joyous time. As the luncheon hour approached, we posted a sentry to warn us of the coming of anyone of importance and carefully closed the flap of the tent. Doghman Chaouch was frying the steak and onions to a turn, Djemel with a forbidden cigarette between his lips was slicing up some hard-boiled eggs, while I was pouring out a couple of tots of rum, when suddenly the sentry put his head through the flap and in agonized tones told us that Sheikh Ali had come back and was making for our tent. We were like schoolboys caught at a dormitory feast! We swallowed the rum at a gulp; Djemel ground his cigarette into the sand, and Doghman hastily thrust the rum bottle into my haversack. The tall, gaunt Arab entered, and Djemel and I rose politely to greet him. He sniffed suspiciously in the air, but fortunately, owing to the savoury smell of Doghman's cooking, he could not detect the tobacco smoke. We came near to shipwreck, however, when he sat down right on my haversack, finding the bottle somewhat hard. Djemel pulled it rapidly away, saying the bag contained medicine; for it must be understood that the sight of a rum bottle would have had the same effect on Sheikh Ali as a glass of beer has on a teetotal fanatic at home.

After all, however, we enjoyed our meal in peace, for when he had informed me that he wished me to see one of his relatives who was lying sick, he picked up his rifle and strode off majestically to his tent.

During these days Djemel was working hard at his business. He procured the necessary labour from Sheikh Ali, and with Doghman's help rapid progress was made with the removal of the large iron telegraph standards. As a rule I was kept busy all morning with my professional duties, but I had usually finished work at midday, so after a light lunch I would have my pony saddled and go and see how Djemel was getting on.

The place selected for the camp telephone office was a large cave situated on the side of a hill. It was an excavation that had probably been in use as a dwelling for many thousands of years. The floor was covered with débris of all sorts—ashes from the fire, pieces of rock from the roof and bones left over from recent meals. To the astonishment of the Arabs I borrowed a spade, took off my coat and commenced to dig into the cave earth. At first the soil was fairly loose, but on getting down a couple of feet it became harder and more closely packed. Up to the present I had found nothing of interest, and was making preparations to go down deeper, when an Arab asked me what I was looking for. As he seemed to be the proprietor of the cave, I explained to him that I was looking for the remains of the former occupants, whereupon he went to a corner and brought out for my inspection some objects that he himself had found. They included several early neolithic implements, a bone carved into a rough knife and half a dozen bronze Roman coins. The sight of these naturally spurred me on to great efforts, and I was just on a floor of stalagmite when Djemel rushed in, pulling with him his telegraph wire. Owing to the crowd that now filled the cave I was forced to leave the excavation to another time. Unfortunately, however, I never had the opportunity to renew the work, so the mystery still remains for the delectation of the first adventurous cave-hunter who happens to pass by.

An eager crowd thronged round Djemel as he fitted the wire to his instrument, and the Sheikh had to shout for silence when the operator rang up Bahrouni. The work had been well done, and the miracle of the human voice passing many miles over a wire was again made

patent in this cave, where perhaps a hundred thousand
years ago a prehistoric people had quarrelled over their
half-gnawed bones.

I think it must have been the first time Sheikh Ali
had ever spoken over the telephone, and he took up
the receiver rather gingerly; but he was far too well
bred to show any sign of astonishment, and conversed
with Bahrouni in the calm tone that distinguishes a
staff officer when, from the safe shelter of Divisional
Headquarters, he tells the infantryman in the trenches
to hold on at any cost.

Sheikh Ali then asked me if I would like to go with
him to a spot where we could see the Italian lines.
Leaving the horses, we climbed to the crest of a hill
from which a good view of the Gharian range could
be obtained. Following the Sheikh's finger, I focused
the glasses on a number of tiny objects, that turned out
to be the enemy's infantry busily constructing trenches,
and a further and more careful scrutiny caused me to
suspect that gun-pits were being constructed.[1]

The fascination of watching the enemy at work was
very great, and I spent hours with the field-glasses,
sweeping the valley at my feet and wondering what
the next move in the game would be. As a rule I sat
on the shattered wall of an old fortress, of which the
arrow-head arrangement of the courses of primitive
bricks strongly reminded me of the work of the ancient

---

[1] In 1918 I had a curious confirmation of this fact. While in the
Kriegsgefangener-lager at Karlsruhe, I made good friends with an
Italian major who had commanded a battery of mountain guns in
Tripolitana. He told me that at the time I speak of he was busily
engaged in finding positions for his pieces.

Phœnicians. I am aware that some eminent authorities
have stated that this interesting people left no traces
of their architecture in Tripolitana, but as the country
has hardly been touched as yet by modern explorers,
doubtless many interesting things will still come to
light.

One morning I received rather a cryptic telephonic
message from Mustapha, to the effect that things were
moving at El Yefren and I should probably find it
wise to return as soon as possible. As I was enjoying
a pleasant holiday at Lossaba and there were still several
places I wished to visit, I was by no means anxious
to return, more especially, perhaps, because that very
morning I had had my curiosity aroused by the story
of an Arab. He had told me that he knew a place
not far off where beautiful "shining stones" could be
seen. Visions of a vast haul of diamonds, rubies and
sapphires filled my mind. I saw myself in a stately
Park Lane mansion, built with the spoils of the East,
in which an army of flunkeys and servants awaited my
beck and call, where, incidentally, I should doubtless
be thoroughly unhappy and miserable! Still, there is
nothing like wanting what you have not got; it stirs
the ambition and urges one on to further adventure.

I found, however, that Djemel was also anxious to
return to Yefren, and he proposed that we should not
go straight back, but make a detour so that we could
see the "shining stones" and perhaps rest a night or
two at a place called Bir-el-Rhulan, where we both had
many friends.

Having completed our preparations we went to say
goodbye to Sheikh Ali, from whom I parted with great

regret, for he had treated me with kindness and courtesy, and was very grateful for the attention that had been paid to his sick. When the horses were brought round I noticed that Djemel's mount looked very thin, and exercising the small amount of veterinary knowledge I possess, I examined the beast and told the postmaster that it was sick and hardly fit to ride. But Djemel, who obeyed my prescriptions in the matter of small doses of alcohol, did not seem to have a great opinion of my skill in this realm, and insisted on riding the horse.

After descending the hill we got on to the desert, where in a few hours we came to some Roman remains. It was easy to see that here had been a fairly important centre. A large, square piece of ground had been cleared and levelled for a market-place, and at one corner of it stood the walls of a little villa. It is reasonable to suppose that this house had belonged to the Roman Governor, and from its windows he had looked down many a time to see that the people under his charge were peacefully going about their business.

Our guide led us into this house, and going down on his knees he shovelled away the drifting sand with his hands. The " shining stones " he had spoken of were nothing but the coloured cubes set in a beautiful tessellated pavement ! With visions of wealth shattered, Djemel, like the rich young man, " turned sorrowfully away," while I, with the assistance of the Arab, cleared away the sand and had a good look at the interesting picture before me. But before I had had time to make a proper investigation I was called away by the impatient voice of the postmaster.

Half an hour later we reached a large, dismantled fortress of Moorish build, and tying our horses up outside we went in to inspect it. It had obviously been an important building in times past, and probably had protected and controlled the grand caravan route from Tripoli into the interior. A large number of skulls and human bones filled up a sort of well, and I looked to our guide for an explanation. He replied casually enough that a band of brigands had once been in residence here, and that they had thrown the bones of their victims into this well. It was a sinister-looking place, and I was glad to get out into the warm light of the sun again.

We now got into country which was covered with large bushes, big enough to give ample cover to infantry, and as I was riding along, thinking of the things I had seen that morning, I was suddenly startled out of my reverie by the sight of a couple of hundred Arabs rising from the ground and rushing towards us brandishing their rifles and shrieking like madmen. The surprise was so complete that for a moment I did not know what to make of it, but when they surged round us and did us no harm, I understood that it was only their rough way of welcoming us. Still, I am afraid to this day that my heart beat a little faster than usual.

After lunching with the Arabs and drinking the correct amount of tea, we set off for Bir-el-Rhulan, where we arrived at nightfall. Djemel's horse—or more correctly Mustapha's horse—looked none the better for his day's work, and when I saw him refuse his evening meal I told the postmaster that the animal was in a bad way. Djemel now begged to be excused for having slighted my opinion of the morning, and asked me to prescribe for the beast; but I was not so foolish as to risk a hard-earned professional reputation in the matter of a sick horse, so I suggested to Djemel that he should call in the local *hakim*. This practitioner arrived and scrutinized the animal gravely. He then blew on the beast's forehead and sprinkled a little powder, that looked like salt, into both ears. For this procedure he charged fourpence, and having received his fee went off, saying he would return in the morning with his firing-irons. Although I did not wish to throw the slightest aspersion on his professional skill or to disparage his remedies in the least, I called out to him as he was going not to forget to bring his skinning knives!

We slept that night in a cave that had been cut out of the silt, which fortunately had been newly made and was awaiting an occupant. It was well fashioned, and was fitted with a door to keep out the wind and undesirable characters. After a good supper we settled off to rest.

At an early hour a gendarme, eager to be first with evil news, poked his head in at the door and announced to Djemel that the horse was dead. As I thoroughly expected the news I saw no reason to be upset, so merely ordered Doghman to put on the kettle and prepare the gunfire tea. Djemel, however, was in a state of consternation, and insisted on going out, half-dressed, to see the body; whether to verify the fact of death or to take a last look at a neglected charger I do not know. Doghman, like a sensible and religious

A BILLET AT BIR-EL-RHULAN

AN ARAB BIVOUAC

To face p. 210

man, murmured that "it was written," and went on calmly with his cooking.

After breakfast I got a trifle tired of Djemel's lamentations, so determined to ride on to El Yefren alone and leave him to finish the journey on Shanks' mare. Picking the best of the gendarmes I rode off, and allowing no unnecessary halts reached the town at dusk.

After supper I learned the news. Bahrouni had determined to take the offensive; the Arabs at Rapta and Lossaba were to strike at Gharian, and Sheikh Sauf to assail the garrisoned towns near the coast. In case of success both forces were to rendezvous at Zan-Zur.

It was an ambitious plan, and one that held out little chance of succeeding. Riflemen, with good cover, can hold up an attacking force with some degree of success, but infantry, unless backed up by artillery, stand a very poor chance against machine guns and field guns. Moreover, I had had my eyes open during my visits to the camps, and had seen for myself the utter lack of any adequate reserve of ammunition.

Still, these matters hardly concerned the Mission; all we had to do was to make proper preparations for the reception and treatment of the wounded. After some discussion it was determined that Mr. Turnbull should remain behind at El Yefren to superintend the hospital, that two of the male nurses should go down to Lossaba to see to the dressing and transportation of the wounded, while I should proceed to the western plains to assist the men under the command of Sheikh Sauf-ben-Nassur.

CHAPTER XIV.

THE news that I was about to leave El Yefren spread far and wide, and as the departure of the last members of the Mission had been accompanied by a lavish distribution of backsheesh, a repetition of this Oriental liberality was expected. In anticipation, Arabs from the neighbourhood, together with their wives and children, flocked into town and encamped near our house.

On the morning of my departure I was awakened early by a confused murmur of voices outside my window. Looking out on to the bank, usually occupied by the village beauties, who threw reproachful and languishing eyes upon us when we refused them alms, I was astonished to see the street and surrounding spaces packed with a mass of jostling people. As soon as they saw me at the window they shouted and gesticulated.

Calling Mohammed, I told him to go to the door and find out what was the trouble; but he laughed, and told me that the people had gathered to see me off and collect their backsheesh. As, however, it would have taken many purses of gold to satisfy so large a crowd, I asked Mustapha to explain to the crowd that there would be no presents except to the blind and crippled.

No notice was taken of the interpreter's speech, and with the patience of the East the multitude sat down and waited to see what would happen.

After breakfast I forced my way through the mob up to the hospital to superintend the loading of the camels; but such was the press that we could not get on with the packing until Hamid Effendi had sent down some gendarmes to discipline the crowd. Having freely plied their whips on the more unruly, order was restored, and we were able to finish our task.

On my return to the house I found that the waiting crowd had been reinforced by a band of music. A pock-marked negro performed on the bagpipes, two men energetically blew reed flutes, and a small coloured boy beat a large drum. Despite my protests and a liberal backsheesh, these men continued to play outside the house for upwards of two hours.

Looking through the window, I now noticed the presence of several blind people, who were regular recipients of a dole. Not wishing to go out and get mobbed, I pointed them out to little Sambo and gave him a few coins to distribute to them as unostentatiously as possible. Unfortunately, however, he was spotted by an eagle-eyed Arab, who raised the cry that the *hakim's* almoner was in their midst. Sambo was knocked down and relieved not only of the money but also of his coat, shirt and braces, and returned to the house in a tearful condition. When letting him through the door I noticed my Arab colleague, the local medicine man, making piteous signs to me that I should not depart before giving him a present, so I signalled to him to come round to the back window. Just as I had handed him a few shillings the crowd surged round the back of the house, and a hundred hands were thrust up to the window. It is fortunate that the bars were firmly fixed and that the house was a solid one, or the whole edifice would have been pulled down.

Three hours after the appointed time the remainder of the camels arrived, and the head man came into the house and started the usual haggle as to price. Although Hadj Ali, the camel-owner, was a venerable and benevolent-looking old gentleman, he thought it no shame to enter into a long and acrimonious discussion with Mustapha and Mohammed with a view to getting a rise on the price that Sheikh Sassi had fixed. Finally all was settled, the camels were loaded up, and the three gendarmes sent by Bahrouni as a protection to the caravan were waiting at the door.

Leaving Hadj Ali to make his way with the camels on to the plain, I rode up to the *gendarmerie* to say goodbye to my good friend Sassi. He seemed very much affected at my departure, and although we spoke hopefully of another meeting in the near future, I thought he felt the shadow of coming disaster. "But in happier days, good friend, we shall meet again in Tunis or Tripoli," I said. "Nay, my son," he replied, "we shall meet no more in this world; but God is good and compassionate, and I shall wait for you at the gates of Paradise, and together we will gather luscious fruits in the golden orchards." Then, seeing that I carried no rifle, he presented me with an excellent Mauser carbine and a bandolier of fifty cartridges, urging me to keep the sand out of the mechanism and always to have it ready.

INTERIOR OF FORT AT EL YEFREN

GENDARME DESCENDING FROM EL YEFREN

To face p. 214

Riding past the house, I again encountered the crowd, who made reiterated appeals for alms. Not wishing to offend against local custom, I scattered a pound's worth of small change amongst them. The competition to secure this money was very great, and a good deal of quarrelling ensued in the crowded street; so much so that later in the day my colleague had to treat two or three men who had been injured.

When I began to descend the hill I found the musicians waiting, and they persisted in playing in front of me until we got on to the plain. No sooner had I paid off the band than a hermit emerged from a cave and called down a blessing from heaven upon me, extracting in return a small backsheesh.

As soon as I caught up with the camels I noticed little Sambo trudging along beside Mohammed. I asked him what he was doing with the caravan, and if his father had given him permission to come. He replied quite unconcernedly that, as his father was a bad man, he had left him and had adopted me as his guardian; that he would be no trouble and would earn his food by looking after my horse. As I had no means of sending him back I was forced to take him along, and I am bound to say I never regretted it. His only garment consisted of a ragged pair of knickers, so at the first halt I got Mohammed to serve him out with a shirt. Later, at Bechoul, an Arab tailor made him quite a good summer suit out of an old pair of my pyjamas.

As we were looking about for a place to camp for the night a rather alarming incident occurred.

One of the camel-drivers lingered behind to mend

his sandal, and was speedily swallowed up in the darkness behind us. Soon we heard loud cries for help, and the gendarmes and I rode back at full gallop to see what was the matter. We found our camel-driver stripped practically naked and suffering from a deep sabre cut down the side of his face. It seems that robbers had jumped out upon him, and when he had resisted being deprived of his belongings, he had been given the sword cut. The gendarmes were anxious to start in pursuit of the bandits, but, as the night was very dark, I thought it would be impossible to find them; besides, I did not want to leave the caravan unprotected on the desert. When, wrapped up in my blanket, I lay down for the night, I could not help thinking that I was marching into a district none too healthy for a man who had goods to protect.

During the second day we came across large patches of barley, which was springing up well. This proved a great temptation to the camels, who kept on halting and cropping it. The Arabs seemed to have very little concern for the cereal property of others, and despite my protests allowed the camels to wander at will amongst the cultivated patches.

I spent the day learning as much Arabic as possible from the gendarmes and Hadj Ali. The latter turned out an interesting character, and entertained me all the morning with tales of his visit to Mecca and Medina. Surrounded as I had been at El Yefren by French and English speaking people, I found I had been too distrustful of my power of conversing in Arabic, and that when I got with men who spoke no other language I could manage fairly well. Hadj Ali, I soon found,

enjoyed considerable fame amongst the other Arabs as
a holy man, and it was not long before he got an
opportunity of displaying his powers. One of the
camels fell sick and kept on wanting to kneel down,
at the same time giving vent to the most doleful cries.
Hadj Ali took off his cap, blew into it, and then had
it rubbed on the camel's stomach and passed several
times round his head. The camel at once showed signs
of improvement, although I should not like to say that
it was due to the remedy.

Little Sambo provided a little comedy during the
afternoon. He had quickly got tired of walking, and
was constantly pestering the camel-men to make the
animals kneel either for him to get on or off. Finally
the men got tired of the constant repetition of the performance and left him perched on the top of the biggest
of the camels. As the animals were rather tired and
I was anxious to reach the wells at nightfall, they
required a lot of driving, and it was amusing to see
little Sambo whacking his camel with a big stick, accompanying each blow with the words " Zan, kelp! " (Go
along, dog!), the patient animal, of course, not taking
the slightest notice of the blow on his thick hide.
Tired at length of this exercise, Sambo begged hard to
be allowed to walk, and so insistent—and piercing—
were his requests, that I ordered one of the drivers to
make the camel kneel. Sambo trudged along contentedly
for some distance, but at length his little legs got tired
of trying to keep up with the caravan, and he began
to clamour to be put back on the camel. As I wanted
to stretch my legs a little, I got off Darkey and put
little Sambo up in the saddle. The pony soon noticed

that there was no very firm hand on the bridle, and
he commenced to stop at every tuft of herbage on the
road. Down came Sambo's stick on Darkey's hind-
quarters, and the pluckiest little pony in Tripoli was
insulted with the words " *Itt, kelp!* " (Get along, dog!).
Off went Darkey like an arrow across the desert, and
little Sambo was picked up a frightened but uninjured
object from the sand.

At dusk we reached the wells, and prepared to halt
for the night. The camp fire was already ablaze, and
Mohammed was rummaging in the provision box to
see what he could put on for dinner, when the venerable sheikh of the place came up and invited me into
his tent for the evening. It was a glorious starlight
night, and I was loth to leave the open air for the
interior of a tent, but Sheikh Abdulla was so insistent
that at last I accepted the invitation. The scene was
typical of many such evenings I have spent with the
Arabs. The low tent, with the carpets and mats spread
on the floor, was completely open on one side to the
little courtyard, railed off for the sake of privacy by
a hedge of dried brushwood. In the centre of the
courtyard blazed a fire, which was fed from time to time
by a servant with a handful of dry sticks; this fire not
being used for cooking, but for the purpose of illumin-
ation and boiling the all-important tea kettle. In the
weird firelight the shrouded forms of the women-folk
flitted to and fro, occupied with the preparation of the
evening meal. Busy as they were, however, they still
had time to throw furtive glances at the first Englishman they had ever seen. Kneeling by the hedge could
be dimly seen the forms of camels, their jaws working

CROSSING THE DESERT

LITTLE SAMBO ON DARKEY

as they chewed the cud with the regularity of those of a New York sales-lady masticating her gum.

The large bowl of *bazine* was now brought in, and after making the customary ablutions I fell to with a good appetite, not before, however, I had earned approving nods from the large company that had now gathered by the loud and pious manner with which I ejaculated "*Bismillah*" before commencing. The *bazine* was very hot, and I burnt my fingers at the first attempt I made to mix up the flour and hot oil. The sheikh, seeing my difficulty, came to the rescue, and mixed the ingredients up for me with a loud squishing noise. He also insisted on putting pieces of meat into my mouth with his own fingers. As soon as we had finished the bowl was pushed on to the gendarmes, Mohammed and the two boys, whose noisy methods of eating would hardly have recommended them to an English hostess.

The water at this place was very bad, and full of dirt and other foreign bodies. On account of this, when the earthenware goblet was handed round the Arabs invariably pulled out a piece of their shirt and covered the mouth of the jar before drinking, so as to filter the liquid. It was rather disconcerting to me to notice how many of the shirts needed the attentions of a laundress; still, the food was highly spiced, and one was forced to drink. "*Bismillah!*"

Sheikh Abdulla seemed delighted with our visit and kept on exclaiming, "*Lila mabrouka!*" (What a happy evening!). As this was a useful phrase I adopted it, and during the rest of my stay in the country often used it with great success.

Among the assembled company was a man who enjoyed some reputation in the district as a flute player, and the sheikh asked me if I would like to hear a tune. On my replying in the affirmative the man tuned up and continued playing a melancholy dirge for the best part of half an hour. "*Lila mabrouka*, Sheikh Abdulla!" I exclaimed, as I applauded perfunctorily, and then asked the man to oblige with an encore. At this Sheikh Abdulla turned to me and said that the performer should continue playing all the night if it gave the Doctor Bey any pleasure. This calamity I was fortunately able to avoid owing to the next artiste on the programme being anxious to start his performance.

While the music had been going on I noticed an Arab who was sitting near the fire, gazing intently in front of him and swaying about to the music. A large pruning knife had been thrust into the fire some time previously; this the man took up, and red-hot as it clearly was to my horror commenced drawing it across his lips and tongue. Finally he thrust the point into his mouth and closed his lips upon it, when a loud sizzling noise could be plainly heard. " What a splendid evening we are having!" exclaimed Sheikh Abdulla in an ecstasy.

The Arab seemed none the worse for the feat he had performed, and a few minutes after was smoking with apparent unconcern a cigarette that I had given him. I felt quite sure that this was no conjuring trick, as the man was sitting so near that I could have leaned over the fire and touched him. I should have asked him to let me examine his mouth, but did not like to be

considered too curious. I complimented him highly
on his skill, whereupon Sheikh Abdulla, who was
delighted that his evening's entertainment was going
off so well, ordered the knife to be replaced in the fire
for a repetition of the feat. It was only by saying that
I preferred another tune on the flute that I was able
to dissuade him. During the last effort of the flautist,
a bowl was handed round the company containing some
live coals on which incense had been sprinkled; a good
sniff of this was taken by each in turn.

As the evening wore on, I gradually found out that
we men-folk were not the only people who were enjoying
themselves. I noticed that each of my lame attempts
to speak Arabic was greeted with subdued laughter and
suppressed giggles from the half of the tent that was
set apart for the women and girls. To prepare for the
evening's entertainment, a shoulder-high partition had
been put up to divide the tent. I was facing it, while
the sheikh had his back to it. Once looking up suddenly, I saw a row of heads in the dim light of the
tent gazing on me curiously over the partition,
while a henna-stained finger was constantly to be seen,
cautiously enlarging a peep-hole just above the sheikh's
head.

One by one the guests slipped away, and after a last
good-night to Sheikh Abdulla I prepared for the night,
lying down with my blankets on the floor of the tent.
I had to scowl severely at my feminine audience before
I could make them understand that I proposed retiring
for the night.

On the following day Hadj Ali, who had been
favourably impressed by the fluent manner in which

AT–H*

I learned to utter the pious ejaculations he had taught me, renewed his religious discourses, evidently under the impression that he was on the high road to making a convert; for even as the poor Chinaman or Indian listens to the missionary for what he can get out of him, so I listened to Hadj Ali in the hopes of improving my Arabic. At all events, his exhortations were given entirely free, and no one could accuse him of trying to make money out of his religious propaganda.

On the evening of the third day we arrived at Bechoul, only to find that Sheikh Sauf had moved off that very morning with his troops to a place near Ajilat, on which town he intended to make an attack. I was in doubt what to do, but after consultation with the Arab officials I determined to fix my headquarters at Bechoul and then, if the attack on Ajilat succeeded, I could move the hospital into that town.

At this time Bechoul was a small collection of tents and huts situated in the middle of the desert. There was one small lath and plaster house, in which Bahrouni's representative kept his books and papers, and round which a small bazaar or market was held every day. As soon as my tent was erected Hadj Ali came in asking for his money, as he was anxious to get off the next morning at daybreak. Although Sheikh Sassi had driven a hard bargain with him over the price of the camels, and I was unable to give him a good backsheesh owing to the small amount of money I had with me, the old man seemed quite pleased.

Before leaving he wrote me a talisman on a piece of paper and urged me to wear it always round my neck, as it was a certain preventive of disease and wounds. To be quite fair to Hadj Ali, I must record the fact that I enjoyed excellent health while I wore it, and I much regret that I lost it before I had been able to test its virtues on a real battlefield.

CHAPTER XV.

THE notables at Bechoul who gathered to meet me proved excellent fellows and hospitable to a fault. Despite the fact that I told them I was well supplied with provisions, no sooner had I unsaddled than some servants came round bringing a present of a sheep, together with tea, sugar and goat's milk. Without being asked, they sent up Arabs to assist in erecting the tents and to make themselves generally useful.

The people I met at Bechoul seemed much better educated and informed than the men in the hills; they had a good knowledge of European politics and took a great delight in discussing them with me. Masroud Effendi, Bahrouni's representative, spoke Djebelli, Arabic and Turkish fluently, as well as possessing some knowledge of Persian and French. He at once constituted himself my professor in Arabic, and in return I was bold enough to help him to improve his French.

As soon as we had unpacked the stores and put up the tents, the usual flock of out-patients began to arrive. In order to attend to these, I had a piece of carpet laid on the sand at the tent door, and seated on this face to face with the patients I would endeavour to find out what was the matter with them. As Mohammed was usually busy in the mornings, either marketing or cooking, I often had to act as my own interpreter. The fun frequently waxed fast and furious, as everyone knows the great temptation there is to speak loudly when anyone obstinately refuses to understand what you are saying. I shouted to make my Arabic more intelligible, while the patient roared his symptoms at me, so as to give the impression that he was very much in need of assistance. Arabs have one great redeeming feature, a good sense of humour, and frequently when I was betrayed into laughter the whole audience would join in heartily.

Sometimes I could make no progress and had to call upon Mohammed for help. Unfortunately, he looked upon it as an insult for anyone not to understand me, and he would assume a distinctly aggressive attitude, often threatening the unlucky patient with the frying-pan or the rolling-pin.

At other times El Khani would come up and assist, but as he had ideas of his own on medical treatment it became very difficult to prescribe through him. His views were similar to those of the Peculiar People, and he seemed to consider prayers of more value than physic. Still, I learned one good thing from him— that the ritual of Moslem prayer is as good for the body as it is said to be for the soul. The genuflections and prostrations form a very valuable physical exercise, and if carried out regularly five times a day they tend to keep the joints supple and also conduce to a regular habit of the body.

During my stay at Bechoul a severe epidemic of whooping cough was sweeping the desert and killing

off many of the younger children; in consequence I
had very many babies brought to me by their mothers.
Unfortunately, even under the best conditions the treatment of this disease is a reproach to the medical profession, and it was very little I was able to do for the
tiny sufferers; but as they were all very feeble and
weak from lack of proper food the present of a
tin of milk was greatly appreciated by the anxious
mothers.

Eye cases began coming in in increasing numbers.
Without in any way deserving it, I had made some
small reputation in this branch of surgery, and the
people I had relieved on returning to their homes gave
an exaggerated account of what I had done for them.
In consequence of this, many poor Arabs travelled very
long distances to consult me, often arriving at the camp
in a state of absolute destitution. It was sad, however,
that one could do so little for many of them. Often
they would come with the eyeball entirely destroyed,
exhibiting nothing but hollow, staring sockets, or with
the sight utterly ruined by trachoma. What could we
do for them? Well, at all events, we could take them
into the hospital for a few days, provide them with good
nourishing food, and then send them home with a new
cap or an article of clothing.

Nor did El Khani neglect the shining hour. Missionary fire burnt fiercely in his breast, and he would
sit for hours in the hospital tent leading the patients in
prayer and reciting extracts from the Koran. I can
picture him now sitting on the floor talking to the sick,
his fierce eyes ablaze with religious zeal, and the sand
of the desert still clinging to his forehead, where it

ARAB WARRIORS

BAHROUNI'S OFFICERS AT BECHOUL

To face p. 226

remained after he had bent his head to the dust. One
hand rested on the hilt of his dagger while the other
beat the air to give force to his argument. A large,
much-used rosary hung round his neck, the beads falling
on to a pair of field-glasses, from which he was never
parted.

There seems to be a general impression that the
Arabs are an ungrateful race. Personally, I did not
find this the case, for my patients showed in many ways
that they appreciated what had been done for them.
Women would very often bring me an egg, a bottle
of milk, or a wisp of grass for my pony to show their
gratitude. Seeing their abject want and poverty, I
refused these gifts as gently as I could, but I must
confess I was touched that people so poor should even
have offered me the food that they needed so badly
themselves.

As I got more familiar with Arabic I began to realize
Mohammed's limitations as an interpreter. Probably
it was largely due to the fact that he did not properly
understand my French, which was either too good for
an Algerian or too bad for a Frenchman. He seemed
quite incapable of putting anything politely or wording
a refusal in a courteous manner. For example, one
evening I was taking a rest when a grave, dignified-
looking sheikh rode up and asked for a consultation.
As the light was fading and I was very tired, I called
Mohammed and asked him to tell the Arab that I
greatly regretted I was unable to treat him that night,
but if he would have the goodness to return in the
morning I should have much pleasure in doing what
I could for him. With a steaming saucepan in one

hand, Mohammed barked out a dozen words at the sheikh. As they were all familiar words, I understood completely what he said. The English equivalent of his translation of my apologetic remarks would read : " Be off, come back to-morrow morning! "

Another day, when I had a large crowd of visitors in the reception tent, I was asked by one of the notables if I thought that if the Arab resistance failed the Italians would severely punish the sheikhs who had taken up arms against them. I answered that all civilized nations appreciated a courageous and fearless enemy and I felt sure they had nothing to fear. In order to illustrate the point, and at the same time to show the magnanimity of my own fellow-countrymen, I told them of the visit that the three Boer generals made to London after the collapse of their gallant resistance. How that when they appeared in the streets they were surrounded by huge crowds, who instead of injuring or insulting them cheered them to the echo.

Mohammed duly interpreted, but instead of seeing the faces of the assembled guests light up with pleasure at the tale of the honour shown to defeated enemies they sat silent and impressed. I asked the cook what he had said. He ran through the tale correctly enough until he came to the last phrases, when to my horror he finished glibly : " . . . The crowd seized the three generals and cut their throats on the spot! "

After this appalling example in the art of interpreting I usually managed to get hold of El Khani when I wished to say anything important; not that his services were completely satisfactory, for he always added any points he wished to make himself, but I could always rely upon my remarks being interpreted in a grave and impressive manner.

My staff now consisted of three people—Mohammed, Sambo Kebir and Sambo Serir. The latter's business was to keep the brazier alight in the hospital tent, as well as to act as a miniature policeman to prevent theft. If I warned a patient overnight that he would be discharged in the morning, he frequently would make up his mind to leave unostentatiously in the night. At first I thought in my innocence that this was a kindly act on the man's part, because he did not wish to throw too much strain on the financial resources of the Mission by accepting the small gift that was presented to those leaving. Later, however, I found that when anyone left secretly at night, a blanket always disappeared with him; hence my having to make little Sambo sleep at the tent door.

In addition to these three servants, I had to employ a grass-gatherer, men to fetch water and girls to bring in firewood. Grass for the pony was picked by a very old Arab, who had served twenty-five years in the Turkish Army. He was a most interesting old fellow and had seen a great deal of active service. He was one of that gallant band who held Plevna for the Sultan; one of the army whose heroic exploits were so esteemed in England, before the days when we sacrificed the friendship of the Turk for the hug of Russia. He had taken part in that heroic sortie from Plevna so well described by W. V. Herbert: " Here a whole division marched cheerfully to certain death, and the feet kept step to the lips, which murmured the Arab prayer,

'*Bismillah Rahmin Rahamin*' (In the name of God the Merciful, the Compassionate)."

He was never tired of telling me how once he carried a message through the historic Balkan town to the headquarters of Osman Pasha. "Did you see Osman Pasha, Achmet?" I asked.

"Oh, yes! Doctor Bey, and I drank coffee with him," replied the soldier. "He wished to know how we were getting on in the trenches, and he called to the sentry to admit me. He was sitting at a table like you, but he looked wan and tired, except that his eyes flashed fire. I saluted him (and Achmet's hand sped from his breast to his forehead in a salute), and when I had answered his questions he called to the boy to serve me with coffee. Ah! that was before the Rumanians came to the help of our enemies; without them we could have kept the Russians from our earthworks."

Poor old Achmet! He took everyone's measure, even Mohammed's. He called the latter "Effendi," and Mohammed was so flattered that the old soldier got many a good meal in our kitchen.

As to water we had considerable difficulty, as the supply at Bechoul was both meagre and bad. It was so highly charged with salts that Mohammed and the boys were troubled with a constant dysentery, while it was almost impossible to wash in it, as soap failed to make the slightest lather. Tea made with it was very unpalatable, and when milk was added it fell immediately in a cloudy precipitate to the bottom of the cup. Moreover, the well was very dirty. By means of a rope and the rough steps cut in the side, I went

WATER TANKS AND GUARD

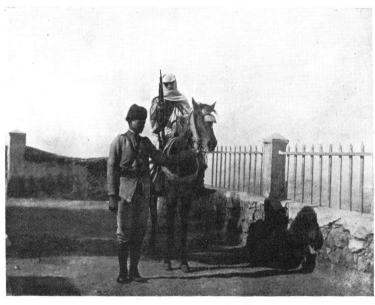

SON OF SHEIKH SASSI

To face p. 230

down to inspect it, and found in the muddy pool at
the bottom a large collection of tin cans and broken
bottles, as well as fragments of improvised ropes made
by knotting old rags together.

As I did not think it right to continue giving this
contaminated water to the people under my medical
care, I spent my leisure hours hunting round for a
proper supply. Finally, I had to go a journey of several
hours to a place called Juesh, situated in the hills, and
the nearest point on the telegraph route from Nalout
to El Yefren. Here I found a spring of delicious water
which was naturally aerated. Comparing it with Vichy
water, of which I kept a few bottles in reserve, I found
a marked resemblance; if anything, the product of
Juesh was the better, owing perhaps to its freshness and
coolness. I should think that if ever Tripoli develops
into a large city a company might do worse than exploit
this mountain spring.

Having ascertained the presence of this water, I
engaged two men with a camel to go up and bring
back a small tankful. About nightfall, on returning
from my evening ride, I found at least a dozen men
waiting patiently at the door of the cookhouse.
I noticed that many of them carried water pots. On
my asking Mohammed what they wanted, he replied
that they were waiting for the water from Juesh, which
it appeared was famous for its sweetness in the district.
I was sorry to have to disappoint them, but I had to
tell them that the water was only for the sick. Thereupon, with common consent, they all laid their hands
on their belts and groaned, wishing me to understand
that they also were sick. In the end I was forced to

give them a draught apiece, although I naturally refused to fill their pots.

However, the next few days we had so many visitors asking for a drink of water—and who can refuse so simple a request?—that after a time I was obliged to tell Mohammed to serve nothing but Bechoul water. On this being done, much to my delight our popularity greatly waned.

As a rule I left all bargaining to Mohammed, who beat down provision merchants and purveyors in a masterly fashion. Whenever I did any buying I was always charged an exorbitant price, as I let my pity for the apparently poor run away with my desire for economy. One day I gave a miserable-looking Jew a franc for doing some small job about the camp. Mohammed asked me why I gave him so much, and I replied because he looked as if he wanted a good meal and was too poor to get one.

" Poor! " retorted Mohammed. " He's one of the richest Jews in Tripolitana and owns two hundred camels! "

The women always looked impoverished and ill-nourished. While their men-folk were away fighting they lived on a miserable pittance of flour, allowed them by the Government. I remember one day, on returning to the tents after a good gallop on Darkey, I saw a large bundle of firewood lying on the ground, and beside it the curled-up figure of an Arab girl; apparently she was weeping bitterly. I asked Mohammed what the matter was. He shrugged his shoulders and told me to take no notice, suggesting cynically that the crying was put on for my benefit.

As he, however, was inclined to be harsh with visitors of the fair sex, I told him not to interfere, but to get back to his pots and pans; for what indeed can a greasy cook know about drying a woman's tears?

" What is it, Fatima? " I asked gently, and she shyly lifted two glistening eyes to mine. (Untruthful Mohammed! This was no make-believe; these were real tears that glittered in her eyes and hung like jewels on her fringing lashes.) Then her veil flashed across her face again.

" Speak, Fatima! " I urged.

Slowly she lifted herself from the ground and sobbed out her story: her father had been killed in the war; she was terribly hungry; she had spent all day gathering firewood, and now—a heart-breaking sob—Mohammed had refused to buy it.

I exclaimed with horror at this brutality and was rewarded by a dropping of the veil and a little, wan smile. The stones of the desert had hurt her feet too, and an arched foot was held up for my inspection; a foot fresh from Nature's mould, with dainty toes, uncramped and unconfined; so different from the tortured, distorted feet the sight of which makes the most hardened of us shudder when a civilized woman takes off her stocking. But Fatima had still another confidence to make—if only the Doctor Bey knew how heavy the load had been, how it had hurt her shoulders. Then a furtive glance round to make sure Mohammed was far away and none but professional eyes could see, and a discreet area of smooth skin was exposed with an ugly scratch across it. I grew indignant.

"Mohammed!" I called sharply. "*Mais, mon Dieu*, what is this? What are we here for? Have we not come to help the poor and unfortunate? This young lady's father has been killed in the war, and yet you refuse to buy her wood!"

Mohammed muttered some libellous remark to the effect that he did not wish to encourage bad characters about the camp, thrust a coin into the girl's hand and marched off.

Fatima clutched the coin in a tiny hand but showed no signs of departing. She looked at me appealingly with her veil caught coquettishly between little white teeth and an arm displayed effectively against the tent pole.

I asked her what more she wanted. Alas! food was so dear—a sob—Mohammed had given her so little; but, praise God!—eyes lifted to Heaven—the Doctor Bey had a kind heart.

I took a hasty glance to see that Mohammed was not a witness of my weakness and then put a piece of money into her hand. She glanced at it, gasped with pleasure and seized my hand to kiss it. I snatched it away as etiquette demands, and calling up my best Arabic I said: "What a pretty girl you are, Fatima!"

An illuminating and satisfied smile crossed her face, and conquering woman went on her way rejoicing.

On the 3rd of March a mounted messenger dashed into the market-place of Bechoul, shouting and gesticulating. His horse was white with foam and the rider's spurs were not innocent of blood. Anxious to hear the news, but unwilling to display undignified curiosity, I stayed in my tent and sent Mohammed down to find out what was happening. He came back, after a few minutes, and told me that the troops under the command of Sheikh Sauf-ben-Nassur had captured the town of Ajilat and had killed and wounded a large number of the enemy.

If this were true, it was of course an important success for the Arabs, especially if it be remembered that that town is only a few hours' sharp ride from Tripoli itself. Still, I received the news with caution, as even in a well-organized army the most absurd rumours fly about as to the doings of some division only a few miles off. Moreover, in reading this account, it must again be remembered that the only source of information I had access to was an Arab one, so that I was quite prepared to hear presently that the facts were not exactly as they were reported to me.

At all events, the next day Sheikh Sauf rode into the town amid great excitement. He seemed very much beloved by the Arabs and they all crowded round to kiss his hand. On top of a camel came El Khani, waving a huge flag in triumph. Behind swarmed a fierce band of soldiers, bringing with them all sorts of spoil—arms and equipment in profusion, a pair of splendid mules bearing loads of clothing and a large supply of ammunition. The Arabs also displayed jewellery and watches, money and bank-notes, and a collection of those little things that a soldier carries in his valise.

I could see at once that Sauf had scored a success, but as he had returned with his troops it was obvious he had been unable to consolidate his gain of ground. Anxious to gather the fullest particulars possible, I asked

El Khani to come into my tent and drink tea. Then I learned how once again the Arabs had allowed their love of looting to prevent them driving their victory home.

In the early hours of the morning of February 28th a party of about 500 Arabs cautiously made their way into Ajilat, just as the moon was rising. At first, not meeting any of the enemy's troops, they naturally started looting the shops. The Italians then hearing the noise and the shouting of the civilian population made a sortie from the barracks, and a furious skirmish took place between the opposing forces. For a time, despite a disparity in numbers, the Italians held their ground well, but at length their ranks were broken and they had to fall back on the barracks. According to the Arab accounts, this building was well fortified, nevertheless it would probably have fallen to a determined attack; but Sauf's men having the alternative before them of assaulting a strong place with small prospect of booty and a good prospect of getting killed, or a chance of looting shops in perfect safety, gave themselves up to the latter occupation.

Unfortunately, however, it did not end in looting, for apparently the Italians had brought large quantities of wines and other intoxicants into the town, and the Arabs breaking into the drink-shops could not resist tasting the contents of the inviting-looking bottles. Being entirely unused to alcoholic liquors, the drink quickly took effect, and the Arabs, getting out of their officers' control, committed the crime of killing several non-combatants.

As soon as daybreak was near they gathered up their

spoils and left the town, carrying with them their wounded.

In this skirmish the Arabs confessed to several killed and between fifty and sixty wounded. They gave probably an exaggerated account of the enemy's losses, but, judging from the large amount of equipment and spoil they brought back, I should imagine that the Italian casualties were fairly heavy for so small an affair.

The moral effect of the affair must have been considerable, as it gave the submitted Arabs along the coast an uneasy feeling that they could not be adequately protected, and every night afterwards we had men coming in from the towns to bring information to Sheikh Sauf.

The officer in authority at Ajilat during this time must have had his knuckles rapped severely, for if the Arab reports were true, no sentries had been posted and the approaches to the town were in no way guarded.

It may be an impertinence for a civilian to criticize the conduct of a war, but it seemed to me that the Italian cavalry were strangely remiss in not dealing a death-blow to the Arab forces on the plains. With his horses in good condition a bold leader would have quickly covered the distance from Ajilat to Bechoul and stamped out the hornets' nest encamped there. Then, by burning the stores and ammunition, he would have completely paralyzed the Arab resistance. I always thought that the Italian failure to penetrate the interior was largely due to a neglecting of the advice of the great Danton : " *L'audace, encore de l'audace, toujours de l'audace!*" Keen soldiers, led by such cavalry officers as the American Civil War bred, would have cleared the country to the hills in a few weeks.

As Sheikh Sauf was very tired after his exertions I made no attempt to see him that day, but busied myself making preparations for the reception of the wounded, who were being carried in by their friends on litters. In Tripolitana we did not make use of the ordinary army stretcher, as I thought even at that date that it was too heavy and cumbersome. We employed light bamboo poles, pushed through the doubled sides of a piece of stout canvas; the handles being kept apart by an iron bar, furnished with rings, through which the bamboo handles were thrust. This formed an excellent means of carrying the wounded and was much lighter and more portable than the ordinary stretcher, which is a heavy burden to carry about even when unoccupied by a casualty.

On returning to the camp after my evening ride, I found to my annoyance that the gendarmes had begun erecting Sheikh Sauf's tents quite close to the hospital. I was therefore forced to go and see him at once, in order to point out that if he persisted in coming so near I should either have to move farther off or haul down the Red Crescent and my national flag. In these days I was still fairly innocent of the effects of shell-fire and aeroplane bombing, but I knew enough to understand that it would not be correct for me to protect a combatant camp with my flags. Fortunately, the Arab leader saw the point at once and immediately gave orders for the erected tents to be taken down and removed to a spot half a mile away.

The same evening the Arab casualties began to arrive; some limping along with the help of sticks and crutches, representing all grades of the class that is rather euphemistically called "walking wounded." Following these came men on horses or camels, groaning with pain as broken limbs were shaken up with the jolting of their beasts. Lastly we received the stretcher cases, which usually demanded immediate treatment.

A small tent was used as a reception-room, and through this the cases passed one by one, every man being provisionally treated pending a more serious examination the next day. It was a long business and the sun had already risen before this part of the work had been done. Everyone was called upon to assist. Mohammed kept the kitchen fires alight all night, in order to provide every soldier whose condition permitted it with a good meal. El Khani acted as interpreter and also, when occasion demanded, undertook the rôle of anæsthetist, occasionally alarming me by the generosity with which he used the chloroform. Big Sambo helped efficiently with the dressings, while the youngster ran about with hot water and saw that the lamps were kept provided with paraffin. Sheikh Sauf kindly placed a gendarme at my disposal to watch the two abdominal cases, as they shouted continually for food, and had we not been vigilant they would have swallowed as hearty a meal as they could have procured.

Looking back, I still view with satisfaction the work we did that night, and it is pleasant to think that, although we treated many severe cases, we never lost a single patient.

Thoroughly exhausted by my night's work, I got into bed (about eleven o'clock) and settled down for a few hours' sleep; but so active was my brain, and so persistently did I follow up trains of thought, that it was a long time before I fell into that delicious state called dozing. Suddenly I was roused up by a loud " *Salaam alikoum* " at the tent door, and, starting up, I saw one of the abdominal cases, who had escaped the vigilance of his guards, standing before me. He looked extremely ill and was supporting himself on a stick. It is almost impossible to secure any privacy at all in an Arab settlement, as anyone feels free to come into your tent after the usual words of greeting. I naturally supposed that the man in front of me was suffering great pain and had come to me direct for relief, so I asked him politely enough what was the trouble. My politeness swiftly vanished when he replied that he would be much obliged if the Doctor Bey would give him a pinch of snuff!

As usual, the wounds produced by the small Italian bullet healed very rapidly; as a rule I only detained the uncomplicated cases about ten days before discharging them to their duties. Some of the wounded, however, appeared to have been hit by large leaden bullets, discharged perhaps by Arab auxiliaries on the Italian side, and these injuries caused me serious trouble.

Life in hospital was made as pleasant as possible for the patients. I am no believer in the advice given to me by one of my old chiefs at Guy's: " Always be grave in the presence of suffering." Certainly there are times when it is necessary and politic to be serious, but the unfortunate and afflicted do not always wish to be greeted with long faces. More especially does this apply to the patients in military hospitals, who have done their duty to their country and do not wish to have it impressed upon them that they are objects of pity.

At all events, our hospital was a cheerful place. Mohammed served the wounded with the best food they had ever had in their lives; the beds were soft and warm, and tea-making was allowed at all hours of the day. After the few minutes' pain caused by the morning dressing, a distribution of cigarettes was made, and the rest of the day was passed pleasantly in eating, smoking and chatting. The night was often enlivened by the efforts of someone to elude the vigilance of little Sambo by getting away with a blanket or a suit of hospital clothing. When one remembers that in addition to these attractions El Khani had appointed himself chaplain and worked as hard at his duties as our own padres do in the field, no one will be surprised to hear that when I wished to discharge a patient I frequently had to call a gendarme to assist in getting him off the premises.

Unfortunately the weather proved very bad during March. It rained heavily at times, and often during the night the wind blew with such intensity that Mohammed and I had to get out of bed and go round tightening the tent ropes. The wind drove the sand into the tents, and it penetrated into all our belongings. Despite the cook's endeavours it forced its way into the cooking-pots and mingled with the food.

Some years ago I was in a mining camp in the tropics,

where a fastidious member of the mess had a genius
for making complaints. One day, alluding to the
number of insects that swam in the food, he facetiously
asked the West Indian butler to bring a little more
of the "ant soup"!

Well, at Bechoul sand became a regular article of
diet—sand in the dates, sand in the soups and sand
in the omelettes. Still, the days passed quickly and
happily. There was sufficient work to make leisure
enjoyable, and sufficient exercise to make going to bed
at nights a pleasure.

Sometimes, despite Mohammed's protests, I would
go into the kitchen and prepare my own dinner, since
I have found cooking an interesting and restful occupation. It is always amusing to try one's hand at another
person's occupation. I remember once running a hotel
bar for an evening, when a harassed woman licensee
was unable to keep an unruly mob of customers in
order. I succeeded better in this line than I did when
I usurped the profession of a hairdresser. It was a wet
afternoon in a Welsh health resort, and I rather foolishly
volunteered to shampoo the hair of a prepossessing
young lady. The draggled and rat-like appearance of
my client after the operation cured me of any desire
to continue in the trade.

As well as my professional work at Bechoul I had
another important duty—receiving and entertaining the
large number of visitors that called to see me. With
these I was frequently in minor difficulties as to procedure and etiquette. Sometimes Mohammed would
come in with tea or coffee and then tell me, in a stage
whisper, that such a man was only a beggar, and ought

not to be allowed to sit in a chair; or he would point to an Arab squatting on the floor and urge that a chair should be given him, on account of his high standing. In order to obviate these difficulties, I had the reception tent entirely cleared of chairs and caused blankets to be spread on the floor, so that everyone was on an equality. Only when Sheikh Sauf paid me one of his complimentary visits did I order the chairs to be brought in.

As soon as I heard that fresh people had come into the camp, I used to send Mohammed down to the market-place to make inquiries as to their standing, so that I was in a position to know how to receive them. This must not be put down to snobbery on my part, but as the representative of the Mission in these parts, I conceived it to be my duty to observe, as far as possible, the correct etiquette.

In the evening, after dinner, I usually went down to the Arab headquarters to drink tea with the notables. They always rose politely to receive me, and treated me with the greatest courtesy. At first I had great difficulty in sitting for long cross-legged on the floor, but by and by I got quite used to it, and in the end even found the position comfortable.

The conversation, of course, at these gatherings was always in Arabic, and I soon began to understand what was being said, and even to throw in a word here and there. The Arabs helped me all they could by speaking slowly and distinctly, and never even smiled when I made the most foolish blunders. At Bechoul I was greatly helped in my study of Arabic by the absolute dearth of anything to read. I soon exhausted the possibilities of Whitaker's Almanack, the only book I had with me, so I had little to divert my attention from a serious study of the language.

At the tea parties we had several forms of amusement. One Arab would recite a long poem, perhaps extemporized, in which I frequently caught the words " war," " Mauser " and " Italian," describing some action in the campaign. Another would give a solo on a sort of piccolo, whilst a third would thrill the audience with an account of how his caravan had been attacked by the Tuaregs.

Friday, the Sabbath of Islam, was always celebrated in an appropriate manner. The poor were called up by a few trustworthy gendarmes to the front of the hospital tent. Then El Khani, at my invitation, would mount one of the provision boxes and harangue the crowd. It was his duty to explain to the people that the Moslems of India and certain charitable people in England were not unmindful of the sufferings of the Arabs in Tripolitana, and had sent out the Mission to help them. As it took El Khani at least half an hour to deliver these few simple phrases, I always concluded that he added a little religious teaching to my remarks, but as the proceeding gave him great pleasure and the audience listened open mouthed, I made no objection.

Then the poor came up, one by one, and received a measure of flour each, to which I added in the case of the blind a few small coins. After this two orphan boys were selected by me to receive a new cap apiece, and finally the two or three most miserably-clad women were presented with wrappers. After a time, however,

I had to abandon this method of distributing clothes to the women, for having learned that the possession of rags constituted a claim on the generosity of the Mission, they vied with each other in coming to the hospital in such tattered gowns that common decency prevented me sending them away without adequate clothing.

As the wounded began to recover I was able to get about the country more, and I frequently went for long rides with El Khani. But in these days he was evidently harbouring a secret, for whenever we went to the house of any important sheikh, he would always politely request me to leave the room for a few minutes, as he had important and secret matters he wished to speak to the master of the house about.

Just as I was leaving Bechoul the secret came out. He presented me with a large testimonial, beautifully written in Arabic and Persian, describing my work in the country in all too flattering terms. It was stamped at the bottom with twenty seals, that had been placed on it by all the notables in Western Tripolitana.

I shall always feel a debt of gratitude to El Khani for the great assistance he gave me in many little difficulties. Fortunately, I was able to return it in some slight degree, when to my astonishment he turned up in London. He still wore the identical costume that I had seen him in at Bechoul, a costume more suitable for a fancy-dress ball than the London streets; but as he always carried himself with a natural air of dignity, he never looked peculiar nor was uneasy in his manner.

A few weeks before the Great War broke out I

received a small parcel from Turkey containing a present from him—a silver-gilt snuffbox set with amethysts. It was a gaudy toy, but welcome enough to me, as it showed I was not forgotten by an old friend.

CHAPTER XVI.

NEWS was now reaching Bechoul daily that Bahrouni was attacking Gharian and was meeting with considerable success in his efforts. We heard that the Italians had been driven out of several of the surrounding hamlets, and that these positions had been occupied and consolidated by the Arabs. However, as it cannot be said that truthfulness is one of the cardinal virtues of the Arab, and as rumours of the wildest description are always rife during a war, it was difficult to be sure of the exact state of affairs. Nevertheless it was clear that my days of usefulness at Bechoul were at an end. I had discharged most of my wounded cured, and the six cases remaining in the hospital could make no further progress until some form of major operation had been performed, which I was quite unable to undertake without some skilled assistance. Under these circumstances I determined to return to El Yefren, taking the cases for operation with me; so I rode up to Juesh and telegraphed to Mr. Turnbull announcing my decision. I then asked Sheikh Sauf to get me the necessary camels at as reasonable a price as possible, and he promised that they should be ready on the afternoon of March 22nd. On this day we were all

up very early, getting down and packing up the tents;
a work which was considerably hampered by a high
wind and frequent showers of driving rain. The
wounded were placed under temporary shelters, and a
good hot meal was served up preparatory to the journey.
About two o'clock, as the camels had not arrived, I
sent Mohammed to make inquiries, and he returned
with the exasperating news that the camels would not
arrive that afternoon, but a start would be made early
next morning, "please God." Could anything have
been more annoying? All the tents were folded and
packed, and consequently there was no shelter for
Mohammed and myself, either from the hot sun or
from the rain that was falling in torrents. Slowly the
day wore on, and I was delighted when at length the
sun set, hoping that at its next appearance we should
be able to start on our journey. But these were vain
hopes, for the sun rose and mounted higher and higher
in the heavens without any signs of the promised
camels; nor could Mohammed succeed in finding the
man who was going to supply them. Just as I was
boiling over with indignation, up came El Khani, to
whom I had said goodbye the previous day; and he,
in the blandest tones, asked me why I had not started.
As temperately as I could I explained the position to
him, and together we went down to the market-place,
where he quickly found the guilty camel-owner drinking tea in a tent. El Khani let fly a volley of abuse
at him in all the dialects of which he was master, and
the camel-driver, in a burst of furious activity, went
outside the tent and handed on the message to a group
of Arabs who were squatting round a fire. It then

appeared that the camels had not yet arrived from Juesh, but "please God" they were sure to come that evening; to-morrow, *inchallah*, we would make an early start. Maddening as was the delay, there was nothing to do but sit down and wait. Mohammed, at least, did his duty by serving up an excellent dinner on the biggest packing-case, and thinking that the circumstances made a little stimulant excusable, I finished off a large flask of rum to combat the wet and cold.

The night that followed was a miserable one. The wind grew furious, and tore up the temporary shelter we had placed over the wounded, who, poor fellows, became drenched with the rain that followed. Dawn found Mohammed and myself thoroughly exhausted after the night's battle with the elements. The sun, however, rose in kindly mood. The wounded, who were shivering with cold, soon got warm and dry, and the ration of tea and cigarettes I served out put everyone in a good humour. About eleven o'clock the camels turned up, and an hour later we were all ready to start. I had asked Sheikh Sauf to supply me with three reliable gendarmes, as during the last month several people had been robbed and assaulted on the road to El Yefren. But when everything was ready only one gendarme turned up, and he was the weediest-looking man I ever saw filling a uniform. His horse, too, was the poorest of beasts, and would have been beaten by Rosinante in the commonest of canters. But, tempting as it is to judge by first appearances, I had good cause later on to look upon this man Selim as one of the most faithful Arabs I ever had occasion to employ. Seeing no signs of the other gendarmes, and tired of exasperating delays, I determined to set out without them, and signalled to Mohammed to start the caravan.

We had been about half an hour on the road when we met a small caravan of three camels coming from the opposite direction, and I soon recognized one of the drivers as a man called Saad, a one-eyed Arab, who was one of the oldest servants of our Mission. He had a letter for me from Mr. Turnbull, and I dismounted and sat down on the sand to read it. Up to the date of his writing, he reported, there had been no fighting his way, and he was sending Saad with a couple of cases that had recently arrived for me from Tunis. One of the boxes contained a good supply of thick winter underclothing, that I had ordered some months previously to combat the cold weather in the hills. This I felt little temptation to put on, as it was now so hot that I was riding in a thin cotton shirt. The other case was filled with a varied assortment of books. Everyone who is fond of reading will appreciate my delight at handling these books after the months of literary famine I had endured. I pushed Pierre Loti's *Roman d'un Spahi* into one of my holsters, told Saad he would have to return with me to El Yefren, and, after the usual tussle with the camel-driver as to price, we started again on our journey, reinforced by the three camels.

The day passed fairly uneventfully, but the wounded suffered cruelly with the jolting of the camels. The sun was very hot, and there were constant stops to supply the sufferers with water. It was annoying, when one wanted to push on rapidly, to have to halt the

camels for this purpose. It would have been easy to
have told them to wait until we reached the halting-
place; but now that I know what it is to suffer the
appalling thirst that an extensive wound causes, I am
devoutly thankful that I never refused a drink of water
either to friend or foe.

We halted for the night near a large encampment,
the Arabs in which had taken part in the attack on
Ajilat. The sheikh invited me to dinner in his tent,
but before I was able to sit down I had the wounded
to dress and make comfortable. I was also called to
several tents near for the purpose of giving surgical
assistance to men of the tribe who had been hit in
the recent fighting. Several of them clamoured to be
taken to the hospital at El Yefren, but as I had no wish
to increase the size of my caravan I contented myself
with leaving a good supply of dressings with the local
hakim, who seemed an intelligent sort of man, hoping
that they would be well looked after by him. I was
surprised on arriving at the sheikh's tent for supper
to see the amount of loot he had secured. Two splendid
Italian mules were tethered near by, while the tent was
piled with all sorts of goods, including rifles and other
arms, packets of chocolates, tins of sardines, cases containing anti-typhoid serum, mouth-organs, picture postcards and a plentiful supply of stationery. An amusing
thing about these picture postcards was that, although
the views shown were of beauty spots in Tunisia, the
names printed underneath were those of places in Tripolitana; doubtless to impress the Italian people with
the progress their army was making in overrunning the
new colony.

The sheikh had just received a letter from Bahrouni, confirming the news of the fighting in Gharian, and also stating that the Arabs had captured several guns. This proved to be a fact, but the success was of little value to the Arabs, as instead of getting away with their capture they had devoted their time to looting.

Early the next morning, when on the march, I saw that three fresh camels had joined our caravan, and on making inquiries I found that despite my prohibition four more wounded men were accompanying us to El Yefren. I called up Mahommed and was about to send them back, when my host of the previous night turned up and begged me to allow them to proceed, as they were his own relations. On the strict understanding that I was not to be held responsible for the hire of the camels I agreed to take them, so we marched forward with six more mouths to fill. But as both the new camel-drivers carried good serviceable rifles and a supply of ammunition, I did not grudge them their food, for they added considerably to the security of the caravan.

During the day we made very poor progress, owing to the constant halts necessitated by the sufferings of the wounded, and when night fell we had not made more than half the distance appointed for the day's journey. I determined, however, to halt for the night and make an early start at daybreak. After supper I took the first watch myself, awakening Mohammed at midnight, as it had been arranged that he should divide the rest of the night with Saad.

I was awakened at dawn by the buzz of conversation between Mohammed and a man who had just arrived

YOUNG CAMELS ON THE ROAD

SOME ARAB FRIENDS

To face p. 252:

in the camp. He brought the news that there had been further furious fighting and that the Arab encampments were full of wounded. Picturing my colleague overwhelmed with work, and seeing the utter impossibility of reaching the town that night with my caravan of suffering, I arranged to take Selim the gendarme with me and ride on ahead to El Yefren, while Mohammed followed slowly with the camels. It was my intention, on arrival at El Yefren, to ask Sheikh Sassi to send a party of gendarmes down on to the plain to protect the caravan, taking with them a couple of good camels with the ambulance stretchers, so that the more severely wounded could do the journey up the hillside without any unnecessary suffering. I communicated my plans to Mohammed, and told him to wait on the plain until I sent for him.

To facilitate my travelling as fast as possible I relieved myself of all superfluous kit, leaving the Mauser rifle with Mohammed; then I started off with Selim, with nothing but a blanket under the saddle and a bag full of biscuits. With the mountains on our right we rode due east towards our landmark, the mountain called Tamalilt. The sun shone viciously in our faces, and Selim, who, like all Arabs, seemed quite unable to control his thirst, constantly begged me to let him have a drink out of my water-bottle. On the understanding that we should reach a well at midday I was foolish enough to let him empty it. One o'clock arrived, but no sight of the well, and as I was now getting very thirsty, owing to the heat of the day and the dry biscuits I had been eating, I asked Selim to look out for a tent from which we could get a supply

of water. The gendarme, however, did not appear to
have much opinion of the honesty of the people in
this part, for he continually made excuses so as not to
approach the Arab encampments. In the afternoon the
desire for a drink got the better of me, and thinking
that as we were so near to El Yefren we should be
quite safe, I rode up to the first tent I saw and called
for some milk. An Arab boy at once brought out a
large bowl of buttermilk which, parched as I was with
thirst, seemed a draught fit for the gods. As the water
offered me was filthy beyond description, I filled my
bottle with buttermilk, a fact which later I regretted,
as I found that, far from assuaging one's thirst, it
merely aggravated it.

Towards evening we got on to the silt at the foot of
Ein Romiya, and I was dreaming of the good dinner
I was going to have with my colleague, when I noticed
Selim looking about him in amazement. Then I
noticed that the whole place presented an unusual
appearance. There were no women washing clothes
in the little pools in the clusters of palm trees that
lay under the frowning cliffs of El Yefren. There were
no herds of lowing cattle being led home from the
pastures, no horses being brought down to water. I
seemed also to hear a queer, unaccustomed murmur
from the town. Something unusual was happening.
What could it be? Suddenly, as we stood there in
doubt, Selim pointed with his finger to the rugged
road that led down from the town. A large body of
men in the utmost confusion were pouring down as
fast as their legs could carry them. In a few minutes
they surrounded us, and I have never before seen so

terrible a rabble. I should imagine that the bands of
wild men and women who swept through Paris during
the Revolution could have looked no more revolting.
They were haggard and travel-stained; all were armed
to the teeth, and many concealed wounds under blood-
stained bandages. Some were walking with the help
of sticks, and others were being half carried by their
friends. They shouted incoherently at Selim and myself,
and pointing to the desert urged us to fly with them.
Slowly we got the story. The Arabs' supply of ammunition had failed, and General Lequio, shelling them
out of the camps at Rapta and Lossaba, had made a
rapid march to Kikla, whence, after a brief halt, he
had advanced on El Yefren and had hoisted the Italian
flag in triumph over the castle. The news certainly
was stunning, and I could not make up my mind
what to do, but the pressing of the unsavoury crowd
round Selim and myself made me anxious first of all
to extricate myself from their midst without being
robbed and perhaps killed. Some of the fiercer-looking
Arabs were eyeing our horses with greedy looks, and
apparently thought we might be easy prey; nor were
they long in putting the matter to the test. A ragged-
looking negro, armed with spear and sword, laid a rough
hand on the bridle of Selim's horse, at the same time
half drawing a curved houghing knife from his belt.
The gendarme, who had his rifle slung, was also armed
with an enormous bell-mouthed pistol, formidable
enough to blow a hole through a wall. Cocking this
appalling weapon ostentatiously, he presented it at the
negro, who drew back muttering. Meanwhile an Arab
seized my bag of biscuits and endeavoured to drag it

off the saddle. Much as I pitied the fellow, for starvation was written plainly on his face, I feared that if I let it go it would only encourage the crowd to further licence, so I whipped out my big army revolver and covered the man. But he, as well as the rest of the crowd, had had their fill of fighting, and he quickly disappeared among the mob. I then noticed an Arab that I had frequently seen at Rapta riding furiously down the road. The blood was streaming from his face, and he was shouting and gesticulating. Coming up to me he pointed to the desert, and urged me to fly with all speed, as the "renegades" were coming. This word was used as a term of reproach for those Arabs who had been recruited by the Italians to fight against their co-religionists. They were well mounted and armed, and were held in considerable dread. At this last item of news the mob moved off quickly, leaving Selim and myself to puzzle out what was to be done. Now I was to reap in full the benefit of the small amount of Arabic I had acquired, for I was able to communicate my ideas to Selim, and I could understand nearly all that he said to me. Personally, I had little fear of Italian pursuit, for if Lequio had really arrived in El Yefren, it seemed fairly certain he would give his troops a good rest before venturing on to the desert, where Sheikh Sauf was known to be in force.

As we were both tired after the day in the saddle, and our horses had had no food since the morning, I called a halt, while I sat down on a rock and thought out what I had better do. Undoubtedly the easiest solution of the matter was to ride up the Ein Romiya valley, leave the horses in a secluded spot and enter

the town by the path up the cliff and then claim the
protection of the Italian conquerors. But this I felt
very unwilling to do. I had been very hospitably
received by the Italians in the drawing-room, and had
no wish now to be sent round to the kitchen. I had
had a fair and courteous warning from General Ragni
as to my position, and did not wish to stand on the
carpet in an Italian Orderly Room. Moreover, I had
been associated with the Arabs for so long that it looked
like a confession of failure to have to go hat in hand
to the Italian General and beg for protection as far
as the frontier. Again, I was terribly anxious about
Mohammed and the two Sambos, for it seemed quite
possible that the fugitives might fall upon the caravan
and loot it; and knowing that my faithful cook would
resist such treatment, I feared the matter might end
in his death and in the other two negroes being carried
off as slaves to Fezzan. Another point that weighed
with me was the fact that I had already lost enough
of the Society's goods during the voyage of the *Boudelblous*, and I had no wish to increase further my
reputation as a loser of stores. So taking it in all, I
determined to start back and find the camels.

We therefore turned our backs on the hills and began
to descend again. After about half an hour we came
across a group of Arabs who were busy making tea,
with a big heap of dates on an old sack lying in front
of them. They asked us to join them, and as it was
obvious we could not go much farther that night Selim
and I sat down with them. They all looked fairly
prosperous, and I felt we could trust ourselves with
them without any fear. Among these men was an old

Turkish soldier who had been a patient of mine at
Rapta. He sat down between Selim and myself. After
we had drunk tea, the Arabs led the conversation round
to the usual topic—their abject poverty and lack of
money. This, of course, was a clear invitation to me
to be charitable, but I knew that to give them anything
would be fatal, for it would only tempt their cupidity,
with the result that they might attempt to rob me of
all I had. I answered that unfortunately I had nothing
with me except a few *sous*, and then informed them
that the object of my visit to El Yefren was to get
hold of the money I had left with Sheikh Sassi. I added
that I was sure they would not be the losers, as God
was sure to reward them for their hospitality to a poor
hakim. They seemed satisfied with this, and when I
suggested to Selim that we should find a soft piece
of sand and try to snatch a few hours' sleep, they let
us go without further comment. We discovered a suitable spot, and having unsaddled and spread the blanket
on the ground, we sat down, smoking steadily, for
tired as we were neither of us felt inclined for sleep.

An hour must have passed, when we heard someone
stealthily approaching. We snatched up our arms and
waited. "Effendi!" gently called a voice that I at
once recognized as that of the Turkish soldier. "Come
here!" I replied softly, and soon the face of the soldier
appeared out of the darkness. He began to speak
rapidly in Arabic to Selim, and it was not until the
latter repeated what had been said to him that I could
grasp the meaning. It seemed that my late patient
had been lying down with his eyes shut and had over-
heard the Arabs planning to wait until we were asleep

and then to come and rob us of the horses and whatever
else they could lay their hands upon. Needless to say,
this news banished all thoughts of sleep, and we started
to saddle the horses as fast and as quietly as possible.
The soldier then suggested that, as the district was
dangerous for all strangers, especially now that Bahrouni's power was broken, I should buy for my protection the little Italian carbine he was carrying. As
I was anxious to reward the good fellow for his services,
I gave him a couple of pounds for the rifle and half a
dozen clips of cartridges. He then said goodbye, and
disappeared rapidly in the darkness.

Selim and I, leading the horses, wended our way
cautiously over the desert, and after a few minutes
came to a deep rift in the silt that had been cut out
by the mountain stream from the Ein Romiya valley.
We descended into this and made our way along for
some distance until we splashed into a pool that the
recent rains had left. Into this our horses thrust their
noses with delight and drank long and deeply; nor did
Selim and I disdain a good drink. The gendarme now
thought we were safe from pursuit, but as the moon
had risen I thought it best still to push on. An hour
or two later, as we were both tired out, and Selim
appeared to have no idea of where we were, I agreed
to a halt. We picketed the horses and wrapped ourselves in our blankets, and then, despite a determination
on my part to keep watch, tired nature asserted itself
and we both fell fast asleep. When I awoke the sun
had already risen, and as I looked round I noticed a
young Arab standing a few yards off, gazing at us
intently. I motioned to him to come forward, as I was

anxious to see if he could give us any news, but he could only confirm the fact that the Italians were in possession of El Yefren and that Bahrouni had fled to Fessato. He added that it was extremely dangerous to sleep in the open desert without guards, as there were many bad characters about robbing and killing all and sundry. Then, seeing that I carried an Italian carbine, he urged me to get rid of it as soon as possible, as, if we were captured by the enemy, it would go against me if I were found in possession of Italian arms. As this young Arab was well dressed and nicely spoken, I suggested that he should come along with us, as the rifle he carried would be an advantage to our party if we should be attacked. To this he willingly agreed, and we started off, taking a south-westerly direction so as to cut the road, in hopes of picking up Mohammed.

Nothing particular occurred during the morning's march, but by midday I had become thoroughly tired of Selim's grumbling. He was always urging that we should make straight for the French frontier without worrying about the caravan, for he and the young Arab seemed quite sure that by this time it would have been plundered. Suddenly, however, while we were discussing the point, we saw three Arabs, all armed with rifles, coming towards us. Glancing at Selim and our Arab, I saw that they did not like the look of the newcomers, for they both got their rifles into a ready position. I, personally, was rapidly becoming acquainted with fear, the sort that dries the mouth and makes one's heart thump at nothing. A bayonet charge, with a tot of rum inside and " the leave and the liking to shout," gives one little time to be afraid.

Moreover, it is comforting to know that the stretcher-bearers are just behind and the surgeons at the Casualty Clearing Station have their knives ready for you in the operating-theatre. But, on the desert, away from the moral support of your own race and hopeless miles from proper medical attention, one is apt to worry somewhat when there seems a chance of getting a handful of nails in the stomach from a flint-lock.

I was just going to dismount when the young Arab rapidly stripped off his leather belt and covertly thrust it between my legs as I sat in the saddle, and from the weight of it I felt sure that it contained money. The Arabs came up close, and proved to be three truculent - looking ruffians. They spoke pleasantly enough, however, and invited us into their tent for a meal. As it was now too late to draw back and we were urgently in need of food, we accepted their invitation and followed them to their encampment. As we went along I succeeded in getting the Arab's money-belt inside my shirt, and later in the day managed to buckle it around me. Nevertheless it was a great annoyance to me for the next few days, as it was far too small, and required a lot of pulling to make both ends meet. We tied the horses near the tent door and sat down with our arms at our sides. I started straight away by telling the owner of the house that I was very poor, but that if he supplied us with food he would doubtless receive the blessing of heaven. I was, unfortunately, often forced to tell this modified untruth, as I had nothing but gold with me and feared to change it, for the sight of such a sum of money would have been a direct inducement to the baser sort of Arab to attempt robbery with violence. I had, however, previously handed Selim some small change, so that our hosts, when they would take money, were amply rewarded for their hospitality.

I then promised my present host a letter to the Italian General that would protect him and his family from being plundered. Letters of this sort caused me little trouble to write and were always received with gratitude. I often wonder if any of them fell into the hands of the Italians, and what they thought of them if they did. The Arab seemed quite satisfied, for he placed a large *bazine* in front of us. Although it only consisted of flour and warm water mixed together, with hot olive oil poured on as a sauce, my hands were soon busy in the bowl. No sooner had I finished a hearty meal than a heated argument arose between the Arabs of the place on the one hand and the young Arab who was with us on the other. The only expression I could catch was a constant repetition of the word *flous* (money). All the time I noticed Selim looking on anxiously. I assumed little interest in the altercation, but drawing from my pocket a battered copy of the Koran that I had acquired at Bechoul, I read it in an open and ostentatious manner, although I was utterly unable to decipher more than a few words. Not that I had any idea of denying my religion and pretending to be a disciple of the Prophet, for this I have always looked upon as a vulgar expedient and adopted only by tourists who are bankrupt of resource; but it was the only book I happened to have in my pocket at the time. Suddenly the discussion came to a climax and the young Arab sullenly threw his purse down on the floor. It was eagerly seized by the other Arabs, who opened it and only found a few small coins. Again followed angry exclamations, which ended in the young Arab suddenly standing up and dramatically stripping off his robes to show that he had nothing concealed.

By this time I was feeling very uneasy and had to take frequent pulls at the skin containing the butter-milk in order to keep my mouth sufficiently wet to be able to articulate. Then the young Arab looked at me and contorted his face as if he wished to convey some meaning to me; I was, however, quite unable to interpret what he wished to say. Putting on his clothes again, he walked out of the tent with the other Arabs, leaving Selim and myself alone. We sat there smoking for perhaps half an hour, when my companion said something to the effect that they were bad men we were with, and proposed we should make a start. I hardly liked running away with the young man's money-belt, but as Selim seemed so insistent we mounted our horses and started off towards the west.

As soon as we were out of sight of the tent we galloped for a mile or two, and then, on the gendarme's advice, turned sharply to the right and made straight for the north. Coming to a clump of trees, we dis-mounted, and in a few minutes Selim pointed to the path we had just left. With the glasses I could clearly see three men with rifles moving rapidly along. I have little doubt that they were our hosts, who were following our supposed trail for no good purpose. Selim now said there was a small encampment not far from this place, where he knew the Arabs well and where we

could get barley for the horses and something decent
to eat and drink for ourselves. After about a two
hours' ride we came to a few very small, ragged tents,
in front of which some articles were exposed for sale.
I bought a good feed for the horses, and while they
were enjoying it Selim and I went into a tent and drank
what was, even for an Arab, an abnormal amount of
tea. After this we held a council of war. It was clearly
impossible to cross the danger-line again that evening
to go in search of the camels, so we agreed to rest
that night with Selim's friends, and when the moon
got up to strike again for the hills in hopes of finding
the caravan. As the gendarme again started grumbling
that I was leading him into danger I told him that,
when we came up with the camels, I should present
him with a couple of Turkish pounds, in addition to
the backsheesh I had already promised him. At this
he wanted to kiss my hand and told me he would not
leave me until he had seen me safely to Ben-Gardane.
Looking back, I think it highly probable that I owed
my life to Selim's fidelity, even though he did consider the financial aspect of the case. Still, as he was
a married man with a family to support, he had them
to consider.

An excellent *bazine*, garnished with a disarticulated
fowl, was provided for supper, after which we settled
down to an hour's tea-drinking and a chat. Selim
seemed to have made out to his friends that I was an
important personage and one having considerable weight
with the Italian Government, for immediately after
the meal the governor of the feast, who with noble
independence had waved aside my offer of payment,

asked me if I would be so good as to furnish him with a pass into El Yefren! This I agreed to do, and wrote him a few lines in French, which I hope served his purpose. Then, not wishing to show ingratitude for his hospitality, I handed him a few potash pellets, telling him to preserve them carefully until such a time as he should have a serious illness, when he was to suck one every day for a week. Having thus rendered myself a *persona grata* in the house, and feeling that I was in good company, I lay down and snatched a few hours' sleep.

As soon as the moon rose we had the horses saddled, and with one of the Arabs as a guide we started in a south-westerly direction in search of Mohammed. Until daybreak we had a very quiet journey, for although we passed several encampments we did not see a single Arab. As soon as it was quite light I dismissed the Arab guide with a good backsheesh, and Selim and I rode forward alone.

About the middle of the morning we approached a poor-looking Arab tent, where we stopped and were successful in purchasing a skin of buttermilk and a good supply of dates. To my great joy, I also heard that my caravan had been seen the day before not very far from this tent travelling in a direction parallel to the hills. Greatly encouraged by this news, we rode forward at a good pace, but the sun climbed into the meridian and began to descend without our seeing anything of the camels. About six o'clock in the evening Selim pointed out that the horses were very exhausted and that we had better look out for a suitable place to camp for the night. The rapidly-failing light made it difficult to see very far over the desert, and I recognized that

it would be useless to continue our search that night,
so with a feeling of bitter disappointment I agreed to
unsaddle. Under a clump of trees we found a decent
spot, and we were just munching a few biscuits when
we were hailed by a party of six Arabs, all armed with
rifles. One came forward to reconnoitre. He told us
that he and his companions had served all through
the war with Bahrouni, but now, seeing that further
resistance was useless, they were making their way home
to Algeria. Seeing that they were good fellows, I asked
them to come and join us for the night, but they said
they wished to press on and reach the French frontier
as soon as possible, as they feared that the starving
Arabs from the coast would molest them. They also
urged me to join them and they would undertake to
protect me. Hearing this, Selim became quite excited
and exclaimed that it was a God-sent opportunity for
us to get away. Finally, encouraged by the others, he
said that he was very anxious about his family, and
unless I agreed to abandon the search for the caravan
and make for the frontier at once he would refuse to
go any further. By this time I was feeling rather shaky,
and my first inclination was to eat my brave words about
finding Mohammed and to take Selim's advice. Still,
I am not without a certain amount of stubbornness, and
although I have little doubt now that Selim was only
taking the line he did to save me, I felt angry with him
for proposing to leave me after he had promised to go
on with me to Ben-Gardane. Leaving the bivouac
I walked a hundred yards on the sand and sat down
on a stone. I was in a panic, which greatly annoyed
me, as I wanted to think things out.

The broad expanse of the desert was lit by the gentle star-shine. Nothing could be heard but the plaintive notes of a ground bird and the horses tugging at the tether. Above, the vault glittered with brilliant stars. I thought again of the caravan. Surely by this time Mohammed had given up his vigil and found his way to the frontier. Surely I was now justified in abandoning the search and making my own way to safety. But I knew Mohammed was a faithful and loyal servant, and . . . *I had told him to wait.* As I sat there thinking it over, suddenly the desert appeared no longer threatening and lonely. It seemed to me that the explorers of old were passing by. There was the great Clapperton, with the lion-hearted Lander at his side; here were Oudney and Denham and Morrison. These were the men who made the sands of Tripolitana holy ground for their fellow-countrymen. To them the south was a country full of mystery and dangers; they marched on soil that was a blank on the best of maps. They were so great, so bold, so dauntless. The poorest man who bears the name of Englishman can at least see that here no blemish falls on the fair name of the country that they adorned.

I told Selim my decision. He saw that argument was useless, so, having said goodbye to his Algerian friends, he insisted on my lying down, generously offering to take the first watch while I went off to sleep. When I awoke the moon had risen well into the sky, and I was horrified to find, on glancing at my watch, that I had slept six hours. Selim was marching round and round the horses for the double purpose of keeping warm and not falling asleep. I apologized to him for

my laziness, and having seen him well tucked up I sat
down and waited for dawn. Soon, however, I was glad
to get up and walk about, for one of the minor inconveniences I was suffering from was that of being cold.
The days were hot enough to satisfy anyone, but at
night time, with nothing but a shirt and light coat to
cover my chest, I suffered intensely. Unfortunately,
Selim had no blanket, so I was forced to share mine
with him at night. As he suffered, like most Arabs,
from a plague of lice, it will be seen that this arrangement was not without its disagreeable side.

At length the eastern sky began to redden, and very
soon the sun shot up, warm and comforting. I woke
up Selim, and together we saddled the horses. The
gendarme now proposed that we should strike nearly
direct south, hoping that even if we could not hear
anything of Mohammed on the way we might possibly
find him encamped at the foot of the hills.

The day proved most wearisome. The horses were
exhausted with hunger, and we both had to dismount
from time to time to give them a rest. Twice we saw
fairly large bands of Arabs moving across the desert,
but on the advice of Selim we gave them a wide berth.
At four o'clock in the afternoon I was beginning
to despair, when suddenly the gendarme drew rein.
He pointed to a speck afar off on the desert.
" Mohammed! " he said calmly.

It would be difficult for me to express the unutterable
delight that I experienced when I heard this word.
Fatigue vanished in a flash, and I spurred Darkey
forward. As soon as we got near enough to see that
it was really our men we broke into a furious gallop,

brandishing our rifles in the air and cheering like madmen. Hurrah! Here is the whole crowd safe and sound rushing out to meet us! Here is Mohammed the faithful, waving the Mauser aloft in triumph! Here is big Sambo with his honest black face wreathed in smiles, and Sambo S'rir running as fast as my cut-down pyjamas permit! Behind these come the wild-looking mob of camel-men flourishing their prehistoric flint-locks. Even the wounded on their stretchers feebly yelp delight, as they see the chance of having their wounds dressed and their pains relieved. In a twinkle Mohammed rears the flagstaff and with a dramatic smile hoists the Union Jack.

Sitting down now and writing it all in peace and comfort, it may seem to have been a small thing to have rejoiced over, but the three days and nights that I had spent on the desert had been filled with indefinite fears—fears that I could scarcely analyse—and now the delight to me of that meeting in the desert! The delight of knowing that here at my side there was at least one man who would stand by me to the bitter end, the delight of having one man by me to whom I could speak in a decent language! In those few moments when I rushed in among my camp-followers, as they surged forward to kiss my hand, I mounted to the very pinnacle of joy.

" Off with the top of that provision box, Saad : there shall be no stinginess to-night in the camp of joy! A packet of cigarettes and a box of matches to each man in the camp, Mohammed, and decorate the three boys with a new cap apiece! "

The flames of the cooking fire mounted to heaven,

and never was there such a banquet as the meal that
Mohammed prepared. Never was there a vintage as
fragrant as the bottle of invalid port that came out of
the hospital stores. Never did I enjoy a smoke as much
as when, after supper, I lay down on the sand with my
head on a packing-case and chatted over ways and means
with Mohammed. The peril was by no means passed;
perhaps the most dangerous part of our journey lay
in front of us, but, as Mohammed put it, "*Main-
tenant, mon docteur, au moins, nous pouvons mourir
ensemble!*"

.   .   .   .   .   .

Night had fallen and Mohammed moved towards the
flag to lower it in accordance with custom. A fancy
seized me and I checked him: "Leave it, Mohammed;
let it fly to-night. The evening is fair, and the flag
will come to no harm!"

CHAPTER XVII.

MOHAMMED, it seemed, had not been without his share of adventure. The fugitive mob from El Yefren, he said, had surrounded the caravan like a swarm of hungry flies, but fortunately—though unexpectedly—the camel-men had stood firm and threatened the would-be looters with their guns.

Now, to what could I attribute this loyal behaviour on the part of the drivers? Certainly not to any moral reluctance on their part to share in the booty of a plundered caravan; for caravans have been looted in Tripolitana from time immemorial, and, so long as the culprits are not caught, the proceeding is charitably regarded and even applauded; very much in the same way that a man at home, who has robbed the railway company of a few cents or the Income Tax authorities of a few pounds, looks upon himself as rather a clever fellow.

For one thing, I carried the money, and they were anxious for nothing to happen until they had received their wages. Moreover, there were two distinct parties in the caravan—the plainsmen and the hillmen; neither side trusted the other, and, in the event of a general looting, who could say if one or the other party would

not only lose their share of the spoil but their own
goods into the bargain? So like wise men they bided
their time and, stimulated by Mohammed's promise of
a good backsheesh, even announced that they would
shed their blood in defence of the stores!

I was now feeling very tired, and Mohammed, taking
the hint from my loud and unchecked gaping, volunteered to do the first watch of three hours. But my
luxurious repose on the soft sand was not destined to
be of long duration; for no sooner had I fallen into
a dreamless slumber than I was awakened by the loud
report of a camel-gun, followed by the whine of rifle
bullets speeding over the bivouac. In a flash we were
all awake, and grasping our arms lay down behind the
boxes and loads, which formed an excellent zareba.

Although the moon had not yet risen the surface of
the desert showed up clearly under the soft light of the
stars. At first I could see nothing; then suddenly the
running figure of a man came into view. As the
fusillade in front of us was growing in intensity and
the bullets were coming unpleasantly close, I felt it was
time for definite action, so lifting my revolver against
the charging man I was just about to fire a round when
Saad yelled out that the Arab was his cousin. Leaping
the boxes he collapsed on the ground, and I could see
at a glance that he was badly wounded; blood was
running down his face from a large cut on the scalp,
and his left arm hung useless at his side. Having
gulped down some water he explained to Saad that he
had heard we were in the vicinity, and on his way to
join us had been set upon by a band of robbers who
were watching the movements of our caravan.

The firing had now ceased, so far without a shot being fired by my men; but suddenly big Sambo shouted out that the enemy were approaching and discharged his blunderbuss. This acted like a lighted match in powder, and at once the camel-men poured a ragged volley into the unseen enemy. Despite the fact that I felt rather annoyed at the loss of sleep, I could not help feeling strangely exhilarated, for it is not every day that one can take part in a scene of this sort.

A cloud of thick, black, acrid smoke overhung the caravan, half concealing the figures of the Arabs as they thrust home the charge with their ramrods. Out of this cloud burst tongues of flame, as the old muzzle-loaders were fired, to the alarm of the camels, who swung their heads in panic. At my feet knelt the chief camel-owner, who chose this moment to beg me to make good his loss if one of his camels should be hit. In competition with him was the shouting of the wounded man, who complained that he was bleeding to death, while a third Arab, well sheltered behind my tin uniform case, seized the opportunity to inform me that he did not wish to continue in the service of the Mission and would be glad to receive his wages and depart!

As " star-shells " were not included in my medical stores I was forced to wait patiently for the rising of the moon before I could tell what there was in front of us. At length Saad volunteered to go out on patrol to see if he could find out anything. He returned after about half an hour, bringing with him an old camel-gun with bloodstains on the stock and a couple of loaves of Arab bread that he had found lying in the desert.

It certainly did not look as if we had inflicted heavy loss on our assailants; and pleasant as it was to think that we had really been attacked by a bloodthirsty band of brigands and had beaten them off, when I reviewed the whole matter in cold blood I came to the conclusion that we had interfered in a vulgar little robbery just in time to save a man's life, and had then got a few rounds from the discomfited thieves, who perhaps hoped to drop a camel or two.   Still, some of my followers held other views, and a few weeks later I heard a servant of the Mission describing to an Arab notable in Sfax how we had beaten off an attack made by a hundred well-armed Tuaregs!   He forgot to add, however, that the enemy were dressed—in buckram!

At daybreak I extracted the charge of filth from the wounded man's arm, set his fracture and made him as comfortable as possible.   In return he gave me rather grave news.   It seemed that the Arabs guarding the coast had heard of Bahrouni's flight, and seeing no further chance of receiving provisions had determined to go home; so, hungry and desperate, they were streaming across the desert, robbing all who were not strong enough to resist them.   This was serious for us, since their line of retreat to the hills crossed our road at right angles.   As he informed me that Sheikh Sauf was still at Bechoul, I determined to march directly on that place, and not to Juesh as I had first intended. I comforted myself with the thought that Sheikh Sauf would know I was somewhere on the desert between Bechoul and El Yefren and would send some reliable men to meet me.

As the wounded Arab had no further use for his Gras

rifle, I purchased it from him, together with a bandolier
of cartridges; with these I armed Saad, after giving
him some elementary instruction in the action of the
piece. Since I now had fifteen well-armed men and
a good supply of ammunition, I had little reason to
fear the result of an encounter with any small groups
of Arabs, always providing the camel-men stood firm;
but I knew from bitter experience that these latter were
a shifty lot of ruffians and very little reliance could be
placed on them.

No sooner had we got the horses saddled and the
loads adjusted than a violent altercation arose among
the Arabs. Together with Mohammed, I rode up to
them to find out the cause of the trouble, and soon
learned that the Arabs from the plains were sure that
the hillmen were concocting some nefarious scheme,
as they were always together in a group and speaking
Djebelli among themselves, a language the others did
not understand. I settled the matter by prohibiting the
use of Djebelli and threatened to dismiss without backsheesh anyone heard speaking it.

At midday the camels were so tired that I was forced
to agree to a halt, eager as I was to push on. We
unloaded near a large patch of young corn, and the
general undoing of the bonds of discipline was clearly
to be seen when the Arabs allowed both horses and
camels to crop freely the green shoots of what they now
contemptuously called " Italian corn ".

The sun was now very hot, so I had my personal
luggage piled as high as possible in order to make a
shelter from the fierce midday rays. I was just squatting
down on a piece of carpet when Saad came up to me

and pointed to an approaching patch on the desert. Getting out the field-glasses, I focused the group, and was soon able to make out the figures of perhaps sixty Arabs, some on foot, others on horseback or on camels. I shouted to the head driver to bring in the camels, who were feeding in the corn, and together with Sambo, Mohammed and Selim, commenced making a rough breastwork with the boxes.

We were in a splendid position. A good well lay within twenty yards of us, and some large boulders together with our stores gave fair protection from rifle fire. We could hold off a large force if only the camel-men remained loyal. Suddenly I heard a sort of groan burst from the head camel-man. He was looking in a dazed fashion at the newcomers; his jaw had dropped and his face was ashen-gray. Terror and amazement were depicted on his face.

I focused the approaching Arabs again and was just about to utter the ill-omened word, when Saad fore-stalled me : " Tuaregs! " The word probably conveys little to the ordinary traveller, but on the Sahara it stands for the very personification of lying, thieving, cheating and murdering. Sex-Bolshevism has dominated the tribe for many years, and the men appear to do exactly what the women tell them. When the stock of luxuries and food gets low in their camp the warriors are urged by their wives to go forth and loot a caravan. Although I had seen a few of this tribe near Zavia, I thought that they had all returned to the interior, but now there was no mistaking their masked faces and the little high saddles on their fast camels.

For a while I looked at them fascinated, and then

turned round to see how my Arabs enjoyed the prospect.
A rough ring had been made by boxes, stones and sacks,
inside which the camels were knelt. To my gratified
amazement the head camel-man came up to me with
Mohammed, made the usual grasp at my hand to kiss
it, and informed me that everyone was prepared to fight
to the end, as we could expect no mercy from these
people. In return I thanked him for his loyalty and
assured him that we could easily beat the enemy off,
if it came to a fight. I gave instructions that no one
was to fire without orders, and in any case the muzzle-
loaders were to be reserved until the enemy was right
on top of us.

In accordance with the custom of the country the
band stopped about two hundred yards off and sent
two of their number up to parley. These halted about
thirty paces away and commenced a shouting match
with Mohammed. Seated as I was on a piece of carpet
outside the zareba, I could hear quite clearly what was
being said. It appeared that the envoys wished to
speak with the foreign doctor. I told Mohammed
quietly to let them come up but to watch them carefully. I had my revolver in the bosom of my shirt
and a rifle at my side. When the two came up I saw
at once that they were ordinary Arabs, but a more
villainous-looking pair of men I never before cast eyes
on. They had left their rifles behind, but carried large
flint-lock pistols and knives in their belts.

For a while I took no notice of them but continued
reading that illuminating advertisement which is given
away with every bottle of Eno's Fruit Salt, as I had
no wish to appear in an undignified hurry. At length

AT–J*

I looked up and asked them what their business was, and in answer one of them started a long harangue, of which I understood nothing and Mohammed very little, owing to the peculiarity of dialect. The other envoy now spoke and he was able to make himself understood. The upshot of his speech was that they were travelling from the coast to the interior and were all dying of hunger—was I prepared to give them something to eat? In reply I said I should be very pleased to do what I could for them, as we had been sent by pious Moslems to help them, but unfortunately it would not be very much as my stock was low.

During this discussion the other Arab had been edging nearer and nearer the ring of boxes in order to see how many rifles we had. When Mohammed under my instructions ordered him away he laughed in an insolent fashion and made some rapid remarks to his comrade. The latter now changed his conciliatory tone and in a hectoring manner told me that they wanted not only food but clothes and money. Waving his hand to the main body in a scarcely veiled threat, he said that they were many and meant to have their wishes. I had just absolutely refused to give them any money, while willing to concede food and half a dozen blankets in order to avoid bloodshed, when matters came to a crisis. The second Arab had now moved to the well, and seeing big Sambo about to draw water he went up to him and asked for a drink. Not thinking what he was doing, Sambo laid down his blunderbuss on the coping-stone and held the skin for the man to drink out of. In a trice the Arab snatched up the gun and started walking away with it, the object of the manœuvre being of course to see if we would show fight. I was unable to do anything myself, as I was completely covered by the little group standing round, but Selim jumped up, covered the man with his rifle and ordered him to halt. The Arab at once threw down the gun, laughed heartily and tried to pass the matter off as a joke. The man in front of me now burst into abuse, and the pair walked away, waving their arms to their friends. This I took to be a signal, and I was just preparing to retreat into the barricade when, quite unnoticed in the general hubbub, two new figures rode up. One was an elderly man with a long grey beard, who sat his horse with dignity and had a look of authority in his eyes. He asked me what the trouble was, and, after Mohammed had translated my reply, got off his horse and sat on the mat beside me. Before going any further I told the cook to make some tea as fast as possible, as I was anxious to secure the support of the old man by the ties of bread and salt.

The old Arab now introduced himself as the sheikh of that district, and said he was very sorry to see us in any trouble, as he had very good cause to be grateful to the Mission for the care we had given his son when the latter had been wounded. But the times were very troublesome and there were a lot of bad people about; moreover, all his men were with Sheikh Sauf and he could not offer us protection. He thought it would be better for us to give presents to the bandits rather than stand the risk of fighting, and he pointed out that it would be easy for the enemy to sit down and wear us out by sniping. In reply I told him it was only a matter of hours before Sheikh Sauf's gendarmes came to escort us, and that I utterly refused to give anything away except food, which it was my duty to distribute by the laws of the Holy Prophet. The sheikh thereupon said that the tribesmen in front of us were very cunning and unmerciful, and if we were beaten would leave no one alive. At this cheerful news I scarcely knew what to say, as the day was so warm, the atmosphere so clear, the sky so blue, that it seemed a distinct pity to leave it all. It ended in my saying to the sheikh that God was Merciful and Compassionate and what was written would come to pass. The sheikh quite agreed with this pious statement, although he was just commencing to qualify it with a phrase beginning with " but " when Saad brought up tea. At first the old man was reluctant to drink, but, encouraged by the loud " Bismillah! " with which I prefaced my own cup, his scruples vanished, and he not only drank the full number of glasses allowed by etiquette, but thoroughly enjoyed a box of fancy biscuits that I had saved for any important occasion. Having accepted a tin of cigarettes and the remainder of the biscuits, he called for his horse, saying he would go across and speak to the bandits. He mounted and rode off to where his fellow-countrymen were gathered.

During his absence I improved as much as possible the defences of the camp. Large stones were rolled up against the boxes as a protection against rifle fire; skins and water-pots were filled and provisions laid out. I promised the camel-owner full indemnity for any camels killed or injured and told the men that if they should be wounded in the service of the Mission they would be properly looked after until they were restored to health, and amply compensated for any injury.

Although I felt quite sure of the position, at the same time I could not help feeling rather excited, and when Mohammed brought me my dinner I found it was all I could do to masticate it; still, I made up by drinking large draughts of tea. As well as the young Arab's money-belt that I was still wearing, I had a fairly large sum in Turkish gold in my pockets, and I was now anxious to make quite sure that none of this should fall into the hands of the enemy in case our caravan should be overwhelmed. With this end in view I picked up the large bell-mouthed blunderbuss that big Sambo usually carried and retired with it to the shadow of some rocks, where one by one I loaded the coins into its huge barrel, ramming on top large paper wads. One shot and the money would have been scattered to the four winds of heaven!

The next hour passed very slowly, and I was indeed thankful when at last I saw the sheikh returning. He told me that he had spoken earnestly with the men and that they had agreed to leave us unmolested if we would supply them with a little food and attend to their wounded. The old man was inclined to be rather apologetic as to the attitude of his co-religionists, and he was greatly relieved when I told him I did not expect a very high standard of morality from soldiers who were perishing of hunger. Anyone who has seen even the best European troops retreating after a serious reverse will, I think, agree that these poor Arabs should not be too severely judged.

Taking with me a large parcel of cigarettes as a peace-offering, despite Mohammed's protests, I walked across with the sheikh to cast an eye over the wounded, little Sambo marching in the rear with a towel and a large galvanized bowl. There is always a certain amount of moral satisfaction to be gained by thrusting one's head into the lion's jaws, and I can quite understand how easy it is for a travelling showman to get a volunteer in any village to be shaved—or even married—in a cage of forest-bred tigers.

At all events, I was soon surrounded by some of the roughest and wildest looking men it is possible to imagine. But except for patting my gloves and scrutinizing my dress generally very closely they treated me with the greatest deference. Protected only by my sacred calling I walked freely amongst these men who a few minutes before had been ready to cut my throat.

Having treated the three wounded men, I made them each a present of cigarettes and then called to Sambo for a bowl of water to wash in. As I had taken the precaution to place crystals of permanganate of potash under my finger nails, the water rapidly became blood-red in colour to the gratified amazement of the onlookers. Then, as the whole band looked so miserable and hungry, I determined to do what I could for them. I bought a sheep from the sheikh to provide them with a good dinner, and added as well flour, tea and sugar. Finally, selecting three who looked the most depraved of the lot, I presented them with a copy of the Koran apiece. Having thus ministered to their spiritual and bodily needs, I was able to leave them with a clear conscience.

A HALT ON THE DESERT

GENDARMES

To face p. 282

The sheikh now invited me into his tent to take food, and although I was most anxious to push on I felt it would be ungracious to refuse after all he had done for us. Inside his quarters there were two men clad in gendarmes' uniform who complained bitterly to me that Bahrouni had paid them no wages for over three months. The sheikh told me that, so far as he knew, they were both good men, and strongly advised me to take them with me as far as the frontier, as he felt sure we should need protection on the way. I therefore agreed to give them thirty francs each and their food to take us as far as Sheikh Sauf's camp, or, in default of this, to the French frontier. I must confess that Mohammed did not like the look of them and urged me not to take them. He proved to be right, for they turned out to be a pair of unmitigated scoundrels and a source of danger instead of a protection.

We started off again, taking the two gendarmes with us, and met with no further adventure during the day. At nightfall we unloaded the camels and settled down to sleep as early as possible, on the understanding that we should move off as soon as the moon rose, in the hope of passing the danger zone before daybreak. I, personally, got very little sleep, both on account of the cold and also because of the swarm of parasites that now infested me. I had long ceased to make any but the slightest pretence at keeping properly clean, and my evening toilet usually consisted in putting a handful of Keating's powder inside my shirt.

At the first sight of the moon I roused the caravan, but the gendarmes refused to budge and advised the camel-men that there was no need to start for an hour

or two.   Seeing that my authority was being openly
flouted, I went up to the gendarmes with Mohammed,
and told them that I was the person who gave orders
to the caravan, and if they did not like to obey they
could turn back at once.   At this they got up grumbling
and began to saddle their horses, saying that their sheikh
had ordered them to go with us, and they must obey.
As we were loading up, it started to rain heavily, and
we were all soaked through before a start had been
made.   Considering that we had gone to bed supperless
and were now unable to make a hot drink before setting
out, it can be imagined that our wounded were suffering
severely, and that it was not a very high-spirited party
who started on this unpleasant portion of the journey.

When day dawned a fresh trouble arose.   One of
the camel-men came up to Mohammed and said that
he and his fellows did not like the way that the two
gendarmes and Saad were always lingering behind
and conversing together.   Although I trusted Saad,
Mohammed did not, but thinking the latter understood
the character of his co-religionists better than I did
I rode back and relieved Saad of his rifle, and then told
the gendarmes that their place was in front of the
caravan and that I preferred to bring up the rear myself.
They looked at me as if they wished to disobey, and
then with an insolent laugh rode forward in front of
the camels.

As I have had to say some harsh things about the
Arabs generally, I must in fairness to them relate a
little incident to show that on the desert true hospitality
may still be found.   Feeling very thirsty I drew up at
a tent and asked a young boy standing by to give me a

drink of milk. He at once brought me out a large
bowl, for which I handed him a small silver coin in
payment. I rode on for perhaps two miles when I heard
a man running behind me, shouting. I stopped until
he came up, when to my surprise he handed me back
the coin I had given to the boy, saying that he could
not allow his son to be rewarded for so simple an act
of hospitality.

At midday we reached Bechoul, and at once I saw
our troubles were far from being over. Sheikh Sauf
had withdrawn with his men to Juesh, and absolute
anarchy was reigning round the old camp. The house
had been broken open and the contents looted; the
merchants had all gone away and the only persons to
be seen about were the beggars and wastrels, who had
persistently haunted our tents when last we were in
Bechoul. The Arabs were walking about armed to the
teeth, and everybody seemed highly distrustful of his
neighbour. If the fugitives from El Yefren had surrounded Mohammed on the desert like flies, at Bechoul
the Arabs hung around us like hungry vultures. I put
down my water bottle for one moment, and in a flash
it was gone; nor was I able to find out who had taken
it. Suddenly I heard little Sambo crying out, and was
just in time to see a big lout trying to rob him of his
cap. Selim, however, rose to the occasion and dealt the
would-be robber a severe blow.

I wanted to go straight on to Juesh to rejoin Sheikh
Sauf, but this the camel-drivers utterly refused to do,
nor would the promise of a larger backsheesh induce
them. They began unloading the camels and throwing
the boxes down on the desert. After a few moments

the chief camel-owner came up and demanded that I should settle up for the camels. He said he could take me no farther, as he required the camels to transport his own family into Tunisia, for he had heard that the Italians were coming, and he feared a repetition of the Tripoli massacres. Obviously to be left stranded on the desert at Bechoul among this gang of thieves would have been the end of all things, yet I was too worn out by lack of sleep to be able to enter into an argument, so I gave Mohammed plenipotentiary powers, telling him to strike as good a bargain as possible. I then went off to attend to the wounded, leaving Selim and the other gendarmes to guard the luggage.

It was now a difficult thing for me to know what to do for the best to help these poor victims of the war. I could hardly take them with me into Tunisia and leave them chargeable on the rates; nor did I know what the French authorities would say at seeing these derelicts dumped down over their frontier. So after some trouble I found the local *hakim* and delivered them into his charge, giving him at the same time a large supply of dressings, some elementary instructions as to how to apply them and a present of a sovereign. I then went round to the wounded, and as secretly as possible gave them each a like sum, urging them not to let anyone know, or they would be robbed. Later, however, two of them followed me to Ben-Gardane, where my French colleague was good enough to tend them until they were well enough to get about.

Meanwhile the argument between Mohammed and the head camel-owner was getting very acrimonious,

THE AUTHOR AT BECHOUL

NOTABLES AT BECHOUL

To face p. 286

and the large crowd gathered round them joined freely
in the discussion. Finally, the old man demanded to
be paid up in full for the journey he had completed,
and agreed that if we handed him half the fare to the
French fort at El Assa he would take us to that place.
I thought, however, that if I gave him so large a sum
of money we should be entirely at his mercy and have
no further hold on him. So I proposed that I should
give him five Turkish pounds in cash and then hand
him all that was due to him the moment we got to El
Assa. I knew that if I could get him to come to this
place the French authorities would probably insist on
his taking my goods on to Ben-Gardane. After another
hour's talk he agreed to my proposition, not that he
wished to help us, but because Mohammed had
informed him that I only had enough cash to settle
for the camels, and if he insisted on the whole amount
and I persisted in refusing it a general scramble for my
property might arise, in which case he would stand a
very poor chance of getting anything at all. We were
putting the packs on the camels when another annoying
incident arose—one of the camel-owners utterly refusing
to start with his camel, unless I paid him there and then
the full charge to El Assa. Naturally I refused, as this
would have meant the tearing up of the agreement I had
made with the old man. As he proved obdurate, I paid
him off without adding any backsheesh, and he drove
off his animal in high dudgeon. As all the other camels
were now loaded up, I suggested to Mohammed that
we should make a start without this load, but my cook
was now obsessed with the idea of getting away with
everything, and made the very sensible remark that if

we started abandoning stores it would make the Arabs think we were hurrying away because we were afraid of them. A man now came up and said he could get us a camel if we would give him half an hour to fetch it. He was a sinister-looking man, but as we wanted the animal badly I sent him off to fetch it, and two miserable hours dragged by until he drove it up.

Just before sunset we started off, but scarcely had we gone half a mile when the two gendarmes approached me and demanded their cash. They had by no means fulfilled their bargain, but I was anxious to get rid of them, so I handed them three *louis* between them; whereupon they both said I had promised them forty francs apiece and that they were determined to have it. The caravan had now moved on, and Mohammed and I were left facing them. They both had their rifles across their knees, while I was carrying my carbine slung. It was, of course, blackmail of the rankest description levied by two thorough-paced scoundrels. It was hard to pay it, but—a few miles off there was the French frontier and safety. I shrugged my shoulders in humiliating surrender and told Mohammed to pay them. I am sorry now that I did, and I regret paying that extra twenty francs as much as anything I have ever done in my life.

Another mile and I was addressed by the old camel-driver; he could see men following us on the sky-line, and refused absolutely to move another step. By this time I was rather tired and rather demoralized, and although it was a dangerous policy I thrust a couple of pounds into his hand and pointed forwards. Just as this argument was finished, I heard Mohammed shout-

ing that five armed men were running up from the
rear. I dismounted, handed the horse into the care
of Sambo Kebir and ran back with Selim, telling Saad
to hurry forward the caravan. I lay down on the sand
with Mohammed and got ready. One man detached
himself from the party and rushed up to us shouting
out something that Mohammed understood. Then in
the dim light I saw that it was one of my Bechoul
patients, who had had a fractured arm and had been
cared for by the Mission. He quickly gave us his
news. He said that the gendarmes had returned to
Bechoul and had told the Arabs there that we should
fall an easy prey if they pursued us. He added that
the old man and the Arab who had recently joined us
were both villains, and in case of attack would drive
off the camels and divide the spoil after we had been
finished. As, however, he was grateful for the attention
I had given him in the hospital, he had brought up
four of his kinsmen, who would see us safely to El
Assa.

I felt that this was the last straw. After the days I
had passed in the midst of suspicion, greed and plotting,
I hardly knew how to act for the best. I gambled,
however, on the gratitude of a grateful patient and on
the honest faces of his four relations. Calling the whole
of the caravan together I told them that it was to the
interest of all to stand by me; that, as they knew,
the cases contained nothing but medicines and that I
had concealed the money in a place where it could
never be found; that if they remained faithful they
would receive the good backsheesh I had promised
them as well as a blanket apiece. Then, turning to the

four new arrivals, I promised them that in case of an attack, if we beat off the enemy I would divide a hundred pounds among the survivors when we got to El Assa. They all seemed very pleased at this offer, and we started off again. My old patient then said he was not strong enough to go any farther and would have to say goodbye. I shook hands with him warmly, whereupon he tried to kiss my hand, and I was glad to return the compliment by making a motion of kissing his. When I come to count up the faults of the Tripolitan Arabs I must not forget to place this exhibition of gratitude on the other side.

Our direction now lay due north, and we marched directly on the Pole Star. I arranged the order of march as follows :—Mohammed led with one of the new Arabs, both armed with Mausers; Selim and a rifleman took the right; on the left were the other two newcomers with good rifles, and myself and Saad shepherded the rear. I gave orders to the old man that at the first shot he was to halt and kneel the camels, then if he liked he could cut and run as fast as he liked.

We could now have done with a dark night, as in the bright starlight the camels showed up clearly. Venus, almost at her full, was blazing away like a ship's lamp, while the big stars in Orion sparkled like jewels. My watch had long ceased work, and I was calculating time by the position of the Dipper. Surely the celestial machinery never moved before with the slowness that it did that night!

Although it was of the utmost importance to keep the caravan together and push on with all speed possible, various irritating delays kept us back; a load required shifting or a man stopped to arrange his sandals. My nerves were in such a frayed state that once, when little Sambo started shouting to be taken off his camel, I let him have such a volley of abuse that one of the Arabs respectfully informed me that I was endangering the safety of the party by using such impious language.

The weary night was slowly passing when suddenly Mohammed doubled back and pointed out to me a white monument showing up clearly in the starlight —it was the boundary post between Tripolitana and Tunisia. It was an excellent thing to see was that post, but we were not as yet out of all danger, for the French frontier encampment still lay some miles off, and our would-be pursuers were not men likely to trouble themselves about the niceties of international law. I may here say that, after we had arrived at Ben-Gardane, I learned that the tale that my old patient had told me was true and that a party actually did set out after us, but hearing that we had been reinforced by four rifles they thought the game hardly worth the candle and abandoned the pursuit.

A couple of hours after we had passed the boundary the old camel-man said that we were now quite safe and that, as the camels were tired, he wanted to halt for a while. After taking the opinion of Mohammed I cordially agreed to this, for I was thoroughly fatigued, and could hardly walk on account of the intense desire I had to go to sleep. Long before the camels were unloaded, wrapped in a blanket I was fast asleep on the ground.

At dawn I got up with great reluctance, as I felt I could easily have slept the clock round. After a frugal breakfast, we loaded up and set out once again. Before starting, however, I dismissed Selim, the gendarme who had accompanied me so faithfully during the preceding days. Selim was sorry to go, and I was sorry to lose him. For a long time he stood still watching us from the top of a hillock, raising his rifle from time to time in salute. As we moved on he got smaller and smaller, until the tiny dot on the hill-top disappeared. Ah, well, I suppose I shall see him no more until we spur together down the golden streets of Paradise!

Another hour passed, and suddenly I spied a horseman surveying the country from the top of a hillock. It was one of the frontier guards of France, and he stood there, a gallant figure with his blue burnous afloat in the morning breeze, with his well-groomed, well-fed horse, his polished sword under the saddle flap, and his carbine resting over his knees. Now, at last, our troubles were over, for this horseman stood for law, order and civilization, for a good, well-cooked meal and the luxury of an undisturbed sleep in a real bed. He galloped up to us, and when Mohammed put our case before him he at once volunteered to take us to the nearest post. After a short ride we arrived at a large tent, when the Arab *chaouch* came out and saluted and asked me to enter the tent and drink tea. I sprawled on the floor in utter content. I felt the load of responsibility lifted from my shoulders by the kindly hand of France.

Then occurred what I had foreseen for a long while;

the *chaouch* and his men commenced relieving the camel-men of their weapons, for the laws in Tunisia are very strict as to the carrying of arms and no one is allowed to enter the colony from Tripolitana carrying rifles. Up to the time of the break-up of the Arab Government the arms of a caravan had always been left at Bechoul, but as it was clearly impossible for my men to have deposited their guns at that place, they had brought them along with them. The Arabs now commenced charging me with perfidy, so I got the *chaouch*, who was an amiable fellow, to give each man a receipt for his weapon, and I promised that when we got to the fort at El Assa I would get a permit from the French officer to enable them to withdraw their weapons on their return journey. This arrangement seemed to satisfy the Arabs, and they begged me to start at once, because they were anxious to get back into Tripolitana as soon as possible, in order to protect their own families.

Having made the frontier guards a present of some cooking-pots and a few other articles, with which they were highly delighted, we started for El Assa, and arrived there just after midday without further incident. When we arrived the hot sun was beating down on the dazzling white walls of the fort, the whiteness only relieved by the patch of colour on the flagstaff, where the tricolour of France floated proudly. As I was very thirsty I had ridden ahead of the caravan, and drawing rein outside the gate of the fort I called to an Arab to bring me some water. This man had been lying half-asleep, and he jumped up, looking at me wonderingly. Seeing myself in a glass a short while after I am not surprised he did not know what to make of me. My clothing was half-Arab and half-European, I had had neither a wash nor a shave for many days, and I was girded with arms like a cinematograph cowboy. At length he recovered sufficiently to go and fetch me some water, which he brought in a watering-can. Despite the vehicle, it was the best water I had tasted for weeks, and I drank long and thirstily. On making inquiries I learned that there was no French officer here, and loud were the lamentations of the camel-men when they learned that they would have to go to Ben-Gardane to get the permit to withdraw their arms. I need hardly say that this arrangement suited me excellently, as I had no wish to have my goods shot down at El Assa and then to have to look for fresh camels to take me on to Ben-Gardane. I promised the Arabs that they should not be the losers by this new arrangement, and at their urgent request agreed to push on with all speed, although personally I wanted no better than to lie down and sleep the day away.

After a good meal in the house of an hospitable Arab, we started off again at dusk, and this last stage proved one of the most wearisome we had experienced. The camels were dead tired, and required plenty of driving to make them move forward. Mohammed and the two boys were snoring loudly, perched high on the loads. I kept on going to sleep on Darkey and twice I rolled off on to the sand. My eyes seemed to have given out, for I saw all sorts of imaginary objects in the road. Once I thought I saw a body of men barring our way and shouted out to the camel-men to halt the caravan; large armies, too, appeared

THE AUTHOR ON DARKEY

A FRENCH FRONTIER FORT

To face p. 294

to be marching side by side with us. Still, all things
pleasant and unpleasant come to an end, and shortly
after dawn we saw the minarets of the Ben-Gardane
Mosque glittering in the rays of the early morning
sun.

CHAPTER XVIII.

At the Hôtel des Colonies I received a hearty welcome from François and his good wife. He greeted me as one risen from the grave, for a few days previously an Arab had come into the town and had announced that both I and my followers had been butchered by the Arab bandits.

Going into the bar for a glass of iced beer, for the possession of which I had to fight with a myriad of buzzing flies, I was greeted by the young Arab who had entrusted me with his money-belt a few days before. I handed it over to him and asked him to be so good as to check the contents. To my surprise, he shook no less than fifty sovereigns out on to the table, and having counted them announced that the sum was correct. Then, after politely thanking me for the service I had done him, he salaamed and prepared to walk away. Before he left, however, I asked him how he had been able to trust his entire fortune to an utter stranger. He replied that his father had told him that the English were honest people and could be relied upon. This answer made me think how careful we all ought to be when travelling abroad to do nothing to undermine the prestige that our forefathers have so firmly established.

The French Resident made no difficulty over signing a permit to enable my men to get their arms from the frontier post, so I dismissed them with my blessing and—which they seemed to appreciate more—with a blanket apiece and good backsheesh. Then after a good meal I slept away fifteen luxurious hours on a bed that a few months previously I had despised as hard and comfortless.

I waited about in Ben-Gardane for several days in hopes of hearing what had happened to Mr. Turnbull and the other members of the Mission, but all I heard were vague rumours and the booming of big guns over the vast plains. Bahrouni and Sassi made their way through a storm of bullets to French territory, having had to fight a pitched battle with Af-Khini's men on the way.

As the Society did not wish me to return to the interior of Tripolitana, as I had suggested, I made my way to Tunis, where I reluctantly said goodbye to Mohammed and the two boys. Ah! Mohammed, when I saw the tears run down your honest black face, and heard the broken words of farewell you uttered, I swore by the faithful service you had rendered me that never again would I apply the contemptuous word " nigger " to a man of your race!

The cinematograph of life flickered bravely for me during the months I spent in Tripolitana. I never remember enjoying a period of travel more; for looking back over the fifteen years spent amongst the pleasures and worries that fall to the lot of a man who has his living to earn, I have found that the great joys are to be found in the rich contrasts that life offers—the cool of the green oasis after the scorch of the desert; the delights of the valley after the ice-locked mountain pass; the fresh breeze of the savannah after the stifling heat of the bush; the lounge by the bivouac fire after the sweating toil of battle; and finally, when the body bends under the weight of years and the drooping head seeks the pillow in repose—the pregnant sleep of Death after the hurried, crowded hours of Life.